More praise for *Celebrity and the Environment*

'More exposé than a tabloid. More weight than a broadsheet ... Brockington lends academic muscle to what, I suspect, many of us instinctively feel about these issues. Extensively researched yet winsomely written and, thankfully, not veering into cynicism which a book on this subject could easily do. Enlightening and easily accessible by the armchair environmentalist.' Terry Clark, St Luke's Church, Glossop

'I was surprised by this book. Anything containing the mere word "celebrity" will normally see me heading for the hills at speed, let alone a whole book on the subject! Dan's book is written with wit and grace. His research was clearly meticulous and the result is a book that is informative and enjoyable.' Robin Barker, Countrycare Children's Homes

'In an analysis that builds on a large literature examining interlinkages between conservation and corporate interest, Dan Brockington turns a new corner, investigating how the rich and famous lend their glamour to the noble goal of saving the planet. In reality conservation is a highly political pursuit with winners and losers. Brockington provides a well-balanced account of the pros of harnessing the razzamatazz of celebrity to the conservation cause with the cons of sanitizing the harsh realities of conservation politics and the insidious danger of commoditizing nature. If you want to embark on the journey into contemporary conservation you would go well with this book.' Monique Borgerhoff Mulder and Tim Caro, University of California at Davis

'A thoroughly stimulating book that made me question my role as a conservation filmmaker.' Jeremy Bristow, director and writer

About the author

Dan Brockington has a PhD in anthropology from UCL and is happiest conducting long-term research in remote rural areas. He is the author of *Fortress Conservation and Nature Unbound* (with Rosaleen Duffy and Jim Igoe), and has undertaken research for several years in Tanzania as well as shorter projects in South Africa, Australia, New Zealand and India. He has worked at the Universities of Oxford, Cambridge and London and is now a senior lecturer at the Institute for Development Policy and Management at the University of Manchester.

Celebrity and the Environment

Fame, wealth and power in conservation

Dan Brockington

Zed Books

LONDON | NEW YORK

Celebrity and the Environment: Fame, wealth and power in conserva-tion was first published in 2009 by Zed Books Ltd, 7 Cynthia Street, London N1 9JF, UK and Room 400, 175 Fifth Avenue, New York, NY 10010, USA

www.zedbooks.co.uk

Set in OurType Arnhem and Futura Bold by Ewan Smith, London
Index: ed.emery@thefreeuniversity.net
Cover designed by Rogue Four Design
Printed and bound in Great Britain by CPI Antony Rowe, Chippenham and Eastbourne

Distributed in the USA exclusively by Palgrave Macmillan, a division of St Martin's Press, LLC, 175 Fifth Avenue, New York, NY 10010, USA

A catalogue record for this book is available from the British Library
Library of Congress Cataloging in Publication Data available

ISBN 978 1 84277 973 6 hb
ISBN 978 1 84277 974 3 pb

Contents

Figures and table

Figures

Table

Acronyms

ATREE	Ashoka Trust for Ecology and Environment
BBC	British Broadcasting Corporation
CEO	chief executive officer
CNN	Cable News Network
DRC	Democratic Republic of the Congo
ESRC	Economic and Social Research Council
HTV	Harlech Television, now called ITV Wales and West
IUCN	International Union for Conservation of Nature
MTV	Music Television
NGO	non-governmental organization
PETA	People for the Ethical Treatment of Animals
RMAP	Resource Management in Asia-Pacific Programme
SECS	Sudanese Environmental Conservation Society
SERG	Society and Environment Research Group
UK	United Kingdom
US/USA	United States of America
USAID	US Agency for International Development
WWF	Worldwide Fund for Nature

Preface

I know something about wildlife conservation. I have written books and articles about conservation, I go to international meetings about it, I enjoy talking to conservationists and wrestling with their problems in conservation journals. I love spending time in rural societies learning about conservation, and listening to people talk about local environmental politics and the impact of government policies or non-governmental organizations (NGOs) on their lives. I have spent nearly three years on such work in rural societies in Tanzania for my PhD and post-doctoral research, and have been able to talk with farmers and conservationists in many other parts of the world about their struggles.

However, I have had only glancing encounters with celebrity conservation and I am not normally drawn to celebrity in a more general sense. I do not dress fashionably and visit the cinema only sporadically. I never fitted in with the groups at school who were keen on the latest trends in music – I did not like the sound of it and could not (cannot) dance. I do not read *Hello!* or *OK!*, or men's (or women's) magazines. I was out of the country when the first *Big Brother*s were screened in the UK, and could not understand the hype when I returned. I do not follow reality TV shows; in fact I do not watch television. When I realized that celebrity was becoming increasingly important in environmental affairs and that I was going to have to take an interest in it and find out how it works, my main problem was that I simply did not know the names of the people involved. And when I found out what they were, I did not know who they were. Early drafts of this manuscript were full of unfortunate mistakes: Brangelina was a woman and I recorded the support of both Harrison Ford and Indiana Jones for conservation causes. I still do not 'get' celebrity. I have had trouble taking it seriously. I have frequently found the world I encountered bizarre and ridiculous.

Celebrity is presented as an all-encompassing, totalizing phenomenon which touches everyone. Most newspapers and magazines are full of details about celebrities' lives and goings-on. Even the more serious publications can be keen to tell us what apparently random celebrities think about various current affairs. However, as we shall see, the media are an unreliable guide to the popularity of celebrity: theirs is too vested an interest. I suggest that some simple statistics will make my antipathetic stance the most plausible and representative one to take. There are millions of us who are not interested in celebrities. In fact, we are in the majority. Over 98 per cent of the population of Britain does not buy *Hello!*; over 80 per cent does not even read any celebrity magazine. Many readers are probably just forced to encounter the publications while waiting for doctors, dentists and hairdressers. Viewing figures for the most popular soap operas in the UK are frequently under 10 million, which means that more than 80 per cent of the country has found other things to do rather than watch them. I admit that celebrity features prominently in British society, and in much of the West, but I deny its domination. And my strangeness to celebrity makes me well placed to write about it. For decades anthropologists have been pitching up in societies they knew little about, and soon learnt enough to write about them. A stranger's eye can be perceptive, even if she dislikes, or wants to laugh at, what she sees.

My methods for coping with, and finding out about, this strange world have been straightforward. I read books and articles, wrote letters and emails, surfed the Web and talked to people. I have explored the literature on celebrity and wildlife films, interviewed celebrity conservationists, read their autobiographies and biographies, and talked to wildlife filmmakers, presenters and conservation NGO staff; interviews and personal communications are anonymized and referred to as 'Sources' in the notes. I have studied the structure of the conservation NGO sector in particular regions. I have examined websites and followed particular conservation campaigns. The result is not an exhaustive survey; it was not intended to be. Nor have I followed the work of particular celebrities in depth. I am more interested in the conservation celebretariat as a whole.

Many people have assisted during the course of writing this book. Mahesh Rangarajan helped to get it off the ground; his enthusiasm for the project and extraordinary memory prompted some wonderful leads. Tamsine O'Riordan and Susannah Trefgarne have been patient at Zed, and arranged for several useful anonymous reviews – my thanks to those readers. I also thank Amanda Stronza, Andrew Mittelman, Ashish Kothari, Barbara Brower, Barbara F. Wolf, Bernardo Peredo, Bram Büscher, Christopher Thoms, Chuck Willer, Crystal Fortwangler, David Hoffman, David M. Hughes, Dian Deva, Dilys Roe, Steve Fraser, Ellen Brown, Fiona Nagle, Francine Madden, Grazia Borrini-Feyerabend, Guillermo Rodriguez-Navarro, Jason Morris, Jessica Budds, Julie Brugger, Ken MacDonald, Lauren Rickards, Linda Robson, M. Ferrari, M. Castelo, Mark Dowie, Matt Walpole, Maya Fischhoff, Michael Brown, Peter Wilshusen, Priscilla

Weeks, Rob Law, Roly Russell, Roy Maconachie, Sandy Gauntlett, Marianne Schmink, Serena Agostino, Shauna McGarvey, Simon Batterbury, Sugato Dutt, Terence Hay-Edie, Tom Blomley, Brendon Bromwich and Will Hurd, who, among others, all suggested names to be considered in a list of celebrity and charismatic conservationists. Numerous employees of conservation NGOs were generous with their time; many wildlife filmmakers, employees of the British Broadcasting Corporation (BBC) and presenters' agents were similarly patient. Particular thanks to Jeremy Bristow, Tim Scoones, Toby Sinclair, Beverly and Dereck Joubert, Brian Palmer, Paul Redman, Jo Sarsby, Joe Yaggi, Bianca Keeley, Martin Atkin, Richard Brock, Steven Fairchild, David Curl, William Goodchild, Ashima Narain, Charlie Mayhew, Vicky Mellor, Mike Rands, Marcus Colchester, Jill Inglis and Cathy Dean.

Colleagues and students at the University of Manchester have been sounding boards for some of my ideas. I would like to thank the Society and Environment Research Group (SERG), especially Noel Castree, Tony Bebbington, Gavin Bridge, Admos Chimhowu and Phillip Woodhouse. I would also like to thank the Environment and Development Reading Group, especially Katie Scholfield, George Holmes, Hilary Gilbert, Emmanuel Nuesiri, Lorraine Moore, Lisa Ficklin, Lindsay Stringer, Rupert Frederichsen and Tomas Frederiksen. The class attending the Conservation and Development course in 2007–08 at Manchester, the best it has been my privilege to teach, made me rethink my ideas about all sorts of things. Emma Casey and the Development Management students in Uganda 2009 worked on the Introduction.

I owe a great deal to Jim Igoe and Katja Neves-Graca for their patient explaining of spectacle to me, and for their enthusiasm for this project and for reading it in various forms. Rosaleen Duffy, Bill Adams, Kathy Homewood, Sian Sullivan, Kit Vaughan, Liz Garland, Lindsey Gilson and Mark Dowie read early drafts. Hassan Sachedina spent three hours in the stacks of the Bodleian Library in Oxford reading *Hello!* magazine with me, and still spoke to me afterwards. Libby Lester, Brett Hutchins, Graham Huggan, Cheryl Lousley, William Beinart, Malcolm Draper, Max Boykoff and Michael Goodman discovered and explored the interaction of celebrity and the environment at the same time as I did. It has been wonderful to be able to share ideas, early manuscripts, projects and leads with them. Their generosity has been as welcome as their criticism. Long may this collegial spirit continue.

The Economic and Social Research Council (ESRC) supported this work through a three-year Research Fellowship on the Social Impacts of

Protected Areas (RES-000-27-0174). I thank Eric Pawson, at the Department of Geography at the University of Canterbury, Christchurch, Colin Filer at the Resource Management in Asia-Pacific Programme (RMAP) of the Australian National University in Canberra, and Kartik Shanker, Meera Oomen and Ravi Chellam of the Ashoka Trust for Ecology and Environment (ATREE), Bangalore, for hosting me for part of that fellowship. I am also grateful for opportunities to test the ideas in this book in presentations at all of these institutions, as well as to Rohan D'Souza of the Centre for Studies in Science Policy at the Jawaharlal Nehru University, the Nature Conservation Foundation, Mysore, DESTIN at the London School of Economics and the IDPM at the University of Manchester for more opportunities of the same. Thanks also to all who attended the symposium on capitalism and conservation which I convened in Manchester with Professor Duffy in 2008, where these ideas were further refined.

Elements of the argument of this book have been explored in previous publications. I thank *Media, Culture and Society* for permission to reproduce parts of my paper, 'Powerful Environmentalisms: Conservation, Celebrity and Capitalism' (2008, 30 (4): 551–68) and *Media International Australia* for permission to reproduce parts of 'Celebrity Conservation: Interpreting the Irwins' (2008, 127: 96–108).

Finally to family and friends: Ilfra Pink's descendants made many useful suggestions on the front cover, and cast even more useful aspersions on the worth of this project. Dr David Gee introduced me to Oscar Wilde; he, my brother and sisters paid far more attention to my interest in this topic than it deserved. My parents read and commented on the penultimate manuscript in great detail. Tekla, Rosie and Emily are just wonderful – the best possible reasons to start, and stop, writing.

To Tekla, Rosie and Emily,
never my celebrities.

1 | Introduction

> The aim of the liar is simply to charm, to delight, to give pleasure. He
> is the very basis of civilized society. (Oscar Wilde, *The Decay of Lying*)

The authorized biography of Sir Laurens van der Post (author and conservationist) caused a stir. Van der Post had been revered by millions
as a sage of wilderness and conservation. He had been a guru to Prince
Charles (British royalty) and an adviser to Margaret Thatcher (when she
was the British Prime Minister). He had been a mystic and a secular
saint. Yet J. D. F. Jones's *Storyteller: The Many Lives of Laurens van der Post*
exposed him as a liar, philanderer and paedophile.[1] Jones showed that
van der Post had distorted many aspects of his life, deceiving the public
and those close to him in pursuit of greatness, sex and popularity.

The sordid details of van der Post's corruption are not the focus of
this enquiry. This is not that sort of book.[2] What I find more interesting
is the way van der Post's followers reacted to these revelations. For the
diehards, their hero was still a great and wonderful man.[3] Van der Post
is significant not because he lied, but because his fabrications had such
influence and because people believed in him so strongly. They owed their
understanding of African environments, wildlife and people to his words
and ideas. Responding to Jones's book, Christopher Booker described
sitting 'entranced while he spoke of the Kalahari or African wildlife'.[4] Dea
Birkett observed that we 'needed to believe van der Post. He pandered to
a part of the Western imagination that longs for the so-called natural – a
pristine wilderness and untouched primitives.'[5]

I find it fascinating that conservation thinking, hopes, fears, plans
and practices can be vested in individuals. Why do their ideas become
so powerful? Why are their audiences so credulous? Why do they cling
so tightly to their captains, and to their captains' beliefs?

Unfortunately Jones's book, as many reviewers noted, could not explain
van der Post's appeal. Jones just demolishes every falsehood that van
der Post created about himself. He does not consider why his subject's
deceptions were so beguiling. Van der Post's supporters insisted that they
realized the stories he spun were embellished, and that 'this tendency to
embroider life into "story" was all part of the magic'.[6] We will not be able
to explain the appeal of falsehoods simply by uncovering the truth.

To answer my questions, we need to see van der Post as but one example of the work of celebrity in conservation. We shall have to forget his deceptions, and look at the public construction and consumption of his persona and writings, and those of others like him. There is a multitude of conservationists who enjoy fame and influence (and without van der Post's inventions). By examining their ideas, actions, claims, consequences and publicity, the responses they elicit and the uses the conservation movement makes of them, we can suggest some answers to my questions about the source and nature of their influence. That is the purpose of this book.

In the process of exploring these issues I have found it useful to distinguish between different varieties of conservation celebrity. I separate those who are already famous, and who lend their fame to conservation, from those who win fame from their conservation work. The latter we can divide into wildlife film presenters, celebrity conservationists and conservation 'celeactors' (fictional characters). Behind the celebrities stand ranks of charismatic, wealthy or powerful individuals who also promote conservation. The work of all of these will be explored in the pages that follow.

I shall argue that the interaction between celebrity and conservation is decades old, suggesting that it has accelerated of late, partly because of changes in the production of celebrity and in the organization and funding of conservation. The growth of conservation NGOs has provided new vectors for celebrity in conservation. They guide celebrities' charitable work, seek celebrity endorsement and support the work of celebrity conservationists themselves. More fundamentally, the flourishing of celebrity conservation is part of an ever-closer intertwining of conservation and corporate capitalism. Companies are greening, with varying degrees of sincerity and effectiveness, because being green enhances sales. Conservation is becoming more commercial because selling commodities provides funds. Far from restricting the activities of capitalism, conservation is becoming one of the means by which profit is generated. Celebrity promotion, the investments of rich executives, and the wealthy social networks of charismatic conservationists are an important, but as yet unremarked, part of this process.

I shall show that celebrity conservation alters the world it tries to save. It can promote an imagined world which may not exist. Yet this very promotion can help to realize such visions. The funding celebrity amasses conjures the dreams into existence. Celebrity also advances particular types of conservation. It can strengthen the conservation of wilderness, charismatic species and work involving indigenous peoples or heroes more easily than other conservation initiatives. This can disadvantage conservation that is not so mediagenic. More subtly, mediagenic conservation can readily promote market solutions for conservation while making certain forms of conservation injustice harder to see.

I shall suggest that perhaps the most insidious and pervasive influence is on countless individuals' relationships with the wild. In industrial urban societies, people seek to reconnect with nature by vicariously participating in the activities conservationists and celebrities support. At a time when conservationists are calling for people to restore relationships with the wild, many can do so simply by following the exploits of celebrities. People need celebrities to get close to nature on their behalf when they themselves cannot.

Celebrity conservation produces images that are commodities in themselves, sold or used to elicit donors' support, and which are consumed with little awareness of these images' origins or conditions of production. It is difficult to imagine an alternative, for celebrity is deeply rooted in the very fabric of modern democracy. As conservation expands in tandem with philanthropy, the challenge NGOs, donors and their critics face is how to encourage investigations of the relationships that lie behind conservation's images.

An outline of the book

Chapter 2 introduces the two main issues that this book examines – celebrity and conservation. Its purpose is to acquaint the uninitiated in either topic with recent writings, in order to prepare them for the arguments in the rest of the book. Thereafter the book falls into two parts. The next three chapters are more descriptive, the final three more analytical.

Chapters 3 to 5 describe the business of celebrity conservation, dealing in turn with celebrities who support environmentalism, wildlife filmmakers and celebrity conservationists. Chapter 3 plots the contours of celebrities' support for environmental and conservation causes, particularly climate change. It considers the charge that celebrities can make themselves vulnerable to criticism by supporting such causes. Chapter 4 looks at wildlife films and the nature portrayed by them. It explores the tension between audience demands that wildlife films be authentic and the requirement of the industry that it produces commodities for sale. Chapter 5 considers the people who have won fame from their conservation work. I examine what their work involves and the social,

3

political and economic forces that have created them. These celebrities' associations with nature are often hallmarks of personal authenticity, but they can only be properly understood as products of forces much larger than their own personalities. Each of these chapters also serves to demonstrate a different aspect of celebrity conservation. Celebrity conservation is strong and powerful (Chapter 3); it is perceived to be authentic and true (Chapter 4), and yet it is a socially constructed world shaped by audiences. Its images and personalities can be understood only in their broader social and historical contexts (Chapter 5).

Chapters 6 to 8 examine the forces that have shaped the interaction of celebrity and conservation, the discontent with this interaction, and the world it creates. Chapter 6 attempts to explain the proliferation of celebrity in conservation. It discusses trends in the nature of celebrity and conservation NGOs which have made them mutually dependent. It also considers trends in the power of foundations and rich individuals as well as corporate needs to support green causes. It examines the implications of recent trends in giving by the wealthy for the democratic nature of conservation work. Chapter 7 looks at a variety of dissatisfaction with celebrity conservation. I consider the charge that celebrities who adopt conservation causes are incompetent at best and often hypocritical. I also examine the role of violence in conservation strategies that celebrities support. I argue that we cannot blame celebrity for the problems at work; they are generic to the conservation movement. Chapter 8 examines some of the more profound consequences of celebrity for conservation. It looks at what these developments portend for popular participation in the environmental movement as a whole. It examines the nature of the mediagenic world in whose image our own world is being remade.

Readers may share my ignorance of the identity and achievements of some famous people. To avoid this I have assumed that no one is so famous that everyone will recognize them.[7] *Whenever a famous person is mentioned for the first time in the text I explain why you might be expected to have heard of them.* I make no exceptions, not for Nelson Mandela (Africa's greatest statesman) nor the late Princess Diana (of the British royal family). If you spot exceptions, then either they are careless mistakes on my part, or these individuals have been mentioned in earlier pages (including tables), or they are academic writers of whom I do not expect you to have heard, but whose writings you will find listed in the Bibliography.

Finally, scattered through the text are several thoughts and phrases of Oscar Wilde (wit and writer).[8] He is a useful author for thinking about celebrity, although he lived in the nineteenth century just before the dawn of celebrity as we know it. Wilde was an attention seeker throughout his adult life, and preoccupied by fame, particularly his own. He understood that for the well-known 'there is only one thing in the world worse than being talked about, and that is not being talked about' (*The Picture of Dorian Gray*). His bitter observation in prison that 'between the famous and infamous there is but one step, if so much as one' (*De Profundis*) captures one of the qualities of contemporary celebrity. He was fascinated, too, by charisma, noting in *Dorian Gray* that '[t]here was something terribly enthralling in the exercise of influence'.[9]

There is also a useful contrast between the respective fates of Wilde and van der Post. Both were writers and each was much concerned with his own greatness. There are some parallels, too, in the pain they caused to those who loved them while seeking their own emotional and sexual fulfilment. There are also key differences: Wilde was vilified in his own lifetime, van der Post was lionized. Most importantly, van der Post represented authenticity. He claimed to be real and to be able to show people 'the real Africa'.[10] Wilde played with authenticity, laughed at it, and questioned its meaning. Van der Post serves well as an example of the role of authenticity in conservation, as well as of liars in society. Wilde proves an excellent commentator.

Wilde's banter should not always be taken too seriously; it certainly was not by Wilde himself. As George Orwell (author) observed of him, one could never be sure if his words, or the man himself, ever meant anything.[11] I sought to include his aphorisms at first because they were funny, outrageous and apposite. I hoped that they might offer some light relief. I found, however, that they became more important than that. The more I examined the world of celebrity conservation, the more I realized that this is a realm that tends to prove Wilde remarkably right. His ridiculous ideas become mere descriptions, or prophecies fulfilled. Wilde's commentary makes it easier to see the antiquity of some of the processes and consequences of celebrity conservation and to see apparently new phenomena as reworkings of much older practices.

2 | Combining celebrity and the environment

The truth about the life of a man is not what he does, but the legend
which he creates around himself. (Oscar Wilde, to Jacques Daurelle)

This book addresses two quite different topics, celebrity and the environment, each of which requires a separate introduction summarizing recent
writings and developments. I shall examine first the spate of writings in
the new sub-discipline of celebrity studies, and look at the nature, causes
and effects of celebrity and its curious relationships with democracy. I
then consider environmentalism and conservation, exploring the changing nature and growing power of the conservation movement and its
social impacts. Finally, I demonstrate why celebrity is so important for
understanding the conservation movement, and vice versa.

On celebrity

The origins, nature and consequences of celebrity are the focus of
a burgeoning sub-discipline: celebrity studies.[1] Turner observes that
celebrities are those whose private lives attract more attention than their
professional lives.[2] They are people who experience a degree of incongru-
ence between the attention normally given to their work and the publicity
their lives receive. In Boorstin's famous phrase, '[t]he celebrity is a person
who is known for his well-knownness.'[3]

Celebrities are generally synonymous with the great and the good,
but, as Rojek notes, what we celebrate is also their power to transgress,
their latitude of excessive behaviour, their profligate consumption of
power, beauty, money and luxury, their dwelling in 'a different world
than the rest of us [which] seems to give them licence to do things we
can only dream about'.[4] Indeed Rojek extends the argument. The desire
and pressure to become famous, the experience of 'achievement famine', have encouraged some people to pursue notoriety. There are people
who have found a place in the celebretariat (the word is Rojek's) because
of their evil deeds.[5]

Scholars of celebrity are united in emphasizing that celebrity is not a
recent phenomenon. One of the principal texts, Daniel Boorstin's book
The Image, was first published in 1961, and remains a fresh and percep-

tive read. Boorstin, Rojek and Gamson trace the origins of contemporary fame to the spread of printing presses and newspapers in the nineteenth century (Boorstin calls it the Graphic Revolution). Contemporary celebrity is characterized by the 'illusion of intimacy, the sense of being an exalted confrère, that is part of celebrity status in the age of mass media'.[6] It begins with the spread of cinema. When Griffith developed close-up shots of stars' faces (1910) it allowed people to observe, and identify with, the actors and actresses much more closely; Griffith called it photographing thought.[7]

Rojek offers a typology of celebrities. He suggests that some people are ascribed fame from birth, such as royalty, some achieve fame through great deeds, such as athletes and sports stars, and some are attributed fame by the media, such as the competitors on *Big Brother*. His categories recall Shakespeare: 'some are born great, others achieve greatness, and some have greatness thrust upon them'.[8] The difference between Shakespeare's time and ours, however, is in what constitutes greatness. As Boorstin observed when quoting those lines '[i]t never occurred to [Shakespeare] to mention those who hired public relations experts and press secretaries to make themselves look great.'[9]

How do we explain fame? One school of thought needs to be discounted straight away. Some people explain celebrity by virtue of celebrities' personal qualities, their beauty and skill or the force of their personalities. The trouble with this argument is that, while possessing such characteristics might ease some of the representational processes involved in creating celebrity, no merit or distinction is strictly necessary. There is little that skilled photographers, clothes designers, directors, speech writers or recording technicians cannot conceal, and even fewer limits to the inventive powers of agents, managers and publicists. There are many people with wonderful qualities who do not win any fame – and others with few who do. It is possible to manufacture celebrity out of little.

The mistake here is to equate celebrity with charisma. It is an understandable mistake, for both, in Wilde's words, deal with legends, but the legends of celebrity and charisma are forged in quite different ways. Celebrities' legends are commercially produced and depend on the media, whereas charisma is recognized through direct personal contact.[10]

Weber considered charismatic authority in his treatise *Economy and Society*, arguing that charisma is seen in individuals with extraordinary or exceptional powers and qualities, and that charismatic leaders can be thought of as superhuman or magical by their followers.[11] Charisma, however, is not a property solely of the individual. Whatever special qualities a charismatic leader may have, charisma is a quality conferred by followers, as much as it is claimed by great men and women. Weber insists that:

> What alone is important is how the individual is actually regarded by those subject to charismatic authority, by his 'followers' or 'disciples' ... It is recognition on the part of those subject to authority which is decisive for the validity of charisma ... The basis [of any claim to legitimacy] lies ... in the conception that it is the duty of those subject to charismatic authority to recognize its genuineness and to act accordingly. (Weber 1968 [1914]: 242)

It follows that if we are to understand the hold that charismatic leaders have on people, we cannot focus on the leaders alone. We also have to examine their followers, the networks and societies of which they are part. Beauty, greatness and excitement lie in the beholder's eye. This is visible in the strongly contrasting reactions charismatic leaders can provoke in different audiences. Jim Jones (leader of a cult which exterminated itself in a mass suicide and murder in Guyana in 1978) was an inspirational leader to a few hundred people, but an evil, manipulative and paranoid deceiver to the rest of the world. The boundary line between a powerful figure who commands respect, and an arrogant, conceited twerp can be thin.

Weber observed that charismatic authority tends to become incorporated into rational bureaucratic rule or traditional authority, or both. As charismatic power becomes more mundane it often becomes orientated towards raising money and providing for the group's needs. We shall explore in Chapter 5 how this process in itself provides the impetus to create new generations of charismatic conservationists.

In order to understand celebrity, therefore, a more convincing explanation than the personal charm of charisma is required. More robust arguments explain fame by analysing the celebretariat as industrial products. Celebrities exist because they make money for others. As one disillusioned and retired celebrity wildlife presenter put it to me, when you are famous you are but a cog in a machine, your fame has nothing to do with you; it is an attribute required by a broader system, not something which you generate yourself.[12] Viewing fame as an industry requires understanding the businesses that produce celebrity, and explaining the forces driving its consumption.

In the early years of the film industry (about 1910 onwards) producers learned that the best way to differentiate their products from others was to focus attention on the actors and actresses of the film. By paying stars outrageous salaries (or even faking their deaths), and releasing tantalizing details about what they were really like off-camera, producers found that they could fill the cinemas.[13] An organized star system for the cinema was in place by the second decade of the twentieth century.[14] The industry of fame has grown as the products that celebrities can sell have expanded from films to newspapers and magazines, television shows and advertising slots, and all sorts of other goods.[15] The growth of celebrity is a product of the growth of mass media and the film industries of Hollywood and Bollywood, the proliferation of newspapers and glossy magazines, television and its channels, and the Internet.

The increasing concentration of ownership of the media industry means that different outlets of the same company will feature each other's products: newspapers may promote celebrities featured in magazines and on television channels owned by the same company. The corollary is the aggressive dismissal, or silence, that rival networks display to each other's celebrity wares. Turner provides two illuminating examples: Paul Burrell (butler to Princess Diana) was wooed by all the tabloids for his story, and then lambasted by all those who lost the competition. Stuart Diver (lone survivor of a landslide in Australia) could only escape the media scrum by selling his story to one outlet, thereby making his experience one company's product, and un-newsworthy to the others.[16]

The weakness of accounts that dwell solely on the forces organizing and producing fame is that they fail to explain why there should be such a ready market for these products. Why do people buy *Hello!* or *OK!* magazine, why are they interested in celebrity gossip and the trivia of celebrities daily lives? The theories I have found most illuminating are the structuralist explanations of celebrity. These emphasize the utility of celebrity for political and economic regimes, and particularly for capitalism. The 'culture industry thesis' holds that celebrity perpetrates false consciousness, expressing 'an ideology of heroic individualism, upward mobility and choice in social conditions where standardisation, monotony and routine prevail'.[17] It promotes an imaginative means of escaping the drudgery of day-to-day life, even the hope of realizing celebrities' incredible lives oneself.[18] It solves 'the problem of slavery ... by entertaining the slaves'.[19] Alternatively, some analysts see the alienations of capitalism as fuelling a need for celebrities, for through them we can vicariously live better lives. We might not be able to enjoy wealth, luxury, glamour or attention ourselves, but we can observe others enjoying it so closely that

9

this provides some satisfaction. From this viewpoint celebrities are less the prescription decreed from above to oil the workings of capitalism, and more a tonic demanded by estranged masses. Both views hold that celebrities exist to facilitate, increase and encourage consumption.

The demand for celebrity is fuelled therefore by continuing inequality. It works best where the lives of a wealthy few are highly visible and appear incredibly wonderful to the vast majority of society (in countries like the USA, UK and India). It is also a consequence of changing social circumstances. Celebrity reflects the predominance of new urban industrial living, 'partly a product of the world of the stranger, wherein the individual is uprooted from family and community and relocated in the anonymous city, in which social relations are often glancing, episodic and unstable'.[20] Celebrity compensates for this isolation, filling the void with 'para-social relations', intimacy constructed by the media, with people we do not know.

As Rojek notes, the difficulty with these structural explanations is that they do not appear to have involved much empirical work with any consumers of celebrity.[21] Post-structuralist accounts collect more data, report more diversity of positions, and refuse to be determined by economic dictat. These explanations show how celebrities are constructed and shaped by audiences and fans. Powerful forces directing audience choice certainly exist, but the end products reflect multiple interactions between producers and consumers of celebrity images.

Gamson's discussions with audiences suggest tensions which structuralist models could not have predicted.[22] He found groups who identified with and fantasized about celebrities, and who largely believed the texts and images presented to them. Others were fully aware of the techniques required to produce and maintain fame and enjoyed pulling apart the publicity stunts and pseudo-events. What he does not quite explain, however, is why the audiences should exist in the first place. In this respect the structuralist arguments are more useful.

A powerful theme running throughout celebrity studies is the quest for authenticity. Many audiences want to know what celebrities are 'really' like. One of the attractions of being famous is that it offers access to repeated personal encounters with other celebrities, thus allowing knowledge of them.[23] The pursuit of authenticity, however, is also a continual source of instability. The fact that fame is not the result of individual desert or effort, but the product of an industry, introduces a perpetual tension in celebrity status, and audiences' relations with celebrity, for it suggests that what they are really like may not explain their public prominence. Gamson's analysis of celebrity texts through the twentieth century shows that they have continually had to devise new ways of challenging threats to the authenticity of celebrity, inviting audiences first behind the image of celebrity to view their real lives in action, and then later to see images in production.[24]

Some commentators on the phenomenon of celebrity are filled with dismay at what they see. Ferris describes a body of writing about it which treats celebrity as pathology.[25] For many observers the rise of celebrity seems to be part of an unintelligent cultural shift, one that 'privileges the momentary, the visual and the sensational over the enduring, the written and the rational'.[26] Celebrities are a manifestation of the lack of authenticity in society. They are people and personalities fabricated by the media for economic and political ends. They numb thought, protest and effective engagement with the reality of our surroundings, 'concealing the meaninglessness of modern life and ... reinforcing the power of commodity culture'.[27] Boorstin complains that:

> This is the age of contrivance. The artificial has become so commonplace that the natural seems contrived. The natural is the 'un-' and the 'non-'.
> It is the age of the ... 'unabridged' novel (abridgement is the norm) of the 'uncut' version of the movie ... Fact itself has become 'nonfiction'.
> (Boorstin 1992 [1961]: 254; italics in the original)

Others defend the way celebrities make news direct and personal, and the way they have to respond to popular pressure. Viewed thus, celebrities are truly democratic creations. Turner reports Hartley's argument that celebrities can be put to all sorts of constructive ends and that television can be used to teach citizenship.[28]

The power that fame gives in contemporary society to speak out on all manner of things is particularly controversial. It is not quite clear to me why celebrities are able to enjoy this influence. When I read about, for example, a debate on more nuclear power stations in Britain, I do not find that the stance of Virginia Westwood (fashion designer) casts any substantial light on the issue.[29] Yet her opinions have been reported in major newspapers. Why are celebrities given this power to intervene in such disparate causes? Part of the answer is that celebrities are symbols, they condense large amounts of information into relatively simple, visible signs. When Beijing handed over the Olympic banner to London in 2008, David Beckham (soccer player) was on centre stage, and who better than he, who personifies success and greatness, to reassure the world that the 2012 Olympics are in good hands? On the other hand such interventions can be risky for public figures. Celebrities' perpetual instability, 'at once real and artificial, spontaneous and programmed, performing themselves and being themselves' is foregrounded whenever they adopt good causes.[30] For here they are obviously not authorities, and clearly performers.

John Street offers a compelling apology for the intrusion of celebrity into political affairs.[31] He examines the celebrification of politicians, and the political acts and stances of celebrities. With respect to celebrified politicians, he argues that representative democracies require politicians to communicate their understanding of politics and issues to electorates. They do this through their dress, their language, their metaphors, their body language and by developing a public persona. Style matters. News coverage of a politician behaving like a rock star may in some instances be a trivializing of politics, the swamping of substance with style, but not always. Nothing substantive can be appreciated without style. Accordingly,

> [a]doption of the trappings of popular celebrity is not a trivial gesture towards fashion or a minor detail of political communication, but instead lies at the heart of the notion of political representation itself. (Street 2004: 447)

Electorates are always evaluating and making decisions on the basis of performance. Without style nothing can be communicated or understood. Perhaps Wilde was right to claim that 'in matters of grave importance, style, not sincerity is the vital thing'.[32] Street observes that all politicians are celebrities of a sort, 'only some are more convincing, more "authentic" performers than others'.[33]

With respect to celebrities' political acts Street argues that their bonds with their fans do give them some authority to speak, for they clearly understand what their fans want and how they think. He also argues that where the political establishment gives no space or credence to particular ideas or actions, celebrities can be the authentic voice of the people. This is most clearly visible where musicians have led opposition to oppressive states (East Germany, Hungary, the USSR), but also applies where states appear to be unable to take effective action, for example in African famines (Ethiopia and Darfur), deforestation in the Amazon, or climate change.

Street is careful to stress that these arguments do not endorse all styles or incidences of celebrity politics. More generally, Turner, Ferris and Gamson advocate neither condemnation nor approbation of celebrity culture. Disapproval risks abandoning a critical analytical stance, and can fail to understand how audiences deal proactively, not passively, with celebrity culture. The enthusiast risks missing the broader structures and choices of which celebrities are part. Turner insists, with respect to the activities and choices that celebrity presents to us, that 'we must first consider the conditions of production that determined what choices are actually on offer in the first place'.[34]

It is essential to examine the choices presented to us by celebrity conservation critically. They appear as free, reasonable, good and even heroic, but they are the product of particular worldviews and particular industries (such as wildlife film-making). They are the result of specific interactions between conservation organizations, consumers, audiences, states and industry. The conservation agenda is not given in nature, it is created by people. We must understand how and why celebrity conservation agendas are constructed.

Analysing celebrity conservation thus will not just explain attempts to save the world. One of my principal observations about conservation is that it does far more than merely preserving the world. It actively creates and remakes it.[35] The images and ideas that inspire these creative processes abound in the work of celebrity conservation. If we want to understand what sort of world celebrity conservation is creating, we will need to pay close attention to the techniques of representation celebrity conservation uses and to the ideals in whose image our world is being remade.

On environmentalism and conservation

There are many different varieties of environmentalism, which makes examining the interactions of celebrity and the environment complicated.[36] Which environment, or whose, should we examine? Limiting the scope of the project makes my task easier. Wildlife, biodiversity and landscape conservation, rather than environmentalism more generally, will be my main subjects, though I shall refer to more general environmental causes as well. The interaction of celebrity with conservation provides quite enough to be getting on with. Conservation seems to have had a much longer and more sustained interaction with celebrities than more general environmental causes. The flourishing of celebrity support for measures to combat climate change, which I examine in Chapter 3, is a relatively recent phenomenon, but the support of royalty for conservation causes, the production of films about wildlife and how it is threatened, and the creation of celebrity conservationists who champion the cause of landscape and wildlife, have been going on for decades.

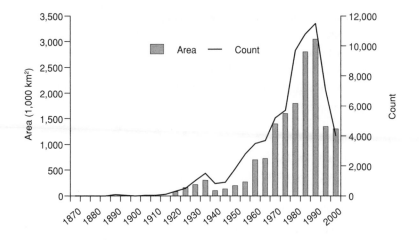

FIGURE 2.1 The global growth of protected areas (*Source*: The World Database of Protected Areas, 2005)

I examine three aspects of the conservation movement in the rest of this chapter. First, I describe its increasing power, influence and wealth, due in part to its changing relationship with capitalism. Second, I explore its intellectual power and public popularity, and the role of science and environmental narratives in making conservation concerns urgent, relevant and important. Third, I look at the consequences of conservation, suggesting that it is not just a good cause that saves wildlife and the environment, but rather needs to be seen to distribute fortune and misfortune. Once we appreciate that, we can then explore who wins, and who loses, from celebrity's support of conservation causes.

Conservation and capitalism The growing influence of the conservation movement is visible in several ways. We can see it in the gradual expansion of the number and extent of protected areas across the planet (Figure 2.1). Protected areas (national parks, game reserves and forest reserves) now cover about 12 per cent of the Earth's land surface, with much of the increase coming in the last twenty-five years.[37] Some of these protected areas exist only on paper, with little monitoring or enforcement, but the underlying trend is unmistakable.[38] There are countries that forbid human residence in more than 30 per cent of their territory. The current generation is living in a much more actively conserved world than any previous one.

We can see it in the growth in size and wealth of the larger conservation

NGOs. I examine this in more detail in Chapter 6, but suffice to say that there are now four large conservation organizations at work globally: the Nature Conservancy, the Worldwide Fund for Nature (WWF), Conservation International and the Wildlife Conservation Society. It is vital to realize the power and scale of these organizations. They are some of the biggest NGOs in the world employing tens of thousands of people and controlling billions of dollars, and with global projects and influence. They are highly visible, particularly in the West; the WWF's panda logo is one of the most successful of all. They enjoy close relations with powerful corporations.[39] One of them (Conservation International) is a relatively new arrival, others have expanded gradually. They are complemented by a continually burgeoning sector of smaller conservation NGOs.

We can see it in the increasing international recognition of the importance of environmental causes. Earth Summits are now held once a decade to plan and enact sustainable development. Earth Days have spread to many countries. Environmental activists are recognized as UN Messengers of Peace. Two of the more recent Nobel Peace Prizes have been awarded to environmentalists (Wangari Maathai in 2004, Al Gore and the Intergovernmental Panel on Climate Change in 2007).

The growth in power and influence of the environmental movement reflects the fact that capitalist policies and values are integral to conservation practice, and that conservation policies are an ever more prominent part of economic growth strategies. The clearest example can be seen in the growth in tourism. National Parks have, since Yellowstone, been recognized as valuable tourism magnets. In poorer economies in particular, protected areas are perceived to be a means of promoting tourism and earning hard foreign currency. Ecotourism is an important business; it has been growing dramatically and is worth billions of dollars annually.[40]

Another aspect is the growth in the mitigation and offset industry. With the rise of Geographical Information Systems, conservation has become more sophisticated and knowledgeable about the extent and importance of particular habitats. It is now possible to assess how serious the loss of habitat to a mine or a dam might be and suggest appropriate alternative areas which can be conserved more adequately in lieu of the damaged areas.[41] Conservation estate thus grows in tandem with development. Finally, many corporations, large and small, want to act responsibly and as appropriately as they can towards the environment, and a great many more want to appear 'green' even if they cannot act it. Corporate endorsement of conservation causes and conservation NGOs is now a major element of everyday life.

I do not wish to overextend these arguments. Conservation has become more important to capitalism, but it is not necessarily integral to it. Business leaders may care about the environment, but they risk destroying their businesses if they do not remain profitable. Environmental causes remain chronically underfunded: the global annual deficit of protected area budgets is about $2 billion, and, as we shall see, environmental charities attract far fewer funds than do organizations advancing human health and welfare.[42] One of the reasons why battles to save particular places from specific developments (Dinosaur monument in the USA, the Franklin River and Jarvis Bay in Australia, the west coast forests of New Zealand) are iconic is that they stand out as exceptions to the general march of capitalist progress and its altering of the surface of the Earth.

Conservation, nevertheless, is becoming an increasingly powerful and influential movement. In the process, as I have argued elsewhere (in *Nature Unbound*), conservation and capitalism are becoming more tightly entwined. The ever-increasing prominence of celebrity within environmental and conservation causes is both illustrative of, and a driving force in, that interweaving. Capitalism requires steady growth; it must continually find new commodities and markets for them. Celebrity, married to conservation, is one of the means of creating and expanding new markets.

Science and power Part of the power of conservation is economic and political, but its greater strength is its intellectual authority. Environmentalism and conservation have the authority of science. There are simply hundreds of thousands of biologists, ecologists, botanists, zoologists, anthropologists, hydrologists, climatologists and geographers whose collective writings provide the foundation for environmental and conservation concerns. Environmental and conservation problems matter because they are urgently true.

Environmental science, however, is powerful not just because it can be true. Its strength does not only depend on its veracity. Indeed, on occasion, it does not need to be right to be powerful. The irrelevance of truth to the scientific power is visible most clearly in cases where scientists and their research have been wrong, but they have been believed, promulgated and applied to policy none the less. In these circumstances truth cannot explain popular authority.[43]

There have been a number of famous cases in environmental science where scientists, indeed the whole policy community including government departments and NGOs, have been profoundly wrong about the nature and causes of environmental change, and particularly anthropogenic degradation. The starkest comes from Guinea in West Africa. Here one of the major environmental concerns was deforestation caused by bad farming practices, until anthropologists James Fairhead and Melissa Leach suggested that there was in fact much evidence for forests being planted by people. They argued that human interventions had tamed a landscape composed of grassland swept by wild fires into a mosaic of woods and grassland which observers mistook for a retreating forest.[44] Another case is the Himalayan degradation narrative. The Himalayas were thought to be a clear case of rapidly changing use by people, overuse and then decline.[45] Population increase and the loss of farmland through poor husbandry were pushing farmers on to ever steeper slopes. Writers portrayed grim pictures of people caught in the midst of unproductive lands, with nowhere left to go to seek good farms and long journeys to travel for firewood from rapidly receding forests. However, investigation by Thompson and colleagues could not find consistent data to back up these claims.[46] They also objected to the fact that these theories said little about local responses to environmental conditions.[47] Ives and Messerli argued that Himalayan landscapes are not a crisis zone, but there is a variety of rates and timings of environmental change, resulting in a mosaic of places with more environmental problems, and places with few, if any.[48]

There are other examples of successful scientific failures. The forces that erroneously institutionalized the theories of deforestation in Guinea, or erosion in the Himalayas, are common to academia and government in all parts of the world. Mortimore and Richards's work in West Africa has emphasized the ingenuity and inventiveness of farmers, which crisis narratives of helplessness in the face of desertification, or want of agricultural expertise, could not properly understand.[49] I have worked on a game reserve in Tanzania from which local pastoralists were expelled in the 1980s because of fears that they were causing environmental degradation due to overgrazing.[50] Yet the data did not add up, for this same supposedly degrading landscape was sustaining an increasing number of cattle, which would not have been breeding so healthily if they were losing condition on an overgrazed range.[51] Then there is the case of the overpopulation of Machakos, a region close to Nairobi in Kenya which was once feared to be an erosion catastrophe incapable of supporting more people, but which experienced a sixfold increase in population and the transformation of its landscape into a productive gardenscape. People and wages from Nairobi combined with new crops like coffee to provide considerable investment in farming.[52] One of the more curious cases is the deforestation myth of Eritrea, for it enjoys not only the support of the policy community but the wholehearted support of many Eritreans. Citizens of this country firmly believe that their country has been severely degraded by poor environmental management by Italian colonizers, and then the Ethiopian military. The difficulty is that early photographs reveal very few trees at all. If there was deforestation in this region then it happened much earlier, and for different reasons, than people remember.[53]

The errors in these environmental crisis narratives are potentially damaging for wildlife conservation causes because they derive so strong an imperative from the widely proclaimed extinction crisis.[54] The common call is that we are now entering an extinction spasm (similar to that which wiped out dinosaurs) which is caused by human activity. Do the problems in previous environmental narratives mean that we should lose faith in the idea of an extinction crisis? There are cases where the scarcity of wildlife has been invented and extinction claims exaggerated, but the short answer is 'no'.[55] Discrepancies exist between the predicted levels of extinction and observed extinctions thus far.[56] This does not mean these high estimates of extinction are wrong.[57] The high figures are based on predictions of numbers of poorly known taxa, such as insects, that will be lost as habitat decreases. However, a number of eminent scientists suggest that measures other than extinction may be better indicators of the state of the planet. Balmford and colleagues have observed that there are plenty of other estimates of habitat decline, population loss and indices of deleterious human influence on diverse ecosystems that could be used.[58] For example, trends in the threat status of birds (the best known taxon) show a persistent decline.[59] Whether or not threatened species are becoming extinct now, the decline in their abundance gives ample grounds for concern.

The broader point is that the fact that previous environmental narratives have proved wrong does not mean that there are no environmental problems. There are all sorts of problems of soil erosion, deforestation, pollution, habitat loss, endangerment and extinction, not to mention climate change, which sceptics (like Bjorn Lomborg) are wrong to dismiss.[60] Nor am I attacking science in general, for it is only through careful research that we are able to present these counter narratives with any authority. Indeed it is quite possible that, through further research, some of the ideas I have described above may well be revised one day.[61] If they are, then the deeper point I am making would still remain: the truth of theories alone cannot explain their influence.

How do falsehoods survive in environmental science? We can consider first to what other agendas they are useful.[62] Following Foucault, where environmental narratives are clear cases of persistent dysfunction we can ask: whose interests are served by this persistence?[63] Scientific ideas are supported by the powerful social networks that scientists form, their allegiances with governments, their control over research funding and their capture of the popular imagination. Science, its philosophers tell us, is meant to be built on conjecture and refutation, but some ideas acquire a status that makes them difficult to question, let alone refute. All too frequently scientists fall in love with their hypotheses, or find that their careers are so intimately bound up with their ideas' success that they develop an excessively close personal interest in their progress.

Environmental narratives also justify interventions. As such they tend to be useful to certain agents – the state which can extend its power and influence, or international NGOs and development agencies which can demonstrate that they are doing good and need financial support to make their work powerful, or to local agents and NGOs who are able to show that they are the proper institutions into which resources should be invested in order to do something about the situation. As Roe has argued:

> crisis narratives are the primary means whereby development experts
> and the institutions for which they work claim rights to stewardship
> over land and resources they do not own. By generating and appealing
> to crisis narratives, technical experts and managers assert rights as
> 'stakeholders' in the land and resources they say are under crisis. (Roe
> 1995: 1066)

Environmental narratives provide legitimacy. They are popularly under-stood. They also often appeal to deeply rooted ideals in the Western psyche.[64] Their consequent fundraising power means that we can reverse the dictum that conservation based on myths is bound to fail. Conservation with powerful money-earning myths behind it may well succeed.

Conservation's consequences Conservation ideas matter because they can have far-reaching impacts. The problem, however, is that conservation's effects are generally just known to be good. Conservation, after all, does all sorts of good things. A healthy environment is beneficial for everybody. Clean air and water are vital. Big trees and mountains are spectacular, large or colourful wildlife powerful and charismatic, and anything that works for them must be a good thing. Furthermore, conservation can promote ecotourism and generate revenue for local livelihoods. National parks and game reserves house biodiversity which is vital for our future medical needs, and insects and ecosystem services on which life as we know it depends. Conservation keeps beautiful places looking beautiful and stops rare and precious things from being destroyed.[65] How can it be anything other than good?

The question is not whether conservation has these good effects. Plainly it does. Conservation is justly celebrated for its work all over the planet. The issue rather is whether that is *all* it does, or whether it also has more problematic consequences. In my experience the benefits are widely known – they certainly are in celebrity conservation – whereas the problems are not. The thrust of this book is to redress the imbalance; it will focus on the problems evaluating the impacts of conservation by looking at the other, less visible, side of the balance sheet.

All sorts of conservation policies have problematic local social impacts. In drastic cases, to establish the pristine wilderness of national parks and protected areas, people may have to be moved. Establishing the Yellowstone National Park depended on the eviction, and killing, of hundreds of Native Americans, and reneging on previous treaty promises.[66] Surveys of eviction literature indicate that in many countries a high proportion of protected areas in Africa and Asia have depended on such moves.[67] There are ongoing attempts to move people from protected areas in Thailand, Botswana, Ethiopia, Tanzania, South Africa and India.[68] Establishing protected areas can also require economic displacement.[69] More pervasively it involves the obliteration of local histories and associations with the land by circulating pictures, stories and images of protected places from which people have been removed. Supporters of the Mkomazi National Park in Tanzania, cleared of people in the late 1980s, proclaimed it 'a restored wilderness' despite the fact that people had been living there for generations before its establishment in 1951.[70] The mountain cattle men of Australia were incensed and depressed when their histories of association with the land, their knowledge, experience and economies were effectively excluded with their livestock from the Alpine National Park in Victoria. The cultural landscape they valued was replaced by another loved by walkers and wilderness supporters.

Many conservation projects try to meet the needs of neighbours of protected areas. They build schools, dig wells, fund clinics, libraries and educational programmes. They encourage participation in protected area management. There are few limits to the good will and intent which conservationists show to the rural poor close to them. In this context many conservation projects again seem to be beneficial – saving the environment for posterity while providing a focus and means for development projects to reach people who really need them. The problem comes when one tries to compare the value of the development projects offered with the costs that people have suffered as a result of conservation policy. In the vast majority of cases this basic comparison has not been made. We have no idea whether or not the education a secondary school offers is adequate compensation for lost access to fuel or grazing from a protected area. Emerton's research in East Africa suggests that the costs are rarely, if ever, met.[71] In some cases poverty can be exacerbated by conservation policies.[72]

The significance and extent of these problems have been visible at recent international conservation conferences (such as the World Parks Congress in 2003) which have been marked by protest and anger by local and indigenous groups.[73] The larger conservation NGOS have been lambasted in the press for their treatment of these groups.[74] There is a substantial body of academic and activist writing which is concerned at the problematic social impacts of protected areas.[75]

The conservation community takes these issues seriously. The World Parks Congress (2003) declared its concern 'that many costs of protected areas are borne locally – particularly by poor communities – while the benefits accrue globally'. The Congress urged 'that protected area management strive to reduce, and in no way exacerbate, poverty'.[76] Similarly, and in response to the Congress's calls, the Convention on Biological Diversity urged that the 'costs and impacts [of biodiversity conservation] – including the cost of livelihood opportunities forgone' should be 'equitably compensated'.[77] Andrew Balmford and Tony Whitten have published a carefully written paper in the journal *Oryx* which detailed how the costs of conservation are concentrated on the rural poor of less developed countries, while the benefits are enjoyed by global elites.[78] Kent Redford and Eva Fearn of the Wildlife Conservation Society has also been producing exploratory collections looking into the issues.[79]

Awareness of these problems does not seem to have percolated into the public domain. For many people the good side of conservation dominates. Its problems are less visible, if noticed at all. Environmental measures are unpopular if they make electricity or cars more expensive, they can be unpopular locally if they threaten livelihoods in timber, mining or farming. However, for the most part, the problems caused by preserving wildlife, particularly in exotic locations, or in the past, are not known. The news that wilderness in Africa, Asia or Latin America is created by removing people comes as a surprise to many. Karl Jacoby's

21

investigation into the exclusions of US national parks was subtitled *The Hidden History of American Conservation*.[80] Recall that people who help protect the environment are given 'peace prizes'. Then there is the Peace Parks Foundation which is promoting the establishment of national parks along the boundaries of states in Africa as a means of promoting regional harmony as well as conservation goals, despite questions about the social impacts of its work.[81] The Millennium Development Goals use protected areas to measure poorer countries' march along the road of progress, even though there is no clear relationship between protected areas and poverty at the national scale.[82] Prominent conservation figures like Jane Goodall (primatologist) appear to have no public critics at all; the positive reviews of her recent biography even noted a tendency towards hagiography.[83]

It is precisely because conservation is not merely good, but distributes fortune and misfortune, that celebrity conservation becomes interesting. Celebrity will not merely support conservation; it will empower particular varieties of conservation. It will not just help conservation save the world; it will advantage some groups and disadvantage others, potentially severely. There can be a dark underbelly to the work of conservation that is rarely discussed in public, and, in celebrity conservation, all the glitz and razzmatazz, the bright lights and glamour, will just obscure the misfortunes all the more.

Celebrity and the environment

What then are the links between celebrity and the environment? Most obviously, celebrity will help to sell the products the conservation movement needs the public to buy. Conservationists and conservation organizations deal in images of famous and charismatic environments, species and people, all of which are carefully produced and packaged. These are used to raise money in advertising campaigns, posters, commercials, documentaries and films. Thus conservation and conservationists, like celebrities, depend on the constructed, attributed, fame and recognition of these images circulated to as large an audience as possible by diverse media. Conservation commodifies and commercializes experiences of nature in order to raise money, promoting ecotourism, commercial hunting, sponsoring discrete portions of protected areas, or chunks of forest to be used in carbon offsets. Conservation encourages particular patterns of consumption such as organic products, eco-friendly power and ecotourist holidays. These endeavours are all the more effective if endorsed and supported by celebrities.

The links go deeper than mere celebrity endorsement: many conservation policies depend on values which can also be useful to disciplinary regimes of nature and society. Conservation can promote them without making the misfortunes involved in those policies explicit. For example, promoting wilderness can require the eviction of people, but this is not always made clear. Similarly, celebrities can insidiously justify certain values. Readers of *Hello!* or *OK!* magazines are treated to beautiful images of celebrities' wealth, with no criticism of the high levels of inequality this profligate consumption necessarily implies. From a Foucaultian perspective both conservation and celebrity promote docile populations, for peoples who accept the existence of high levels of inequality, or restrictions on use of resources by scientists in the name of nature, are easier to control.

Conservation also enables people to cope with the inevitable alienation from nature that life in an industrial urbanized world entails. It offers the possibility to reconnect to the natural world by supporting conservation activities, watching conservation or wildlife films, or following the work of celebrity conservationists. Doing this allows people to live conservationists' achievements vicariously and fulfils a need to reconnect with, and relate to, the wild. Just as para-social relations with celebrities help people to cope with social isolation, so para-social relations with nature, through supporting conservation and watching wildlife films, help people to cope with separation from nature.

Nature and the environment can be important markers of authenticity in celebrity representations. Gamson warns that celebrity risks continually being undermined by awareness of the artifices that produce fame.[84] The markers of authenticity have to be used carefully, they age and lose their authority, but nature and the environment have weathered remarkably well. As we shall see in Chapter 4, despite repeated revelations about the techniques behind wildlife filming, it remains a highly trusted product. It enjoys the authority of scientific endorsement. While celebrities are actively deconstructed by audiences, some of their props will not be, and some conservation causes provide that security.

The role of celebrity becomes particularly interesting where factors other than truth explain the power of ideas about the environment. Appreciating the work of celebrity in the environmental and conservation movements can help us to understand how wrong ideas gain hold. Celebrity can infuse environmental myths with greater vibrancy. The symbolic power of wilderness, nature and charismatic animals can be married to that of celebrity. The narratives provide celebrities with the language and imagery they need to communicate their environmental

23

concerns. Celebrity can become a means by which environmental narratives appear truthful. Celebrities help ideas to gain credibility, to raise money, and through these funds to become real on the ground. They are a substantial force in conservation's remaking of the world.

Understanding the role of celebrity in conservation will help us better to appreciate the ways in which conservation distributes fortune and misfortune. For celebrity works best with mediagenic images, and it will empower these forms of conservation most, even if their social impacts are highly questionable. The problems of conservation are not mediagenic. They are often complex and intricate. They rarely make good copy, or fit into the narratives and expectations of readers. Understanding celebrity's influence on conservation requires knowing what is being hidden by all that is visible.

3 | Conserving celebrities

My dear young lady, there was a great deal of truth I dare say, in what you said, and you looked pretty while you said it, which is more important.
(Oscar Wilde: *A Woman of No Importance*)

Harrison Ford (actor) walked cautiously but resolutely into the room, fixed the camera with a concerned face, and warned us succinctly of the dangers of tropical deforestation. 'When rainforest gets slashed and burned,' he intoned, 'it releases tonnes of carbon into the air we breathe.' He began to take off his shirt and continued, 'it changes our climate'. He lay down on the treatment couch of a beauty studio. 'It hurts,' he said, and a beauty technician began applying adhesive wax to his chest. Ford continued the commentary: 'Every bit of rainforest that gets ripped out over there,' he paused, and the beauty technician briskly tore out a neat square of hair from his chest with the waxing cloth; Ford sucked in his breath sharply at the pain and looked in bemused shock at the dark sward of hair covering the cloth, 'really hurts us over here' he concluded, his brows furrowed. The message was: 'lost there, felt here'. The clearing on Ford's chest was reminiscent of the hard-edged clearing of tropical rainforest for soya bean farms or cattle ranches in the Amazon. Ford's torso became, for a moment, the Amazon basin. It was no longer distant, too far away to affect us. The pain was real to Harrison Ford. It was part of our collective experience.[1]

In this chapter I examine the work of people who are already famous, and who lend that fame to support conservation's cause. I hope that you will come across some people whom you do not recognize. I have dropped as many names as I could into the text from diverse parts of the world to illustrate how rich a field this is. I have taken the view that anyone famous deserves some sort of coverage.[2] In the plethora of people mentioned below I will doubtless have missed many important names, but it is not my purpose to provide a complete overview. The variety demonstrates that it is just not possible to keep track of all that is going on (and what purpose would that serve?). Similarly, I do not focus on particular individuals unduly, for I do not want to get distracted by the performances of particular people, but rather examine the work of the celebretariat as a whole. My goals are to spot more general patterns at work.

My concern in this chapter is to demonstrate the power and strength of celebrity conservation. Wilde suggests that beauty (and I would add celebrity) can lend authority to an argument; I argue that some conservation causes can similarly compliment the celebrities who support them. Most people's encounter with conservation issues is heavily dependent on media representation; they are experienced only indirectly, obliquely or vicariously, not directly or personally. This can be endlessly frustrating for activists trying to connect with disinterested (urban) audiences physically removed from the natural world most conservationists value, but it can also make environmental causes safer for celebrities. While celebrities can be attacked for their environmental stances, many environmental and conservation issues are perceived to be peculiarly apolitical, simply good causes in the public mind. This is especially true if the causes concerned are remote or exotic. The complexities and politics inherent in environmental and conservation problems can be harder to understand from afar.

We shall consider first the kinds of celebrity who support environmental and conservation issues and the types of causes they support, focusing particularly on climate change, and briefly review the history of celebrity involvement with conservation. Then we will consider conflicting positions about the vulnerabilities of celebrities who support conservation and environmental causes.

Celebrity support for the environment

Celebrities' work in environmental affairs is now a fecund and varied phenomenon. They have provided help in a number of ways and do not always have to suffer such personal discomfort as Ford did, in order to support conservation causes. David Gower (former English cricketer) serves as patron to conservation NGOs such as the Bat Conservation Trust and World Lands Trust. Kit Chan Kit Yee (musician) and Cindy Burbridge (model) have added their public endorsement to the NGO WildAid and its attempts to reduce demand for products made from endangered species. Joanna Lumley (British actress) donated enough money to set up a research fellowship in issues of public concern, including environmental issues, at Green College at the University of Oxford. Sylvester Stallone (actor) has purchased thousands of hectares of land in Patagonia. Fat Freddy's Drop (band) has released a video remix of one of their songs featuring pictures of the deep sea in support of campaigns against the impact of bottom trawling. The Duke of Kent (British royal family) has supported conservation fundraising galas at the Dorchester Hotel in London. Douglas Adams (author) was sponsored to run for conservation causes in Kenya. Jon Snow (television presenter) contributed a tie for a WWF auction in support of Borneo. The late William Holden (actor) bought land in Kenya and turned it into a wildlife sanctuary with a foundation to support it. The entire squad of the Benfica soccer team (one of the biggest clubs in Portugal) collaborated in a promotion for the WWF, pretending that the emblematic eagle on the club logo had disappeared, to raise awareness of the importance of eagle conservation.

There are some patterns in the types of celebrity who interact with conservation causes. Royals are favourites. Queen Noor (of Jordan) plays a prominent role in the World Conservation Union IUCN. Prince William (British royal family) is patron of Tusk Trust and Friends of Conservation, among others.[3] Carl XVI Gustaf (of Sweden) is a patron of the WWF and Prince Philip (British royal family) was its second president. The late Prince Bernard (Dutch royal family), the first president of the WWF, set up the prestigious 'Order of the Gold Ark' medal which has been awarded to many of the world's leading conservationists. Prince Charles has established the Prince's Rainforest Project to try to reduce tropical deforestation.

Actors and actresses have been particularly visible, perhaps because they command such widespread audiences. Amitabh Bachchan and Shahrukh Khan (both from India) have spoken out in favour of conservation causes in Asia. In general, Bollywood actors have offered support to conservation causes only relatively recently, but many joined a national campaign to support tiger conservation early in 2008. Stephanie Powers (from the USA) continues the work of the William Holden Foundation. Robert Redford, Pierce Brosnan, Leonardo DiCaprio (all from the USA) have been particularly vocal in their support of diverse causes in the US including protecting the Arctic National Wildlife Refuge, the Sea Shepherds and climate change. Martin Clunes, Helen Worth and Amanda Holden (all from Britain) support the work of the conservation NGO Born Free. Joan Chen (from China) has voiced her opposition to the illegal trade in wildlife parts.

Acting celebrities and television personalities can present natural history programmes (often associated with conservation themes), despite apparently having little scientific expertise, their only qualifications being photogenic smiles, good speaking voices, acting ability, experience and panache before the cameras, mediagenic personalities, good communication skills and popularity with viewers. In the early 1990s

Tigress Productions produced a long series called *In the Wild* in which actors and actresses such as Timothy Dalton, Julia Roberts, John Cleese, Meg Ryan, Anthony Hopkins, Bob Hoskins and Debra Winger presented films that were usually about popular animals (wolves, tigers, pandas, elephants, bears, lemurs, orang-utans). Another example of this genre, in which Amanda Burton (actress) helped nurture orphaned black bear cubs back to the wild, was one of the most popular wildlife films of 2001.[4] Some of these films can have a strong conservation message. Cameron Diaz (actress) made a series called *Trippin'* (2005) for Music Television (MTV) in which she invited various celebrities (Eva Mendes, Jessica Alba – actresses; DMX, Redman and Justin Timberlake – musicians) to threatened environments to promote their problems to junior audiences. The BBC hosted a series called *Saving Planet Earth* (2007) in which different celebrity presenters such as Will Young (musician), Saira Khan and Graham Norton (television presenters) examined particular wildlife and conservation projects, and the public were invited to phone in their commitments of support afterwards.

Athletes and models have been less prominent but still play a role, particularly in their endorsements. Sachin Tendulkar (Indian cricketer) supports the work of WildAid. Gary Lineker (former English soccer player) supports the education programmes of the David Shepherd Wildlife Foundation. David Campese (former Australian rugby player) has named an albatross in BirdLife International's sponsored celebrity bird race. Anton Oliver (former New Zealand rugby player) is patron of the Yellow Eyed Penguin Trust. Kriss Akabusi and Sally Gunnell (both former athletes) have donated items to celebrity auctions held by WWF. Models are noted more for their support for animal rights and welfare (see below) than for conservation issues per se, but Ana Paula Araujo (Brazilian model) has posted a video in support of Conservation International on their website.

Then there are the explorers. The late Sir Edmund Hilary (mountaineer from New Zealand) championed conservation projects in Nepal. Mike Fay and Sylvia Earle are both notable explorers and conservationists in their own right, in Africa and the oceans respectively. Sir Ranulph Twistleton-Wykeham Fiennes (British adventurer) has lectured in support of lions in Africa. Colonel John Blashford-Snell (eccentric British explorer) has supported numerous conservation causes. Mark Shand (travel writer) founded Elephant Family, which supports the Asian elephant.

Conservation and politicians have long enjoyed close relationships, although rarely as close as most conservationists would like. Former US president Theodore Roosevelt's campfire conversations with the famous Californian preservationist John Muir are legendary within the North American conservation movement. President Julius Nyerere (of Tanzania) famously gave a speech shortly after his country won independence, in which he insisted that '[t]he survival of our wildlife is a matter of grave concern to all of us in Africa.'[5] Key phrases of the speech, which is known as the Arusha Manifesto, and which was ghostwritten by the WWF, are continually repeated by wildlife professionals or hung on office walls in many parts of East Africa. Indira Gandhi (prime minister of India) was the driving force behind Project Tiger and the expansion of protected areas in India.

Conservation is now becoming one of the factors in the celebrification of politics, both in the sense that, as we have seen above, celebrities take the authority to speak out as politicians on environmental matters, and in the sense that politicians are behaving and performing like, and with, celebrities.[6] Arnold Schwarzenegger, the Governor of California (and a former actor) has stayed in the public eye following his pronouncements about global warming, but perhaps conservation and environmentalism are most visible among retired statesmen. Nelson Mandela endorses the 'My Acre of Africa' campaign, which is raising money to expand and strengthen protected areas in South Africa, and he is also a founding patron of the Peace Parks Foundation, the fifth largest NGO in Africa.[7] The Wildlife Conservation Foundation of Tanzania was set up with Benjamin Mkapa (former Tanzanian president) and George Bush Snr (former US president) as patrons and Valéry Giscard d'Estaing (former president of France) as its president. It has recently donated three land cruisers to support anti-poaching operations in Tanzania.[8] Tony Blair (former British prime minister) is active in his support for measures to combat climate change.

We must be careful not to conflate celebrity support for animal rights and welfare with support for conservation. A great many celebrities are keen on animals. The green celebrity website 'Ecorazzi' dedicates a page to celebrities' support for them. Celebrity endorsement is particularly well used by the group 'People for the Ethical Treatment of Animals' (PETA) whose promotions have seen beautiful people posing nude to endorse campaigns against Kentucky Fried Chicken, and actors, actresses, athletes and particularly models demonstrating their preference to go naked rather than wear fur. PETA also makes extensive use of celebrity support for diverse animal anti-cruelty campaigns such as anti-vivisection. The pro-vivisection movement in the UK has countered by announcing support from Stephen Hawking (physicist) and Esther Rantzen (British TV presenter), among others.[9] However, this issue does not fall within the purview of conservation. Many conservationists specifically insist that they are concerned with population and habitat health, not the fate of individual animals. Conversely the Brigitte Bardot Foundation (set up by the French actress) insists that it is concerned with animal welfare, not conservation. There are also a number of general environmentally associated causes that have celebrity backing, such as advocacy of locally produced and organic foods (endorsed by diverse celebrity chefs and Prince Charles), sustainable agricultural policies (Prince Charles again) and vegetarianism (advocated by Paul McCartney, a British musician, and his late first wife, Linda). These causes have important environmental benefits, but will not be the focus of this book.

Generally speaking, conservation still plays only a minor supporting role in the publicity surrounding celebrities. Most is concerned with money, relationships, diverse scandals, dress, achievements, everyday activities, consumption patterns and the physical appearance of the celebretariat at parties, on the street, beach or shopping. Only a minority of the *Forbes* 100 list of most powerful celebrities are known for their support for conservation. The conservation work of people like Angelina Jolie (actress) or DiCaprio did not deserve mention by *Forbes*, even though Jolie received a full-length feature on the impact of her other charity work on her career on the front page of the 2006 list.[10] The regular column 'Celebrity Watch' which appears in the journal *Third Sector* and monitors the work of the famous for charity, only occasionally mentions celebrities' support for environmental or conservation causes.

This pattern is clearly visible in the pages of *Hello!*, a popular celebrity magazine in the UK. With a colleague I examined 237 copies of it in the stacks of the Bodleian Library in Oxford. These comprised 138 issues between December 2003 and August 2006 and a random selection of ninety-nine from previous years. The magazine is resoundingly committed to presenting celebrities in a positive light, and is quick to report work for charity, but we found only fifty-one articles (out of nearly 7,000) that referred to conservation, and in some of these the references were indirect. For example, Sigourney Weaver (actress) was covered working with gorillas for the film *Gorillas in the Mist*. Virginia McKenna (actress) is given space to talk about her love for wildlife. There are also occasional pieces about wealthy wildlife ranches. In general, conservation causes are notable for their absence. Even the travel and holiday section mentioned safaris only rarely. *Hello!*'s diary reports about conservation fundraisers are infrequent, though wildlife film presenters have started appearing recently, with a feature on the wedding of Saba Douglas-Hamilton (British presenter).

However, one environmental issue – climate change – is beginning to become a more prominent and persistent staple in celebrity diets. Boykoff and Goodman report an astonishing increase in news items that mention global warming and the names of a select group of celebrities, from between one and 400 in the early 2000s, to nearly 1,500 articles in 2006.[11] The prominence of climate change in the news and public discussion has made it much more central to celebrity life. There has been more coverage of environmental issues in the celebrity-focused media. *Access Hollywood* (National Broadcasting Corporation) and *Planet Green* (Discovery) are cooperating to produce a new show called *Hollywood Green*. Oprah Winfrey (US chat show host) has been interviewing celebrities like Sandra Bullock (actress) about their conservation work. *Vanity Fair* produces green issues dedicated to diverse environmental causes. It was now possible to click a green button on the *Vanity Fair* website to find out how to support environmental causes (or as they put it 'where you can click to save the Earth').[12] The 'Ecorazzi' website is typical of the media attention now given to celebrities' green consumption. It chides those caught shopping with plastic bags and cheers signs of environmental awareness and conscientiousness.

Perhaps the most visible figure in climate change publicity is Al Gore (former US presidential candidate), who was awarded a share of the 2007 Nobel Peace Prize for his campaigning against anthropogenic climate change. He released the Oscar-winning film *An Inconvenient Truth* (2006), and organized the Live Earth concerts on all seven continents in 2007 which were watched, with variable ratings, across the world. Gore topped a recent global survey of leading spokespeople (selected from a given list) on climate change.[13] Runners-up were Kofi Annan (former UN Secretary General), Oprah Winfrey, Bill Clinton (former US president) and Nelson Mandela. David Beckham was ranked tenth and popular with young voters. DiCaprio (seventeenth in the survey) has been vocal in his support for action on climate change and presents videos about the problem on his foundation's website. The Cable News Network (CNN) list of heroes of the environment includes several groups and individuals who are celebrated specifically for their work on climate change, such as Frederic Hauge (environmental activist), Tim Flannery (Australian scientist), the design team of the Toyota Prius (a car) and Tulsi Tanti (Indian businessman).

The alterations to our lifestyles which action on climate change requires are eminently well suited for celebrity promotion, given that so much attention is already focused on celebrity lifestyle and consumption. Matt Damon, George Clooney and Josh Harnett (all actors) promote energy-saving cars. Cate Blanchett (actress) lives in a solar-powered home and restricts the duration of her showers. Brad Pitt (actor) has narrated a film about environmentally friendly architecture. Soleil Moon Frye (actress) has started a sustainable children's clothing company. Lindsay Lohan (actress) promotes clothes swapping to reduce waste and energy consumption.

Parties, concerts and beauty contests are becoming climate conscious. Music groups like Razorlight, Radiohead and Hard Rock are making their concerts and/or travel arrangements climate neutral. The Miss Earth beauty pageant requires competitors to be knowledgeable about their country's culture and environment; winners travel the world promoting clean environmental living. Miss Earth UK's 2008 competition is being sponsored by Club4Climate, an organization which deliberately promotes both environmental awareness and hedonism and encourages people to dance to save the world. Club4Climate has recently opened the Surya eco-nightclub in London which will generate electricity from the movements on its dance floor.[14]

Climate change is interesting not because of the work of individuals, but because of the way in which concerted efforts are being made to organize celebrity action systematically. Here is a cause that is not fighting for celebrity attention, but rather faces the challenge of how best to marshal the ranks of celebrities wanting to support it. Climatestar.org features a variety of celebrity endorsements, insisting that 'Global warming isn't cool. Stopping it is', with stars appearing on posters with headlines like 'Dangerously Hot' (next to actor Esai Morales) or 'Not Cool' (beside actor Orlando Bloom).

The organization Global Cool, launched by the British prime minister at Downing Street in 2007, is dedicated to promoting low carbon lifestyles through celebrity support and endorsements. Their mission is to persuade a billion people to reduce their own CO_2 emissions by one tonne by making 'tiny lifestyle changes' (turning heating down, televisions off, driving less and more efficiently, taking showers and public transport, not using plastic cups). Each aspect is converted into tonnes of CO_2 per year saved (plastic cups are worth 0.144 tonnes); these pledges are added and the total displayed on Global Cool's website.

Global Cool casts itself in populist terms. Its T-shirts proclaim messages such as 'The people versus global warming'. The key to the organization's work is, as KT Tunstall (musician) puts it, 'to make being anti-green very uncool'. It throws Green Globe parties at the Golden Globe Awards. Supporters such as Nick Baines (musician) urge people 'Don't leave your telly on standby overnight and don't watch so much crap'; Ana Matronic (musician) is quoted as saying 'Global Cool is an amazing programme and all it takes is for you guys to shut your shit off at night.' KT Tunstall is more direct: 'Stop completely twatting your planet, because we haven't got anywhere else to live.' Global Cool has partnered with the International Indian Film Academy to produce a movie starring, among others, Amitabh Bachchan, Heather Graham (actress) and Tony Blair, in which people from the future with special powers come back to our times to persuade us to produce less carbon dioxide. Amitabh Bachchan's special powers are to encourage people to use public transport; Tony Blair's are to encourage a switch to low energy light bulbs.

The climate change issue is also remarkable for having adopted its own animal celebrity – Knut the polar bear. Knut, a polar bear cub abandoned by his mother at Berlin Zoo and raised by his keeper, won celebrity in 2007 after suggestions from animal rights activists that he be killed. The protests that followed made him a household name, and a major money earner for Berlin Zoo. Knut's fame has made him a suitable icon to represent the problems that polar bears may face in a warmer world. He appeared on the front cover of *Vanity Fair* next to DiCaprio in May 2007.

How much is new in all of this? It is tempting to lump conservation's interactions with celebrity together with celebrity involvement in other good causes and declare that this is an activity that has mushroomed only recently. Events like Live Aid in 1985, in which a large number of musicians performed in aid of famine victims in Africa, have signalled a step change in the way in which celebrities interact with worthy causes. The appearance of a polar bear on the front cover of *Vanity Fair* does seem to indicate a significant new development in the symbolic vocabulary of celebrity culture.

However, the conservation movement is unusual for the length of time it has been interacting with and producing celebrities. Contemporary forms of celebrity and the modern conservation movement both developed during the early years of the twentieth century. Both began much earlier, but during this period their development gathered pace and momentum. As we have seen, most commentators suggest that the present celebrity phenomenon became possible with the growth of the cinema in the early years of the twentieth century. The Society for the Preservation of the Wild Fauna of the Empire was inaugurated in 1903, with the goal of promoting game conservation in British colonies in part through prom-ulgating national parks, which had recently been invented in the US.[15] Its members were nicknamed 'the penitent butchers', for the society was driven by the concerns of wealthy big game hunters who feared for the future of their trophy specimens. The society enjoyed substantial support from the aristocracy of Britain, many of whom hunted, and the Prince of Wales became its patron. The Royal Society for the Protection of Birds received its royal charter in 1904. Conservation has thus been a worthy cause for worthy people to support for many decades.

It is difficult to say when these two phenomena, celebrity and conserva-tion, combined. Wildlife film presenters such as Martin and Osa Johnson were winning fame for daring clips of them killing charging wildlife in the early 1920s. Celebrity conservationists were active in the 1930s when, for example, William Beebe, of the New York Zoological Society (as the Wild-life Conservation Society was then known) was broadcasting radio from a bathysphere and reaching record depths beneath the sea. Before them, charismatic figures like John Muir were lobbying for the preservation of the Sierra Nevada in California. The interactions notched up a gear again after the Second World War when the Grzimeks (German conservationists) wrote popular books and films in support of African conservation, and lobbied particularly effectively for the Serengeti National Park in (then) Tanganyika. Subsequently, in the 1960s, the extraordinary reception of *Born Free* (see Chapter 5), signalled the power of the Western market for heart-warming stories from the African wilds. Sir Peter Scott, the son of the famous explorer Captain Robert Scott who died in Antarctica, was a main feature on BBC wildlife programmes by the time he helped to launch the WWF in 1961.

Conservation has been associated with the rich and famous since before the times when the rich and famous became synonymous with celebrity. It has been producing its own famous names long before other good causes were thought of. The associations described in this chapter are but the latest stage of a rich and long-lasting tradition. Thus the events of recent years are not a qualitative break from the past. Nevertheless, as we shall see in Chapter 6, when we look at the changing nature of celebrity and conservation NGOs in recent decades, there is good reason to suspect that the connections have become increasingly vigorous.

Vulnerabilities and the celebrity bubble

Why do celebrities support conservation causes? There are three reasons: because they believe in the causes and want to make a difference, because it is good for their image, and because it is enjoyable. The first is fundamental. Harrison Ford is a strongly committed conservationist; he has made substantial donations of time, money and land to different conservation causes, and received several awards in recognition of his efforts. He explained that 'I was looking for an organization to become involved with to be able to give back a little payback for all the good fortune that had come my way. I was embraced by Conservation International.'[16] He serves on the board of Conservation International as Vice Chair, and on their executive committee. Rula Lenska (actress) has said that she was 'already a member of most world conservation movements but none of them seem to be making any real difference'. She dreamt of 'fighting with poachers and single-handedly trying to save animals like a sort of Francis of Assisi'.[17]

The second reason is also vital. It is a celebrity's job to stay in the public eye and their agents must evaluate opportunities to serve conservation causes in terms of their publicity value. Boykoff and Goodman call celebrities' endorsement of climate change 'conspicuous redemption'.[18] The third just gives conservation an added edge when seeking publicity. Support for conservation causes can provide enjoyable benefits to the celebrities who work with them, which helps when lobbying for a slice of their celebrities' time. The Miss Earth beauty pageants are exciting for the contestants and pleasurable for the spectators. Wildlife conservation, particularly in protected areas, and where high-end safaris are available, provides an adequately beautiful backdrop for celebrities' social activities, while also providing unusual privacy. A collection of large fierce animals roaming free can do a good job of keeping the paparazzi at a distance. Prince William's penchant for Africa was forged in part through the extraordinary free life and dramatic landscapes that can be enjoyed on tens of thousands of acres of private wildlife estate in Kenya.

Supporting environmental causes is not simply an easy and pleasant task. The few writings that have examined the interactions of celebrity with environmental causes have noted the vulnerabilities of the celebrities who join forces with environmental causes. Meyer and Gamson produced one of the first studies.[19] They argued that media-produced celebrity, which does not depend on achievement or institutional status, is unstable. The authenticity of the stars can be instantly questioned and their authority to speak is continually scrutinized. Partly as a result, celebrities tend to shy away from confrontation and promote more consensual politics. Meyer and Gamson argue that they are most likely to engage in, and gain credible attention in, issues in which they can claim legitimate standing. They may also redefine the movements in which they engage such that their standing is viewed as legitimate. (1995: 190)

One of their case studies examined the involvement of Don Hedley (musician) in saving Walden Woods (made famous by the writer Henry Thoreau in his book *Walden*) from building development. Hedley took up the cause of local (wealthy) residents who were concerned about the impact of a proposed office and housing development (including some social housing) near Walden Pond. The only way to prevent the development was to buy the land. To raise the money he persuaded a host of other actors (Don Johnson, Mike Myers) and musicians (Bob Seger, Gordon Sumner – known also as Sting, Billy Joel, Arlo Guthrie) to support the cause with their time and money but he had to cope with two sorts of criticism. He and his colleagues were accused of having no mandate to lobby for the Woods, since he lived in Hollywood. They were also accused of opposing the provision of affordable housing. Hedley had to defend his involvement by claiming authority as an environmental activist concerned with global causes. Walden Woods held important symbolic value to the wider environmental movement. He also expanded the remit of the plans to include provision of affordable homes at another location. In the process the original locally based opposition to the developers was completely swamped by the energy (and effectiveness) of Hedley's campaign.

Hutchins and Lester examined the 1980s blockade by the Wilderness Society of Tasmania of the construction of the Franklin Dam (a defining moment of the green movement nationally and internationally).[20] This campaign helped to create new celebrities in Australia as Bob Brown, the leader of the Wilderness Society, was named Australian of the Year and elected to the Tasmanian parliament, and later federal senate. It also attracted the involvement of international celebrity conservationists such as David Bellamy (British ecologist).

Like Meyer and Gamson, Hutchins and Lester were struck by the vulnerability of celebrities to criticism once they had taken a stand on environmental issues, but they note that the difficulties celebrities have in winning legitimate standing to speak in the first place have receded. Instead, Lester insists that '[w]ell-knownness is now a legitimate criterion for participation in political debate'.[21] Turner and colleagues have similarly argued that celebrities' involvement is valued as a means of reducing complexities, and summarizing the overload of information available in the public domain.[22] Hutchins and Lester observe that celebrities' symbolic value and authority can still be contested, but that it is the content of their statements, rather than just their visible association with causes, which is examined. By virtue of being given more authority to speak, what celebrities say matters more.[23]

Hutchins and Lester located the source of celebrities' vulnerability, not in the nature of celebrity itself but, with respect to environmental issues, in the more general marginality of the environmental movement in society. They argued that environmentalists are usually up against a news-making machine which is 'in closer alignment with the dominant powers [of society] than with those individuals and groups dedicated to advocacy for, and protection of place'.[24] Environmentalists face 'different rules of engagement'.[25] Whereas stage-managed pseudo-events and publicity stunts are an accepted part of the publicity machines of industries and politicians, it is less acceptable on behalf of the environment. Hutchins and Lester observed a contest between the media on the one hand, and the Wilderness Society on the other. They showed that the media were not content to let the protesters define the news agenda and became increasingly resistant, even hostile, to the inauthenticities media events ('pseudo events' in Boorstin's terminology) can entail. Instead the media demanded that environmental protest be authentic. The Wilderness Society continually had to find new ways to maintain media space in the face of increasingly cynical coverage.

In my survey, in contrast, I have been struck not so much by the weaknesses and vulnerabilities of celebrities' work for environmental causes, as by their strength. In part the difference is explained by the types of environmentalism we have concentrated upon. Hutchins and Lester were concerned with environmentalisms that resist global capital, basing their work on Castells's characterization of the environmental movement as a fight against the reorganizing logics of dominant society.[26] These environmentalisms protect the special places from which people derive meaning, pleasure and identity, and which are continually threatened and reshaped by dominant economic and elite social interests. Environmental NGOS fighting such developments have their 'feet, hands, minds and hearts firmly in and on the ground'.[27] Burgess and colleagues adopt a similar position when they note that 'the depth of anger and grief many people feel when they see *their* part of the natural world destroyed for new development is part of the force driving the environmental movement'.[28]

As we have seen in Chapter 2, environmentalism is not always marginal to larger economic and social agendas. In more recent years some forms of conservation and environmentalism have become increasingly important in producing profit, winning votes and good publicity.[29] There are many strands of environmentalism that are not about resistance but cooperation and collaboration with powerful forces to achieve their agendas.

Environmental movements, and particularly conservation movements, do not have to be grounded in specific places or rooted in people's everyday realities. The place-based conflicts that Meyer, Gamson, Hutchins and Lester analysed, in which different groups of locals were contesting the wisest use of their own backyards, with the intruding influence of exotic celebrities, are not necessarily the norm. International conservation organizations, for example, spend much of their energy protecting environments far from the everyday experience of their supporters. Moreover, they use concepts and principles (such as biodiversity, hotspots, endemism, ecoregions, cost-effective conservation interventions) which can be alien to the experience and identity of the people living in those places designated for conservation. The establishment of some of the most iconic protected areas has required eviction and dislocation, displacing people from places they loved as their homes.

Celebrities can be cushioned from criticism by the distance and exoticism of their environmental causes. This can work in several ways. First, local contests over conservation issues are often poorly understood, if reported at all. The detail of the political fights over facts and representation is lost when communicated to international audiences. International causes can, in that respect, be simpler. Local disagreements merit fewer column inches and news time.

Second, and as a result of the first, international environmental causes are often cast in apolitical terms, as a general good benefiting humanity, rather than creating fortune and misfortune, favouring some groups over others. In Meyer and Gamson's language, celebrities can claim 'legitimate standing' for causes perpetrated for the good of the global community. Their involvement in many environmental contests is facilitated because these are already presented in such generally charitable terms.

At bottom, celebrities' involvement in environmental causes may be facilitated by the fact that in industrial capitalist societies many people's lives and encounters with environmental causes tend to be characterized by a *lack* of contact and interaction with the environments they value, or they are characterized by infrequent, highly staged and carefully framed encounters provided by wildlife and nature documentaries, tourism trips or safaris. To understand the popularity of ungrounded environmentalisms we have to understand how people come to love particular *representations* of nature. In this context celebrities can enjoy greater security because the symbolic power of the causes they represent is wedded to their own, creating a more substantial edifice.

The third factor at work is the celebrity bubble. David Giles, who worked as a journalist and had to interview diverse musicians, said that:

> The really interesting thing about pop journalism was the subsidiary (and subservient) industry surrounding the stars themselves. The entrance of a band or artist into their record company offices is like a papal visit. Those who can get near offer flattery ... Criticism only takes place behind closed doors out of earshot of the stars themselves ... No one interrupts a star, however banal the verbal content; the mildest witticism issued by one of the band is greeted with gales of laughter from the assembled company. (Giles 2000: 7)

He noted that there was nothing innate in the character or quality of these people which demanded such obsequious behaviour. As a psychologist he wondered what the consequence of all that sycophantic behaviour could be, a question that was all too easy to answer in the 'flagrant disregard for social conventions' which he witnessed all the time.[30] The effects of the cushion of distance, with its simplifications of complex politics, and its diminishing of the volume of opposing voices, can be further accentuated by the bubble of approval and affirmation which can surround celebrities and thus shape their view of themselves and their work.

When celebrities and conservation meet, celebrities are presented with particular constructions of the world on which they are invited to act. They represent their own responses to it in specific ways to fans, the press and the public. The consistency between the problems they are presented with and the solutions they offer makes it difficult to question the validity, usefulness or attractiveness of what they are doing. And it is virtually impossible to suggest that what they are doing is harmful or problematic, which, on occasion, it may be.

Conclusion

Celebrities have embraced the opportunities to serve environmental and conservation causes, and environmentalists and conservationists have lapped up the publicity they provide. The prominence of the climate change agenda in recent years has multiplied the mutually enjoyable benefits celebrities and environmental causes provide to each other. Where they are promoting conservation in remote places, and perhaps particularly where these remote places are poor and do not have their own vigorous well-paid press corps, it could prove difficult to represent the complexities that inevitably surround conservation issues. This type of conservation is easier to pass off as worthwhile and unproblematic, making such conservation causes more attractive to celebrity sponsors, for they offer security from public criticism.

This sort of celebrity interaction with environmentalism and conservation is probably the least interesting form of celebrity involvement with the environment. It is only a minor part of celebrity affairs and, important as it can be for the business of conservation, there are more significant fields to explore. Conservation produces its own media products, even its own celebrities, which can demonstrate more influential forces at work within the conservation movement. We will examine these in the next two chapters, considering first the wildlife film industry and wildlife film presenters.

4 | Wildlife presenters and wildlife film

For what is Nature? Nature is no great mother who has borne us. She is our creation. It is in our brain that she quickens to life. Things are because we see them, and what we see, and how we see it, depends on the Arts that have influenced us. (Oscar Wilde: *The Decay of Lying*)

One of the world's most famous wildlife presenters is Sir David Attenborough, and I had at least to try to interview him for this book. He was kind enough to reply to my letter, but unfortunately was not able to see me. Indeed, it is possible that my request to interview him for a book about conservation and celebrity may have nettled him. He informed me that he was not interested in celebrity, and that he did not consider himself to be a celebrity 'when defined in today's terms'.[1]

I disagree with Attenborough – he is a celebrity – and people like him, the presenters of wildlife films and natural history programmes, are some of the most prominent names associated with, and influencing, conservation and the broader environmental movement today. Celebrity wildlife presenters are not just famous in conservation circles, they are some of the most influential and widely known of all celebrities. When Steve Irwin (Australian presenter) was killed by a stingray in September 2006, his demise was the most searched for news article on Google for that year. David Attenborough was voted Britain's most trusted celebrity in 2006. David Suzuki (Canadian presenter) was voted the greatest living Canadian by his compatriots in 2004.

In this chapter we will examine wildlife presenters and the wildlife film industry of which they are part. Three themes stand out. First, there is a huge demand that films be true to nature, but the nature which these films reveal is also quite clearly a product of other audience demands and commercial pressures. Second, wildlife films and presenters display well the general pattern of celebrity, namely that their fame is a means of selling commodities (films and books), and the more commodities they can sell, the more famous they will be encouraged to become. Finally, it will become clear that wildlife film is a vital means by which people experience nature or, more accurately, watch while other people experience it for them. Wildlife film presenters are a central part of the vicarious enjoyment of nature that characterizes celebrity conservation more generally. This could have significant consequences for people's enjoyment and expectations of nature beyond their television screens.

I review first an authoritative literature on the constructions and history of wildlife film, which has explored the question of the authenticity of natural history programmes. Second, I focus on contrasting styles of wildlife film presenters, taking Attenborough and Irwin as the archetypes, and consider the influence of changing styles on the industry as a whole. I argue that there are some similarities between Attenborough and Irwin, but that the impact of Irwin's type of programme upon the industry recently has been significant. I then consider the variety of other commodities that wildlife presenters can get involved in promoting and the significance of wildlife presenter brands.

Producing wildlife films

To understand properly the influence and impact of wildlife and nature documentary presenters we must first explore the wildlife film, and closely related conservation film, industry of which they are part. Fortunately some excellent works have already tackled these subjects. My principal sources for this section are two classic works, Greg Mitman's *Reel Nature* and Derek Bousé's *Wildlife Films*, along with William Beinart's and Luis Vivanco's essays.[2]

Beinart notes that film and photographs became a popular means of finding out about and seeing Africa's wildlife from an early stage. Films such as *Jungle Adventures* (1917) and *Wild Cargo* (1934) made stars out of filmmakers such as Michael and Osa Johnson and Armand Denis. Before the Second World War the emphasis tended to be on hunting, chasing and capturing animals, and on all that was dangerous about them. Martin Johnson induced elephants, rhinoceroses and lions to charge at his wife Osa to heighten the thrills on show. Bousé's distaste at the number of animals that had to die for such showmanship is palpable. Later films, beginning with Armand and Michaela Denis's release of *Savage Splendour* (1949), tried to be more 'true to life', and record aspects of animals' behaviour that were interesting simply because they were not normally seen – such as hippos under water. However, this attempt still begs crucial questions, as Bousé puts it: 'Do wildlife films "get" the realities of nature? Do they convey the natural world to us on its terms, or on theirs?'.[3] In other words, in what sense can natural history programmes be described as 'authentic'?

Both Bousé and Mitman emphasize that one of the most important aspects of wildlife films is their continual tension between the need to be authentic and the need to be popular. Films have to tell the story well, a task not always made easy by reality. Mitman shows how, from the earliest days, makers of wildlife film in the US struggled between their desires to produce authentic, accurate natural histories, and the competing commercial needs of filling cinemas and producing a return on revenues.[4] The latter generally won.

One of the more prominent figures at the start of the business was William Burden, who was deeply and personally committed to producing natural history films that were authentic, and strongly critical of others who were not. His film *The Silent Enemy* (1930) portrayed the race of the Ojibwa people to find the caribou migration before they starved. Burden went to great lengths to convey authentically something of the wonder of the wildernesses he dwelt in while shooting the film, which he was sure that the mass of tourists missed in their rush. His difficulty, however, as Mitman noted, was that he depended on that selfsame mass to appreciate their mistakes and turn out to view the film.[5] *The Silent Enemy* was not a commercial success. *Ingagi* (1930), about a purported expedition to the Belgian Congo by Sir Hubert Winstead, enjoyed a different reception. Its final scenes featured a group of half-naked women who lived with gorillas; its publicity posters showed a gorilla fondling one of the women. It broke box office records. Wildlife filmmakers and critics condemned it not so much for its bestiality and nudity as its lack of authenticity, for it was filmed in studios using actors, gorilla costumes and stock footage of primates, yet claimed to be real. When Burden later tried to make his own wildlife film about gorillas in the Congo that was true to nature, it inspired a blockbuster but Burden lost control of the project at an early stage, and the film resulting was called *King Kong*.[6]

Wildlife filmmakers and audiences generally insist that natural history films should be real. Marlin Perkins (who presented *Zoo Parade*, 1950–57) actually struck an investigative reporter who questioned the authenticity of his work. Attenborough argued that filmmakers 'must be allowed to manipulate images and use all the devices that recent technological advances [permit]', but that they must also be true to the 'biological facts'.[7] Audiences demand veracity. When Marty Stouffer (who presented the popular show *Wild America*) was accused in 1996 of staging some of his sequences there was a minor national outrage. In the late 1990s Philo and Henderson reported that many members of focal groups in the UK greeted the suggestion that captive animals were used in films 'almost with shock'.[8] Since nature does not act, and cannot dissimulate, it follows that wildlife filmmakers must be revealing the truth. Part of the reason why David Attenborough is so well trusted is that he is the voice of films about nature that appear to be so self-evidently true.

Yet revealing truth is not always a straightforward task. Wildlife films have involved staged encounters from the very beginning. Cameraman James Gray's book contains several references to 'cheating'.[9] Even adherence to the biological facts can be a problem. When Disney filmmakers told the story of lemmings' apparent collective suicide for the True-Life Adventure *White Wilderness* (1958), they presumably thought they were being true to the biological facts when they collected captured lemmings and pushed them over cliffs into a river for the camera.[10]

Focusing on such extraordinary cases alone risks obscuring the point that wildlife film by its very nature, and throughout its history, has always involved careful constructions that interpret nature, rather than reveal it. Wildlife presenters do not just speak for nature. As Wilde recognized at the beginning of this chapter, they give nature her attributes. They speak for the versions of nature produced by the wildlife film industry and that have particular qualities. Mitman brilliantly captures the importance of understanding the devices of wildlife film thus:

> 'Wilderness,' Aldo Leopold wrote, 'is the raw material out of which man has hammered the artifact called civilization.' Longing for the authentic, nostalgic for an innocent past, we are drawn to the spectacle of wildlife untainted by human intervention and will. Yet, we cannot observe this world of nature without such intervention. The camera lens must impose itself, select its subject, and frame its vision. The history of nature film reverses Leopold's claim. Cultural values, technology, and nature itself have supplied the raw materials from which wilderness as artifact has been forged. (Mitman 1999: 4)

Wildlife films are commonly characterized by anthropomorphism. This is partly achieved through the storyline, which is told in human terms. Vivanco notes that 'the archetypal narrative is biographical and individualistic, tracing the individual from birth, through the perils of youth, trials of adolescence, adulthood, and death'.[11] Bousé observes that another common anthropomorphic device is to portray group behaviour in terms of Western nuclear families, with fathers, mothers and children carrying out expected roles. This can be in complete disregard to the prevailing scientific wisdom and much more in accordance with what the scriptwriter thinks families are like. As part of this exercise animals' thoughts are inferred and voiced, again usually in ways that Western audiences would understand. He also argues that the use of close-up shots further creates a 'false intimacy' between viewers and wildlife, reinforcing impressions that wildlife subjects think and feel like humans.[12]

One of the achievements of wildlife film is its ability to communicate intimacy with wildlife, and so encourage affection for the animals. As Beinart notes, this affection and intimacy are a hallmark of successful wildlife films, and filmmakers. A great many wildlife films, be they documentaries or feature films, encourage their audiences to form an emotional bond with the animal subjects (think of *Free Willy*, *Big Cat Diaries*, *Elephant Diaries* and many others). And as such they are remarkably successful in inducing a passion for nature, and persuading people, as Attenborough set out to do, that wildlife is absorbing and beautiful.

Some of the most successful films in (and creators of) this tradition were Disney's *True-Life Adventures* which ran from 1948 to 1960. These films showed pristine nature, but were presented using classic storytelling techniques from other genres. They followed the lives of their animal protagonists in anthropomorphic ways which propounded traditional American values. Mitman noted that Disney's films produced 'a nature tempered by an admixture of family and religious values, a sentimental nature for all ages'.[13]

Wildlife films are not necessarily the same as conservation films. Although there can be much overlap between them, the latter are defined by their strong conservation message while the former can (and some lament that they often do) ignore conservation concerns altogether. Vivanco has examined conservation films and noted two common tropes.[14] The first portray conservationists as saviours; warriors fighting the 'ignorance, greed and overpopulation of local people'.[15] Representations of people in them tend to be 'insultingly simplistic'.[16] Indeed, it is remarkable how many programmes about Africa and Asia are also characterized by their lack of mention or portrayal of people. Many are filmed in national parks and protected areas from which local histories and human presence have been removed (or in studios where the same impression must be given). They invoke ideals of nature and wilderness which depend on the absence of people.[17] George Monbiot (environmental activist) has vigorously attacked Attenborough and his genre for failing to show the unhappy human histories that lie behind the Edens the film crews visit.[18] Beinart, ever sensitive to the nuances and complexities of the historical record, qualifies this critique with numerous observations of the varied roles that Africans played in early films of the continent.[19] However even he concludes, 'this phase of natural history film and literature was ultimately a drama played out between African animals and white men and women'.[20]

The second trope overcompensates the other way, portraying 'the ecological[ly] noble savage living in harmony with nature'.[21] This is the characteristic representation of indigenous people, as in films such as *Blowpipes and Bulldozers* (1988) and *Tong Tana: The Lost Paradise* (2001). As Vivanco observes, such people are rarely allowed any voice or agency other than to fulfil the functions of their category.[22]

More complex films do exist. Vivanco also analyses *The Shaman's Apprentice* (2001), narrated by Susan Sarandon (actress), which examines the nature and reproduction of shamanic knowledge about healing and plants. The main character is ethnobotanist Mark Plotkin, who casts himself as a renegade scientist-hero fighting for the most endangered species in the Amazon – the shaman. Vivanco notes that the film is popular because 'it offers a carefully crafted win-win vision of conservation and sustainable development'.[23] However, like so many such visions its clarity is obtained by obscuring several vital components of the shaman's world. In this case Vivanco complains that it does not pay adequate attention to the problems of bioprospecting and biopiracy.

Examined as a genre, wildlife films, and their conservation cousins, appear to be a distinctly social creation. Bousé notes some common features, describing seven characteristics of the classic 'blue-chip' wildlife film.[24] Such films were visually beautiful, filmed in 'primeval wilderness'; about charismatic species; followed a dramatic storyline; had no overt mention of science, or politics; no historical reference points for they had to appear timeless, and an absence of people. They also tended to have a good dose of sex and violence, be full of courtship rituals and their consummation, and contain exciting footage of predation, where possible in slow motion. Bousé notes that the genre is remarkably unrealistic for these reasons. Rare and infrequent events are compressed into short films, making them seem part of everyday life.[25]

These elements have not always coexisted. In the 1950s footage of violence, sex and birth was edited out. Films in the 1920s and 1930s contained considerable staged violence, indeed one of the first films of animals ever shot (in 1884) is of a meeting between a buffalo and a tiger at Philadelphia zoo, with a predictable outcome.[26] These days the drama is essential. Mitman calls them 'animal snuff films',[27] Bousé writes:

> predation scenes, with or without blood, proved to be audience pleasers and have been as necessary to the success of blue-chip films as obligatory

sex scenes have to R-rated motion pictures. Indeed, the scene of the big kill can be compared to the obligatory 'cum-shot' in XXX-rated films; each serves as a guarantor of authenticity. (Bousé 2000: 182)

Bousé and Mitman both report the Time-Life advertisement for videos of the BBC series *The Trials of Life* (1990). The trailer consisted of rapid sequences of the most exciting and dramatic cuts from the series, a compressed compression. It also added an enticing warning that 'some scenes may be too intense for younger viewers'. Attenborough, who had narrated the series, was reportedly so upset about the advertisements that he considered legal action. However, Bousé argues, the advertisement showed merely a difference of degree, not kind, from the original footage. The ad-makers had simply selected images from much longer footage which they knew would be suitable for their audience, and for their sales figures. The original documentary makers had done exactly the same thing.

Presenting and selling wildlife films

Wildlife films and documentaries, as the Johnsons demonstrate, have been producing famous names for a long time but the genre grew dramatically after the war with the creation of the Natural History Unit at the BBC. Sir Peter Scott became a household name presenting the BBC's first natural history programme in 1953, and on radio before that. His series *Look* ran for twenty-six years. David Attenborough won early acclaim for *Zooquest* in 1954, which filmed animals being captured in the wild and then discussed and presented in the studio on their return to the UK. Jacques Cousteau (French diver and filmmaker) won the Palme d'Or at the Cannes Film Festival in 1956 for *The Silent World*. The Denises (husband-and-wife team based eventually in Nairobi) came to British public attention at roughly the same time.

There are now a great variety of wildlife presenters, of various degrees of fame. An abbreviated list of those who have shone, or are now rising, in the business is shown at the end of the chapter (pages 58–61). It is a scene dominated by some towering (male) figures, and most recently by two men of utterly different personal styles, David Attenborough and the late Steve Irwin. A comparison of their approaches reveals some important differences, and essential similarities, in the nature of their work.[28]

Since *Life on Earth* (1979), David Attenborough has presented and written some of the defining, classic 'blue-chip' natural history programmes.[29] Indeed, that genre seems to have waxed and waned in tandem with his career. The plethora of wildlife presenters now working with the BBC could almost be interpreted as resulting from the corporation's quest, and inability, to find someone who could replace him. Throughout his commentaries he expresses a calm, scientific, understated passion. He makes little attempt to add excitement by what he does or says. When he appears on screen he is either stationary, or else walking slowly. His articulate whisper whenever close to wildlife emphasizes the fact that he is but temporarily intruding in this world, which he is simply observing. His disregard for himself and his enthusiasm for wildlife enhance his stature. He is the model of decorum, well behaved, well spoken, passionate about and fascinated by his subjects, devoting complete attention to them, yet in control of his behaviour. As a result he could even appear dignified while being groomed by a wild gorilla. His pleasure is, like that of the viewers, in watching.

Steve Irwin's first film was in the early 1990s, but his success came with *The Crocodile Hunter* (1996), a series released in Australia and then in the US in 1997. By 1999 he had won widespread fame for a style which was defined (at least by his viewers) as partly in opposition to Attenborough's approach. Irwin typically appeared in safari shorts, often much the worse for wear; his habit of jumping on or picking up animals, particularly if they were dangerous, his everyday language and unscripted expressions and exclamations were the antithesis of Attenborough.

Attenborough demonstrated his closeness to nature by getting himself, or the camera, as close as the wildlife or technical wizardry allowed, as well as commentating, *sotto voce*, on intimate aspects of their lives, seldom witnessed by most people. Irwin adopted an in-your-face approach to wildlife that demanded they accommodate his presence in their world. He demonstrated his close relationship with wildlife by his control and mastery over it. When he was criticized for feeding a captive crocodile with one arm while cradling his infant son in the other, Irwin insisted that he was 'in complete control' and that it would take an earthquake or asteroid strike to have destabilized him.

Irwin had a great impact. His brash and boyish antics, simplicity and verve were lucratively popular in the USA and Britain, particularly with children. Focal group research on young audiences in the UK in the late 1990s suggested that Attenborough and the blue-chip genre were negatively associated with school and compulsory viewing of films. Such audiences thought that traditional blue-chip films were deliberately selected for schools because they were not funny.[30] Members of these groups tended to prefer Rolf Harris (comic Australian presenter). One watcher even said, 'I just can't listen to David Attenborough's voice.'[31]

Irwin's style and panache were not new to the industry. The Armands got as close to wildlife as they could, with the glamorous Michaela ensuring (on camera) that her make-up and coiffure were perfect before the final yards. Frank Buck wrestled with a tiger in *Wild Cargo*, although admittedly only one that had drowned the night before when a rain storm flooded its pit.[32] Irwin's style was just another variant on one end of the continuous tension between entertainment and educational aspects of wildlife film. Parsons recounts how Peter Scott's style in *Look* appeared to appeal to older, more traditional viewers. He experimented by using Johnny Morris (British presenter) to narrate *The Unknown Forest* (1961), only to have to ask him to tone down some of his more colourful remarks.[33]

It would also be a mistake to let the differences in presenters' personal styles conceal the strong commonalities between the sorts of films they produce. Attenborough is just as significant a presence on screen as Irwin, and in some ways as captivating a personality, for his presence is so understated, without all the diverting antics.[34] Parsons noted before *Life on Earth* was released that he pinned his hopes as much on Attenborough's charisma as on the outstanding photography to make it a success.[35] Both presenters' programmes hinge upon bringing remote, exotic places close to home. Their audiences' delight is in watching others being there in real wild places and interacting with real wildlife. As one member of a focal group noted, presenters go 'to all these weird and wonderful countries, places that you would only dream about, you've never seen and you are not likely to anyway'.[36] Sean Cubitt observed of David Attenborough:

> A sense of daring has always surrounded him with a glamorous aura ... Attenborough's presence seemed to prove not only the reality and size of his specimens, but a kind of guarantee that we too were part of this far-flung scientific endeavour. (www.museum.tv/archives/etv/A/htmlA/ attenborough/attenborough.htm)[37]

Attenborough and Irwin's genre shares most of all an obligation to produce films that will be watched and sold. The BBC's Natural History Unit, as a public service, is cushioned from the need to ensure that everything it produces is profitable, but it keeps a close eye on the ratings. Attenborough delighted not just in making a beautiful and intelligent film in *Life on Earth* but in its widespread popularity (weekly audiences reaching 15 million).[38] Moreover, the high production costs of blue-chip films mean that they now have to be jointly funded by several companies, and thus create products that will satisfy commercial considerations.

Commercial requirements can substantially affect how films are presented. Cottle argues that the current collection of personalities presenting wildlife films is part of a bid by commercial filmmakers to improve ratings, and that the new generation of presenters in wildlife films and other genres are all young and attractive, or already minor celebrities.[39] Focal group studies found that young viewers approve of the use of celebrities to present films: 'celebrities like John Cleese and Julia Roberts [are] kind of interesting because you see the celebrities being themselves', or audiences could identify with them because 'they knew a little but not too much, like us'.[40]

Commercial requirements also alter the content. The key to making profitable films is the American market, which consumes most wildlife film and repeats the films often.[41] Aldridge and Dingwall have suggested that there is a surprising lack of explicit references to Darwinian evolution in blue-chip films, and more frequent reference to processes consistent with intelligent design.[42] They argue that this shows the influence of the US market where belief in evolution is weak but faith in intelligent design, and creation, is strong. Mitman notes that none of Disney's True-Life Adventures ever mentioned evolution, but rather supported divine creation.[43] Cottle has noted that the need to maintain shelf life and sustain repeated airings over many years has meant that wildlife films have generally tended to avoid controversies, lest they become dated or split their audiences.[44] Jeffries suggests that natural history programmes on the BBC are now treated as a more or less separate genre from science programmes, with separate space on the website. The non-natural history science programmes can examine similar issues to the wildlife programmes but in quite different ways, particularly with respect to controversy. Of one Horizon programme on sustainable use of elephant ivory and trophies Jeffries observed that:

Elephants are stalwarts of wildlife television but are routinely anthropomorphized as sentient, named family members, not as dangerous wildlife or a source of money. The elephants portrayed by Horizon might as well be a different species to those of the natural history programme. The science portrayed in Horizon works within a different paradigm characterized by change, crisis and challenge. (2003: 531–2)

Filmmakers and presenters can resist the market, as artists defending their creations, or activists committed to environmental causes. Attenborough declined to let the network with first refusal rights over Life on Earth have his commentaries redone by a Hollywood actor, possibly Robert Redford. This decision cost him and the BBC substantial sums.[45]

Mike Pandey's (Indian filmmaker) award-winning films were not produced for sale but to promote conservation agendas. He also produces the *Earth Matters* series aimed at rural audiences across India because of the environmental benefits it may promote.[46]

These are unusual exceptions. It is essential to appreciate that wildlife films are commodities produced for sale, for therein lies the key to understanding recent changes in the industry. The 1980s and the 1990s were the heyday of the wildlife film industry. There seemed to be a constant demand for good (expensive) blue-chip films that required patience and bushcraft on behalf of the cameramen and women, which produced new insights into the wildlife and ecology that audiences seemed to love. Filmmakers were having a wonderful, well-paid time producing products in which they believed. A whole specialized industrial sector, known as the green Hollywood, had sprung up in Bristol in the UK where the BBC's Natural History Unit was based.

The halcyon days of wildlife film-making ended abruptly due to a combination of changing technology, company organization and market demands. Until the mid-1990s the natural history film market in the US was dominated by the Discovery Channel (launched in 1985) and National Geographic, whose explorer series began in 1986.[47] Gradually during the 1990s a series of changes took place. First, more film-making companies and buyers appeared on the scene. The 1990 Broadcasting Act required the BBC to contract 25 per cent of its programmes from independent producers, resulting in fewer BBC staff and some leaving to set up their own companies.[48] National Geographic Television became a taxable subsidiary (and profit-seeking) company, separated from the (non-profit) National Geographic Society in August 1995. The Discovery Channel launched Animal Planet in 1996. Then the companies got bigger and began to merge or form partnerships. In 1994 Devillier Donegan, an American company, formed a partnership with Capital Cities/American Broadcasting Company giving it more capital to invest in quality films, and yet more still when the American Broadcasting Company was bought by Disney in 1995. Harlech Television (HTV) took a majority stake in Partridge Films in 1992, and was then bought by Grenada in 1997, which also acquired Survival (based in Norwich) in 2001, merging both to form United Wildlife.[49] In 1996 National Geographic Television formed National Geographic Channels Worldwide in conjunction with the National Broadcasting Company. In 1999 the Fox Entertainment Group acquired a 50 per cent stake in the National Geographic Channel. Fox, which is owned by News Corporation, a US$62 billion dollar company run by Rupert Murdoch (media magnate), also acquired Natural History New Zealand in the late 1990s. The BBC formed a partnership with Discovery in 1998, with the former providing archival footage and film-making expertise, and the latter finance and marketing skills and first refusal on BBC programmes.[50]

There is nothing in these changes which alone was likely to herald major reorganization in the lower levels of the industry. Indeed, the market remained buoyant. Basset and colleagues observed that throughout the 1990s the BBC's Natural History Unit 'continued to grow as the market for wildlife films expanded in parallel with the proliferation of new channel outlets and growing overseas demand'.[51] Cottle explained National Geographic's and Discovery's acquisition of programme rights and libraries as driven by their desire to 'satisfy the insatiable multi-channel TV environment'.[52] With the finance and marketing large companies can provide, and with viewers increasing, the growth ought to have continued. Bousé reported in 2000 that Discovery was broadcast into 150 countries and National Geographic into 130. At the time of writing they now reach 170 and 166 countries respectively.

Despite all this growth, what actually happened was that the market for expensive films declined dramatically, with jobs lost and company closure. The offices of Survival in Norwich, which had been a respected producer of award-winning blue-chip films requiring months of fieldwork, were closed and production moved to Bristol. Smaller independent companies such as Café Productions, Green Umbrella and Zebra and others based in Bristol have been cutting costs and staff. Among the contributions of all the industry insiders who wrote in Piers Warren's book *Careers in Wildlife Film-Making* in 2002, the sense of shock is palpable.[53]

The collapse was caused by a move out of blue-chip programmes and into the presenter-led style that Irwin had championed. There were three main factors behind it. First, industry executives realized how popular the Irwin style was. The market for traditional blue-chip programmes was declining, its audience was ageing, and younger people responded better to the personality-driven programmes, reality-TV-type programmes and (in a recurrence of the Disney True Life Adventure series) to natural history films with strong storylines. As the director of United Wildlife stated in 2000: 'They want identifiable stories and strong people-based narratives.'[54]

Second, industry executives realized how cheap presenter-led films were to make. This is the most important difference between Attenborough and Irwin's genre of film. The presenter's style, mannerism, dress, character or propensity to handle wildlife is ultimately superficial compared with the importance of the different budgets within which they worked. Blue-chip films cost hundreds of thousands, if not millions of dollars: *Blue Planet* (2001) was £850,000 per episode; *The Private Life of Plants* (1995) £752,000. A whole series of Irwin-style films can be made for less money, and much less time, than one blue-chip film. Cottle reported that *Safari School* (2001) shown on Animal Planet cost just £15,000 per episode. Such programmes are cheap because each one can be padded with footage of the presenter talking to the camera or travelling to the site. Encounters can be prepared quickly, sometimes using captive animals which are released for the presenter to pick up; they involve less waiting time and less time paying film crews in the field. With less money coming in for each hour of film produced, the industry simply could not sustain so many jobs.

Third, in the context of presenter-led programmes and increasing diversity of film styles, the multitude of channels available on which to present natural history programmes no longer served to increase the market; instead, it fragmented it. Each channel could pursue its own brand, differentiating it from others in the market. This means dividing the money to buy programmes, not pooling it. While blue-chip programmes were the only ones available, the different channels had limited choice as to what to air. Each was competing to present the most majestic and insightful film; it was a sellers' market. Now there is a continual quest for new angles and new ways of adding to the excitement. Irwinesque presenters are swimming with great white sharks, without cages, and crawling up to lions as they feed.

The speed with which the industry lurched into presenter-led programmes and away from the blue-chip model is remarkable. Gerry Martin (herpetologist), whose presenting career spanned both the blue-chip and presenter-led models, found the transition dramatic. Shekar Dattatri, an Indian filmmaker, was offered a contract by one major company for a US$600,000 film and asked to review it over three weeks. When he returned to sign it he was asked to do the same work for US$300,000. Rom Whitaker (herpetologist) was asked to turn a film he was working on into a presenter-led film in mid-production, resulting in an unsatisfactory hybrid.[55]

The blue-chip genre has not collapsed, as the success of *The Blue Planet* demonstrated, but it no longer dominates the market. Irwin's primary impact was thus not aesthetic, introducing a new style of presenter interaction with wildlife. After all, that was not new. His main impact was on wildlife film budgets. The timing of his arrival on the scene, at a moment when the blue-chip audience and its archetypal presenter were ageing, combined with the low cost of making films like his, triggered substantial change in the wildlife film industry.

Bousé and Mitman's books about wildlife film were written before this shock occurred. We are yet fully to comprehend the impacts of these changes and we should not assume the change will be permanent. Dramatic, presenter-led formats have been popular before. Their popularity may wane again. As one newspaper commentator recently observed:

> When did people making wildlife programmes get to be more important than the animals? Gone are the days of the hushed voiceover; now you are lucky if you clap eyes on anything other than camera-hogging naturalists using tarantulas, piranhas or anything else they can lay their hands on to help demonstrate how wild and wacky they are. (Watson 2008: 31)

The prevalence of presenter- and celebrity-led films does not mean that the products have been dumbed down.[56] Aldridge and Dingwall suggest that presenter-led films can allow more complex storylines. Filmmakers, however, lament the loss of bushcraft and skill, which are now superfluous to so many wildlife films. Alan Root (British filmmaker) once said that 'a wildlife filmmaker must be a naturalist first, and then a filmmaker'.[57] This may no longer be true. Beautiful and unusual photography requiring good fieldcraft is now not always the measure of a good programme. If there has been any dumbing down, it is in the production process. The interactions with wildlife which were once the staple of making wildlife films, and the joy of which fills the pages and reminiscences of those who were part of it, are no longer an industry requirement.

Selling wildlife film presenters

Films are not the only commodities that the wildlife film industry produces. There are the books and DVDs from major series, but the industry also produces a variety of other products. Tony Soper (British presenter) offers signed copies of his book on his website. Marty Stouffer, despite his fall from grace, offers diverse products on his Wild America website with different goods available at the Wild School, Wild Cabin, Wild Mart, or visitors can be 'inspired by the peace and serenity' of the Wild Chapel which advertises a limited edition range of sculptures Stouffer has created. Marlin Perkins used to build the advertisements for Mutual of Omaha in the *Mutual of Omaha's Wild Kingdom* into the commentary on his show.

Wildlife presenters also lead interesting lives and can sell stories about them. Numerous such presenters can be hired as after dinner speech makers, but one of the key attributes that wildlife presenters can use to promote their wares is closeness to nature. Dereck and Beverly Joubert (filmmakers) have formed a company which promotes light impact tourism. Mike Penman (South African presenter) runs luxury tented safaris in Botswana. Jonathan Scott (Kenyan-based presenter) and his wife Angela (award-winning photographer) offer people the chance to come with them on safari where they can enjoy both the beautiful sites of remote parts of the world and the Scotts' insights into them.[58]

All this activity is rather small beer compared with the industry that sprang up around the Irwins. They have shown exceptional business sense in establishing and marketing a brand and producing a host of products which are sold using that brand. The products on sale via their website range from clothes to toys, books, souvenirs and games. They include the 'Steve Lives Surfwear' range, so called to emphasize the fact that he was still alive despite constant rumours that he had been killed in his encounters with wildlife. The line is still on sale at the time of writing. Steve Irwin expanded and reinvented his father's wildlife park from a small operation with a handful of staff to a multi-million-dollar business employing hundreds of people and renamed 'the Australia Zoo'. He released a feature film (*The Crocodile Hunter: Collision Course*) which grossed millions; had sponsorship deals from Toyota, and set up his own whale-watching business and his own conservation company, Wildlife Warriors Worldwide. The Discovery Channel teamed up with the toy retailer Toys 'R' Us to sell products based on Irwin's series.[59] Steve Irwin became a tourism ambassador for Australia, promoting the country abroad, particularly in the USA.

The commercial aspects of wildlife presenting become yet clearer in the events following Steve Irwin's death and the greater prominence of Bindi Irwin (Steve's daughter). At the superficial level Irwin's death produced macabre new products, such as Halloween costumes of wetsuits complete with a bloody stingray barb. More profoundly, Turner argues that the great public displays of grief shown at his death represent the response of consumers, who had become accustomed to the presence of a particular commodity (someone's life as relayed in the celebrity press), to that commodity being taken rudely and prematurely from them.[60]

Bindi Irwin, just eight years old when her father died, has continued to take a prominent public role, following in her father's brand. She sports safari-style clothing and promotes a strong conservation message, underling the importance of saving wildlife and wildlife habitat. Like her father, Bindi Irwin's leitmotif is her childish enthusiasm for wildlife. But where Steve Irwin's childishness was out of place in an adult, though part of his charisma, Bindi's childishness is the rather more expected result of her being a young child. It works because she is mediagenic, pretty and charming, and because it is associated with Steve Irwin, and delivered with the same approach to touching and handling animals. Bindi sleeps with her snakes and walks around with them on her neck. There are differences too: while Steve Irwin controlled and dominated animals, Bindi is united to them by her innocence and harmlessness.

Fear of commercial exploitation has produced some public anxiety about Bindi Irwin's work after her father's death. At her father's memorial she won instant acclaim for the speech she wrote and presented about him, but there was also concern at the scale of her work in the few months following her father's death. Citizens and politicians were contacting authorities and setting up campaign groups, urging that the child be allowed to develop out of the public eye. Some queried why she had to enthuse about wildlife in front of a camera instead of living out these dreams privately.

Bindi Irwin's work in wildlife film, however, did not begin with her father's death. She was already being groomed for this role, and its attendant publicity, while he was still alive and they were working on father–daughter productions together. Irwin died while looking for shots of sea-life that would have been useful for his daughter's series. While Steve Irwin worked with dangerous wildlife with titles like 'Ocean's Deadliest', his daughter would film the cuddlier, cuter animals. Since his death she has launched a fitness DVD for kids; her own TV show (*Bindi the Jungle Girl*); a regular piece in *The Australian Women's Weekly*; performed with the children's group The Wiggles; appeared on US chat shows, and followed in her father's footsteps as an official tourism ambassador for Australia. A variety of Bindi dolls (bendy, talking and rag) are available, and there is a range of Bindiwear clothing.

Bindi's work has been lucrative, especially since her father's death. Allegations of exploitation have been made, but the industry and Bindi's family have not been deterred by the public anxiety; they and her agents insist that this is something she wants to do. There can be little doubt that she is keen on her work; she is merely continuing the life she led before her father died. Her mother was named Queensland Business Woman of the Year in 2007 for her handling of the family business which must necessarily include strong marketing. However, her family and agents had to convince a sceptical public that commercial considerations play no part in their decision to let Bindi pursue her desires.

The Irwins are perhaps an extreme case. Few, if any, other wildlife presenters have entered into the commercial aspects of their operations so enthusiastically. Others may wish to but lack the business sense, for demand for Irwin-style products does not just exist, it has to be forged. These days, given the variability in demand for wildlife presenters, it can be difficult for them to build the stature that Attenborough or Suzuki enjoy, or that Irwin won. This means that there are fewer commercial opportunities, as few individuals can enjoy the iconic status required for successful product endorsement.

Conclusion

Wilde once quipped in *Phrases and Philosophies for the Use of the Young* that 'The first duty in life is to be as artificial as possible. What the second is no one has yet discovered.' The surprise, on investigating the wildlife film industry, is how apt it makes Wilde's words appear. Many wildlife films accord as closely as possible to entirely human constructions of what nature is and should look like. If people believe in wild, people-less savannas, or pristine rainforest, then that is what audiences will be shown, especially if the filmmakers themselves believe in those concepts.

Yet many are unaware of all this. Wildlife films live on a pedestal. They are believed to be true. They belong to the realm of nature which does not lie or pretend, it simply reveals its truths to those with the camera and bushcraft to film it. As a source of such authority wildlife films are a great boon to the conservation movement. They provide the public with a constantly repeated battery of images about what the natural world should look like, and a litany of (controversy-free) investigations of wild places. Many conservationists have been inspired to join their causes by wildlife film.

However, as we shall explore in Chapter 8, there are also tensions. Wildlife film shies away from the controversial issues on which so many conservation battles need to be fought because they do not make good television. Wildlife film promotes a vicarious enjoyment of nature, which is satisfied by letting others get close to wildlife and wild places instead of oneself. Demand for wildlife film is both a product of our alienation from nature, and one of the forces that produces and enhances that alienation.

If wildlife film and wildlife film presenters are not the straightforward allies of conservation that they at first appear to be, surely the same cannot be said of celebrity conservationists. These are the people whose job it is to be famous for promoting conservation causes. Some have become famous partly as a result of their wildlife film work (Jane Goodall, Gerald Durrell), but such presentation work is a secondary aspect of their careers. Their primary concerns have been conservation itself. Is their collective impact as a branch of the celebretariat as conducive to good conservation outcomes as their individual work? It is to these people that we now turn.

An abbreviated list of wildlife film and nature documentary presenters

David Attenborough The foremost wildlife presenter on the BBC for several decades. He wrote and/or presented some of the defining blue-chip films including *Life on Earth* (1979), *The Living Planet* (1984), *The Trials of Life* (1990), *The Private Life of Plants* (1995), *The Life of Birds* (1998), *The Blue Planet* (2001) and *The Life of Mammals* (2002).

Chris Baines A landscape architect who makes programmes about urban wildlife and wildlife gardening including *The Wild Side of Town* (1980s) and *Bluetits and Bumblebees* (1985), and continued presenting until 2000 with *Charlie's Wildlife Gardens*.

David Bellamy Originally an academic, he is a botanist, author and charismatic presenter of numerous documentaries. He was particularly prominent in the 1970s to early 1990s and co-founded the Conservation Foundation.

Bill Brady Herpetologist who presents and makes numerous films for National Geographic.

Frank Buck Made several films in the 1930s about collecting wild animals involving diverse staged encounters. His book *Bring 'Em Back Alive* was a best seller.

Jeff Corwin Hosted *Going Wild with Jeff Corwin* (1997–99), *The Jeff Corwin Experience* (2001), *The Corwin Experience* (2005).

Jacques Cousteau One of the greatest natural history filmmakers, Cousteau was a pioneering diver (he helped to develop the aqua-lung) and a leading light in marine exploration for many years. He made award-winning films from the 1950s onwards including *The Silent World* (1953) and *World without Sun* (1964) and many television series from 1966 (*The World of Jacques Yves Cousteau*) to 1994 (*Cousteau's Rediscovery of the World*).

Armand and Michaela Denis Armand was making films in the 1920s, directing *Wild Cargo* (1934) starring Frank Buck. He married his second wife Michaela in 1948 and both won fame in Britain presenting *Filming*

Wild Animals (1954) which featured them getting as close to wildlife as possible and several other popular films into the 1960s.

Saba Douglas-Hamilton Daughter of elephant expert Iain Douglas-Hamilton. Saba is better known for her work *Big Cat Diaries* which began in 2002.

Gerald Durrell Zoo-keeper and author and founder of the Jersey Wildlife Preservation Trust (now the Durrell Wildlife Conservation Trust). He presented *Two in the Bush* (1963) for the BBC.

Jane Goodall First came to public attention with *Miss Jane Goodall and the Wild Chimpanzees* (1965), and presented *Jane Goodall and the World of Animal Behaviour* in the 1970s.

Nick Gordon Made *Tarantula!* (1991) and *Jaguar – Eater of Souls* (1999) which were about people's beliefs about wildlife as much as the beasts themselves.

Hans Hass Prolific author and filmmaker, especially, but not exclusively, about marine life.

Kate Humble Worked in television since 1990, starting off with the car programme *Top Gear* but moving on more recently to *Springwatch* (2005–).

Steve Irwin Rapidly became one of the most famous names in the business with his hands-on approach to wildlife presenting in *The Crocodile Hunter* (1996–). He was killed by a sting ray in 2006.

Martin and Osa Johnson Pioneers in the business, their films of the Pacific and Africa came out 1918–37 as silent movies and early 'talkies'. Their films were as much about the Johnsons' adventurous and glamorous lives as the places and wildlife around them.

Dereck and Beverly Joubert Explorers in residence with National Geographic and prolific award-winning filmmakers, including *Eye of the Leopard* (2006).

Simon King Began wildlife presenting as a thirteen-year-old child in *Man and Boy* (1976) and has continued in prolific and precocious vein since, with his first TV film at sixteen years. He has worked out of the BBC's Natural History Unit since 1992 on projects such as *Big Cat Diaries* (1996–), *and Spring Watch* (2005–).

Ruud Kleinpaste Dutch entomologist known as the Bug Man, who hosts *'Buggi' with Ruud* on Animal Planet.

Miranda Krestovnikoff Began presenting with *World Gone Wild* in 1999 and *Coast* (2005).

Steven Leonard A presenter since the mid-1990s he began with *Vets'*

School and then a number of wildlife programmes with *Steve Leonard's Ultimate Killers* (1999–2001) a particular favourite.

Gerry Martin Retired presenter who worked on *World Gone Wild* with Fox and *Wild Things* with National Geographic.

Nigel Marven A television presenter since the late 1990s with an Irwinesque approach to getting close to wildlife, including swimming with great white sharks without cage potection.

Johnny Morris A talented mimic and narrator most famous for *Animal Magic* (1962–84).

Terry Nutkins Worked with Gavin Maxwell and his otters in Scotland. A presenter in *Animal Magic* and the *Really Wild Show* in the mid-1980s.

Bill Oddie Famous first as a comedian with the Goodies, he is a keen birder and has produced many series with the BBC including the popular *Britain Goes Wild* (2004) and *Springwatch* (2005–).

Chris Packham A presenter since the 1980s including *The Really Wild Show* (1986–95) and *The X Creatures* (1998–99).

Mike Pandey An award-winning Indian filmmaker who has created and presented several winners of the Panda award including *The Last Migration* (1994), *Shores of Silence* (2000) and *Vanishing Giants* (2004).

Mike Penman Half of the double act *Mad Mike and Mark* (2004) with Mark Tennant on Animal Planet in which they seek out particularly close-up shots with wildlife in the field.

Marlin Perkins A successful zoo-keeper who hosted *Zoo Parade* (1952-57) and *Mutual of Omaha's Wild Kingdom* (1963–85), he was one of the foremost wildlife presenters of his era.

Julian Pettifer A journalist with keen environmental interests (he is President of the Royal Society for the Protection of Birds), working on environmental issues since the 1980s.

Alan and Joan Root A highly successful independent husband-and-wife team. They produced the first British Natural History to be sold in the US (*Enchanted Isles*, 1968) and produced many iconic images of wildlife in Africa, filming from balloons. They divorced in 1981. Joan was killed violently after taking a stand fighting illegal fishing in Lake Naivaha, in Kenya.

Jonathon Scott Began his presenting career on *Mutual of Omaha's Wild Kingdom* in the early 1980s; best known for *Big Cat Diaries* (1996–), and *Elephant Diaries* (2005–). Also an award-winning photographer.

Peter Scott Acclaimed as the father, and patron saint, of conservation. He co-founded the WWF, designing its Panda logo, and serving as its first chair. He presented wildlife programmes for the BBC from the early 1950s to 1980s.

Tony Soper Co-founded the BBC's Natural History Unit where he worked until 1962. Most well known as an ornithologist and his programmes on birds including *Birdwatch* (1980–).

Austin Stevens South African presenter of *Snakemaster* and *Most Dangerous* on Animal Planet.

Marty Stouffer Most well known as the presenter of the highly successful show *Wild America* which ran on the Public Broadcasting System in the USA from 1982 until 1996. The show was cancelled after allegations of staged encounters. His life inspired a feature film *Wild America* (1997).

Michaela Strachan A presenter since the 1980s and a wildlife presenter since the early 1990s (*The Really Wild Show*, 1993) and *Elephant Diaries* (2005–) more recently.

Tanya Streeter A record-breaking free diver who has turned to presenting recently releasing *Dive Galapagos* in 2007.

David Suzuki A presenter since 1970 on nature and science issues in Canada, he is still revered and most well known for his series *The Nature of Things* (1979–present) which is syndicated internationally. He is an active advocate for taking action on global warming and of plans to set up interconnected networks of wild lands.

Mark Tennant The other half of the *Mad Mike and Mark* duo featuring Mike Penman (see above).

Alan Titchmarsh Best known as a heart-throb presenter of gardening programmes, he hosted *British Isles – A Natural History* in 2004.

Charlotte Uhlenbroek Trained as a primatologist and began presenting in the late 1990s. Most popular programme was *My Life with Animals* (2007).

Rom Whitaker American presenter based in India well known for his work with king cobras.

5 | Celebrity conservation

Most people are other people. Their thoughts are someone else's opinions, their life a mimicry, their passions a quotation. (Oscar Wilde: *De Profundis*)

In the 1930s a man known as Grey Owl, an Ojibwa elder from Canada, enjoyed phenomenal success as a champion of the North American landscape and its conservation. Between 1929 and his death in 1938, he produced books, films and wrote newspaper articles. He was employed by the National Parks Service of Canada to promote their parks and win them publicity. His renown was great. His works sold thousands of copies every month in Britain; they were translated into several languages. He was entertained by the Canadian prime minister and toured England in 1935 and 1937, giving public lectures and having tea with the British royal family.[1]

At the height of his powers Grey Owl's influence was unsurpassed. No environmentalist or conservationist was to have such international influence until Rachel Carson wrote *Silent Spring*. He emerged just as the era of celebrity was first flourishing. His appeal on the stage, screen and in print was as an exotic savage, with a wonderful command of English. He is not so well known now because of his fall from grace when his origins were revealed. Grey Owl's original name was Archibald Stansfield Belaney and he was born in Hastings in England, in 1888. As a child he was deeply excited by stories of 'Indians' in North America, just as his audiences were captivated by the image he embodied. Emigrating to Canada as a teenager, he adopted an Ojibwa identity, which he then lied about to his publishers. His real origins were known to many, including a local newspaper, which suppressed the story until he died, fearful that the influence of his writings would be lost. The fears were justified, for the world's press seized upon the deception, as well as his alcoholism and polygamy. His writings, and cause, suffered heavily. He has only recently been rehabilitated as one of conservation's earlier celebrities and was the subject of a not very successful film in 1999 starring Pierce Brosnan and directed by Richard Attenborough.

I call figures like Grey Owl 'celebrity conservationists': they are people who win fame from their conservation activities. As with wildlife presenters and wildlife film, the main theme here is that celebrity conservationists allow many people vicariously to enjoy being close to nature. They provide entertaining insights into animals and places which we would never otherwise be able to enjoy. I will argue that celebrity conservationists are often people who have forged their own path in life, but the route of each, and the stances they adopt, also owe something to the public appetite for the products (experiences and stories) demanded of such people. While they are commonly perceived as wonderful individuals who have made a great personal difference, it is more helpful to understand that they are part of networks, and partly the product of audiences.

I begin by examining early celebrity conservation authors and more recent manifestations of 'celeactor' (fictional) conservationists, particularly Tarzan. I then look at what being a celebrity conservationist involves – their lives have to be enviable, entertaining and, if possible, heroic. Finally I consider some of the problematic aspects of celebrity conservation, namely the role of race and charisma in constructing great conservationists.

Varieties of celebrity conservationism

Grey Owl (1888–1938) was but one of a group of highly influential North Americans who have won fame as a result of their passionate and inspirational writing about nature.[2] The other names, undisgraced, are more familiar; a small sample might include Henry Thoreau (1817–62), John Muir (1838–1914), William Hornaday (1854–1937), Aldo Leopold (1887–1948) and Rachel Carson (1907–64).[3] It is difficult to overestimate the influence of these authors and their colleagues. Hornaday was the first director of the Bronx Zoo (created by the New York Zoological Society). Earlier, as a taxidermist, his lifelike dioramas had transformed the way wildlife exhibits were presented in museums. His writings and campaigning for the American bison and the seal helped save both from extinction, and he was a strong lobbyist against excessive wildfowling.[4] Thoreau won immense fame after his death for *Walden*, which describes the deliberate simplicity in which he lived for two years at Walden Pond, next to Concord in Massachusetts. He is heralded as a prescient visionary for many aspects of his writings, but conservationists celebrate particularly his championing of wildness when subduing nature was the Zeitgeist. Leopold, who cofounded the Wilderness Society, was likewise ahead of his time with his advocacy of the land ethic, of maintaining whole biotic communities, and in seeing the interconnections of ecology. Muir, although strongly influenced by Thoreau, has arguably been the most influential of them all in North America. His passion for the Sierra Nevada mountains in California, and particularly the Yosemite and Hetchy-Hetchy Valleys, saw him campaign vigorously for their protection and co-found the Sierra Club. His preservationist stance, opposing the use of resources on protected lands advocated by Gifford Pinchot, chief of the US Forest Service, set the tone of conservation debates in the US, and globally, for decades after. Rachel Carson was already an award-winning author of *The Sea Around Us* (1951, also an Oscar-winning film) when, in 1962, she published *Silent Spring*, which attacked the widespread use of pesticides and chemicals in the environment.[5] At a deeper level the book challenged the authority of industrial science and its vision for humanity. Although she died two years after the book was published, her work was influential in the establishment of the Environmental Protection Agency (1970), and the banning of DDT (1972). There are many more (Burroughs, Emerson, Seton, etc.), but my point is made. Collectively these writings have inspired, and continue to inspire, millions of environmentalists and conservationists.

It may not be strictly accurate to call all of these great people celebrities. Thoreau lived and died before the era of celebrity proper. Moreover he won recognition only posthumously. Nevertheless the interest he arouses now is akin to that which many celebrities experience during their lifetimes. People visit his former home. His famous haunt, Walden Pond, is sacred to many environmentalists, as we have seen from the efforts of other celebrities to protect it. Likewise Leopold's influence has been greater after his death than while he was alive (*The Sand County Almanac* was published posthumously). The shack which inspired so much of the *Almanac* is a place of pilgrimage and retreat and is the focal point of the Leopold Memorial Reserve guarded by the Sand County Foundation, an NGO which advocates Leopold's visions. Muir and Hornaday enjoyed the most influence while they were alive, but exercised it through their writings and personal charisma, which is not how celebrity normally works. Of them all, only Carson and Grey Owl were fêted in a manner akin to celebrity when alive.

Whether or not it is anachronistic to call some of them celebrities, these authors belong to an era when it became possible to win fame from conservation work. Their works have great appeal for several reasons. They write beautifully, often with simple directness. Consider, for example, the clarity of prose in one of Leopold's most famous aphorisms: 'A thing is right when it tends to preserve the integrity, stability and beauty of the biotic community. It is wrong when it tends otherwise.'[6] Likewise his encouragement that readers learn 'to think like a mountain', is now an oft-repeated slogan.

The power of the writing lies also in its ambiguities, and openness to different interpretations. Thoreau's observation that 'in wildness lies the salvation of the world' is a rallying call for the conservation movement, although it is often invested with meaning different from the author's intention, and frequently misquoted as 'wilderness'.[7] Thoreau in fact delighted in human landscapes, and believed that wildness had to exist first in our imagination before we could find it in nature. Simon Schama noted that Thoreau wrote in his diaries that:

> It is vain to dream of a wildness distant from ourselves. There is none such. It is the bog in our brains and bowels, the primitive vigor of Nature in us, that inspires that dream. I shall never find in the wilds of Labrador any greater wildness than in some recess of Concord, i.e. than I import into it. (Thoreau, quoted in Schama 1996, prelims)

Advocacy of wilderness now rarely recognizes such sentiment, which is partly why Schama re-examined Thoreau's work.[8]

Perhaps most importantly, all enjoyed a close personal communion with the wild and were brilliant at communicating it. When Muir urged Americans to 'climb the mountains and get their good tidings, nature's peace will flow into you as sunshine flows into trees, the winds will blow their own freshness into you and the storms their relevance while cares will drop off like autumn leaves' his words resonated, and resonate still, with the experience of millions of people. Finally, they were all also fighters for conservation causes, and had the attraction of being the underdogs, taking on the might of industrial capitalism. One of Hornaday's books is called *Thirty Years War for Wild Life*. Carson took on the massive chemical industry; both she and Thoreau questioned the wisdom of growth for growth's sake. Muir fought, and lost, the damming of the Hetchy-Hetchy Valley, but the battle inspired and strengthened conservation movements. Nash argues that it aroused preservationist sentiment across the nation, showing for the first time the political power of defenders of wilderness, and that the scale of the fight was remarkable in a country which earlier would not have noticed the damming of such a river.[9]

Present-day celebrity conservationists wield the same charms. They are passionate advocates of nature, champions of the wild and effective communicators. Moreover, these days their charisma is augmented by all the power of mass publicity machines which their predecessors lacked.

There appear to be many more celebrity conservationists at work now than in previous years (an abbreviated selection of prominent names is given at the end of the chapter on pages 83–9), but this may mean that some have just been forgotten. Whether or not they are more numerous than before, conservation celebrities today have many more ways of winning fame. In addition to film, books and the newspapers, there are also documentaries, conservation campaigns, glossy magazines, *National Geographic*, conservation NGOs, websites and blogs. The stages on which to be famous, and communicate a passion for nature, have proliferated.

As the conservation movement has grown, some conservation dynasties have emerged. Family connections are clearly useful in constructing the networks fame requires. The Leakeys are a good example. Richard Leakey is a prominent Kenyan conservationist, his wife Maeve an explorer-in-residence with the National Geographic Society, as is their daughter Louise. Richard's father Louis was a famous palaeontologist who sent Jane Goodall, Dian Fossey and Biruté Galdikas (primatologists, together known as Leakey's Angels) into the field. Also in Kenya there are the Douglas-Hamiltons. Iain is an elephant expert (and founder of the NGO Save the Elephants); his daughter Saba is a presenter of wildlife programmes.

One relatively recent addition to the list of celebrity conservationists are the celeactor conservationists. Celeactors (the word is Rojek's) are fictional characters who achieve fame, such as Sherlock Holmes, Miss Marple, Calvin (and Hobbes), or Yogi Bear. Conservationist celeactors include figures like Tarzan (whose creator may have been influenced by Kipling's Mowgli). Admittedly, Tarzan was not originally much of a conservationist. The orphaned child of aristocrats lost in the jungle, Tarzan was adopted and raised by a band of great apes. His creator had him killing off all sorts of wonderful beasts with knives and his bare hands. Early Tarzan films showed him wearing fur, but later representations emphasized his special closeness to nature and wildlife. By the late 1930s the films of Tarzan and his family show them communing with (Asian) elephants, in the 1950s he ventures to ride a rhinoceros (although it was clearly an uncomfortable venture) and in the 1980s Tarzan and Jane are caught frolicking in darkest Africa with an extremely lost orang-utan. These days Tarzan is the 'consummate ecotourist', he conveys intimacy with, and mastery over, Africa (both its people and wildlife). In Gordon's words he is a 'white man whose noble civility enabled him to communicate and control savage peoples and animals'.[10]

Tarzan requires mention because he can be emulated by, or his qualities are attributed to, a surprising number of conservationists. He fits well the heroic pose many conservationists adopt in their fight for nature. The Tarzan figure is a trope which flatters them, and which is easily comprehensible to the public. Russell Mittermeier, the president of Conservation International, is an ardent Tarzan fan; Bruno Manser, who fought loggers with the Penan people on Sarawak (and disappeared during the struggle), was called the Swiss Tarzan; Iain Douglas-Hamilton has been described as a cross between Tarzan, Clark Kent and Dr Dolittle; Jane Goodall insists that the inspiration of characters like Mowgli and Tarzan that she received as a child, encouraged her to live with apes later in life.[11]

In addition to inspiring conservationists, Tarzan is partly responsible for the proliferation of other conservationist celeactors who exhibit similar character traits. Zembla is the love child of a French adventurer and an African princess who was raised by lions in the fictional country of Karunda. He is a French comic book character, designed to compete with the market share of another Tarzan-like figure called Akim. These days Zembla is very much a modern conservationist, secretly funding the work of a UN conservation force, called the World Safety Unit (also staffed by heroes), from the profits he earned by exploiting Karunda's magnificent mineral deposits. The Phantom shares many similarities with Tarzan, by whom his inventor was partly inspired. He is a white man based in Africa, and blessed with immense strength and prowess. The series featuring the twenty-fourth Phantom (the task of being the Phantom is inherited) had a strongly environmental storyline with the Phantom battling to save the Earth from ecological death at the hands of a large company. The Phantom was particularly popular in India, in the days before television, and inspired a number of the conservationists I met there. Diego Márquez is aimed at the pre-school market. He is the cousin of a better-known television cartoon character called Dora the Explorer. He spends most of his time saving cuddly animals in the jungle with the help of his baby jaguar. As he sometimes swings through the jungle on vines it is clear who inspired his creators.

The conservation celeactors do not just thrive on the pages of comic books and television screens, or in the minds of conservation protagonists. They are also beginning to populate the landscape. This is obviously the case in theme parks, such as Disney's Animal Kingdom.[12] There is also a Phantom theme park in Parken Zoo in Sweden. The Pench Tiger Reserve in Madhya Pradesh makes much of the notion that it and the surrounding lands inspired Kipling, and that therefore the Reserve was Mowgli's home. Tourists can go on Mowgli trails and stay in Mowgli's den. Cartoon characters from the Disney film about Mowgli decorate its signs.

Celeactors' conservation beliefs can be contested. Banjo Paterson (Australia's greatest poet) created an iconic figure in 'The Man from Snowy River', his most famous poem after 'Waltzing Matilda'. Set to a fast and dancing rhythm, 'The Man from Snowy River' describes the brilliant skill and daring of an anonymous young horseman chasing a herd of brumbies (wild horses) on forbidding terrain in the Australian Alps. The poem is important for it celebrates the courage, ability and pioneer spirit of the settlers. Many Australians can recite portions of it by heart. It has been made into a major film, with other Paterson poems to form sequels.

The Australian Alps, however, are contested grounds. For decades conservationists tried to remove herders from the high pastures, where they grazed their stock in summer. They succeeded first in Kosciuszko National Park in the early 1970s, but were thwarted for some time in the neighbouring state of Victoria because of the public support the herders enjoyed. The mountain cattlemen, as they are called, embody the image of 'The Man from Snowy River', riding their horses through the mountains after cattle and brumbies. They provided the extras and the stuntmen for the film of the poem whenever skilled horsemen were required. Although the Victoria National Parks Association was ultimately successful in its campaign to have grazing licences in the Alpine National Park removed, it could not get a celebrity actor to support its cause because of the sensitivities surrounding the heritage of 'The Man from Snowy River'.[13] Conservation icons, be they celebrities or celeactors, are never simply enrolled in support of the conservation cause. They can only ever be incorporated to support a particular type of conservation. We will explore the sorts of (mediagenic) world most conducive to their work in Chapter 8.

The work of being a celebrity conservationist

Celebrity conservationists can live well. They can travel widely, or dwell intimately with amazing scenery and wildlife. The holidays which the rest of us save for years to enjoy, and which may not provide the views of kills, landscapes, great migrations or particular species we hoped to see, they experience repeatedly. Theirs is an enviable existence. It has to be; that is the staple diet of celebrity. Beautiful actors and actresses are paid generously to enjoy each other's company on screen. Popular musicians are similarly rewarded for the privilege of being revered on stage before hordes of adoring fans. Conservation celebrities enjoy close relationships with animals and nature in the midst of beautiful landscapes and are paid to do so. Amid all the glamour there are two aspects of their work that deserve particular attention. First their relationship with wild nature, and the value that this can realize for the conservation cause, and second, their heroism, fighting for the wild.

Early celebrities tended to be famous for their close relationship to, and understanding of, particular places and landscapes (Muir with the Sierras, Grey Owl with the forested wilds of central Canada), rather than particular animals, although Grey Owl was known for his close relationship with two beavers. These days it is more common to win fame for a close understanding of particular (charismatic) animals, or occasionally taxa. Consider Jane Goodall (chimpanzees), George Schaller (gorillas, tigers, pandas, snow leopards), Rodney Jackson (snow leopards), Iain Douglas-Hamilton and Cynthia Moss (elephants), Laurie Marker (cheetahs), Ruud Kleinpaste and Martin Rapley (insects – they are both known as the Bug Man), Dian Fossey (mountain gorillas) or Biruté Galdikas (orang-utans). The charisma of these individuals is all the greater for their close association with charismatic wildlife.

There is nothing particularly significant about this change. It reflects the growing power of wildlife science to understand and communicate the natural history of wonderful wildlife. More importantly, whether these people are champions of wildlife or places, their deep understanding of exotic strange worlds is appealing because it is so apparently authentic. They are dealing with, and representing, nature, which does not dissimulate; indeed, it is likely to kill imposters. Timothy Treadwell, already known while alive for his work with bears, won more fame posthumously after he and his girlfriend Amie Huguenard were killed and eaten by a grizzly bear in Alaska. Treadwell had spent many seasons trying to habituate the grizzlies and believed he was trusted by the bears, which he could approach and occasionally touch. His life and death were turned into the award-winning film, *Grizzly Man* (2005).[14] As Grey Owl is rehabilitated in the public domain one reviewer observed that, '[i]n a lifetime of deceit, love of wilderness may have been his only genuine emotion.'[15] Wildlife film presenters enjoy the same appeal. Cubitt noted that Attenborough was 'so prepossessed by his fascination with the subject at hand and unconcerned for his own dignity in front of the camera that he seemed to sweat integrity'.[16] Irwin's encounters with wildlife relied, fatally, on the drama of reality, of swimming with crocodiles and being licked by poisonous snakes.

One of the best accounts of intimacy with nature is Joy Adamson's book *Born Free* (1960). This is the story of the Adamsons' friendship with a lioness cub, Elsa, which they adopt after George Adamson shot her mother for attacking a pastoral homestead. They care for her as she grows up, and aid her return to the wild. The success of the book was remarkable. Beinart notes that it sold one million copies in English, five million overall and was translated into thirty-three languages.[17] A film of the same title followed, and two more books (*Living Free* and *Forever Free*) as well as the Born Free conservation foundations in the US and UK set up by the film's actors Virginia McKenna and Bill Travers. However, as Beinart describes, it was the intimacy reported between people and lions that made it so successful.[18] There are also many remarkable photos of the lion accompanying them in their everyday lives. When Elsa finally leaves with a mate, she first comes to say goodbye; she later brought her cubs back to meet the Adamsons. Mitman reports a reviewer in *New Yorker* proclaiming that the book 'fulfilled the irrepressible human dream of entering into wild nature'.[19]

I suspect that the appeal of these genuine relationships reflects partly a weariness with spin and deception which are so common in human societies, and partly the alienation from nature that so many in the audience feel. Many would like to spend more time with wildlife and in the wild than their lifestyles permit; others enjoy the emotional connections and authenticity accounts of such relationships offer. Full-time conservationists can tell them what they are missing. It also reflects the skill and passion with which these communicators allow their audience to identify with the animals portrayed. The anthropologist Kay Milton describes Jane Goodall moving half her audience to tears, including Milton herself, with a talk about chimpanzees.[20] Entitled 'Chimps: so like us', Goodall's talk endearingly portrayed 'the triumphs and tragedies of chimpanzee life' and received a standing ovation. Milton attributes the dramatic impact to the audience's identification with the chimpanzees through Goodall's words and pictures: 'they imagined sharing their experiences, suffering as they suffered, and so felt *for* them'.[21]

By providing such a moving talk Goodall was also fulfilling another prerequisite of good celebrity conservation, indeed celebrity in general: she was entertaining. Celebrity conservationists must be able to amuse, divert and stimulate their audiences. It helps that they are preaching to the choir about beautiful places and amazing creatures, but they have to tell their stories well. Gerald Durrell wrote books that entertained millions, as well as being a successful television presenter. Van der Post enthralled his audiences and readers.

One of the main commodities that conservation celebrities can offer is closeness to nature, and experience of the same. In addition they have to come across as interesting and charismatic people and have a good, entertaining means by which their supporters can discover and learn about nature. The fees from speeches and meetings can benefit both the individuals concerned and the larger cause. When the individuals themselves already work full time for the cause, then it will benefit both. A substantial part of some organizations' fundraising depends upon these encounters. The gala dinners and fundraising events, the sponsored bike rides, walks and runs are all enjoyable, and will be all the more spicy if they offer the opportunity of meeting a real conservationist. For example, the Wildlife Conservation Network, a California-based organization, runs annual Wildlife Conservation Expo events, including a Gala Reception and Dinner, with tickets costing up to US$1,500 each, which is branded as 'a celebration of wildlife heroes' and offers the fortunate diners a chance to mingle and eat with conservationists such as Goodall, Douglas-Hamilton and Moss.

The second key aspect of celebrity conservationists' work is their fight to save places from degradation, or species from endangerment and extinction. In many cases they take on the role of heroes, which can have several meanings. On the one hand, conservationists can deal with dangerous people or groups and expose themselves to considerable risk in the process. Dian Fossey, George Adamson and Joan Root were all killed making a stand for their conservation causes. Chico Mendes (who championed rubber-tappers in the Amazon) was killed by one of the ranchers he opposed. Ken Saro-Wiwa was executed by the Nigerian government in 1995, among international protest and outrage, for his opposition to the environmental destruction caused by Shell Oil. David Chain won posthumous fame when he was killed during a sit-in against tree-felling in the USA by a tree aggressively felled by a logger. More anonymously, Greenpeace activists frequently endanger their lives, and are occasionally killed, in the course of their protests. One died in 1987 when the French government blew up the ship *The Rainbow Warrior* which was set to protest against nuclear testing in the Pacific.

The term 'hero' can also have a broader meaning. It can refer to in-dividuals fighting great causes for the good of others in ways which do not necessarily imply such personal risk, although the costs in time, effort and opportunities forgone can be considerable. Heroes in this sense are often the publicly visible figures of much broader networks. There can be at least as much emphasis on the role of the individual, fighting on behalf of humanity, as on the team behind them. Taking this stance makes good marketing sense, for heroes are often no more than idealized images of ourselves. We see in others what we would like to be ourselves, and so we proclaim them our heroes. Adopting a heroic pose therefore invites audience participation in, and identification with, the hero's cause.

We cannot make audiences and organizations alone responsible for creating conservation heroes. Some seek that status themselves; there are prominent conservationists who spell 'conservation' with a capital 'I'.[22] Others, consciously or not, turn themselves into heroes by making their battles personal. Richard Leakey co-wrote an autobiography sub-titled *My Fight to Save Africa's National Treasures*. When he was appointed head of the Kenyan Wildlife Department he found that its cars were dilapidated, there was no fuel, and his department could not borrow the funds or equipment they needed to travel. So he personally took on loans of US$100,000 (for fuel) and US$500,000 (for cars) such that 'within a week, the Wildlife Department was mobile again'.[23] Equally, a sizeable ego is no hindrance in the pursuit of heroic status. When Leakey interpreted continued poaching in two Kenyan parks as evidence of poachers 'testing his resolve' he was probably underestimating the hunger and poverty that can drive poaching, and taking these actions too personally.[24] Valmik Thapar feels bitterly that he has failed in his objectives for tiger conservation in India, and as a result he assumes the cause of tiger conservation to be generally lost. His personal failure must also be that of the movement.[25]

A good illustration of the conservationist's heroic pose is demonstrated in the trailer for a film called *Hotspots* released by Conservation International. The film concerns the areas of high biodiversity and habitat change which Conservation International prioritize. It portrays a unique team of conservation scientists whose unmatched international experience allows them to identify and save the most valuable parts of the planet. It focuses heavily on Russell Mittermeier, the dynamic president of Conservation International. The trailer to the film begins with a series of disaster images while a deep bass voice-over asks 'Is this the end of the world?', and reassures us 'Not according to Dr Russell Mittermeier', who is then pictured promising viewers that he will be there in twenty minutes. The next shots show him in diverse locations, in command in office meetings and in front of computers, or, camera in hand, in the jungle. Towards the end the trailer loses grip of itself somewhat, making the grandiose claim that this is about 'the mother of all wars'. Indeed, it draws heavily on imagery associated with troops venturing into exotic tropical locations to fight battles in the jungle. With the voice-over

Five

72

warning 'it's a war', and fast sequence shots of skeletons and human-like skulls, all combined with rotor blades thudding in the soundtrack, you only have to replace the cameras with guns (and the movie camera in the helicopter with a machine gun) and you would have a typical soldier action movie unfolding.

The conservationist as hero is saving the planet for us. They are, in a sense, real-life superheroes. Hughes has argued that superheroes in comics are appealing because they live beyond the control of the state's coercive or ideological power.[26] They are free of all the trappings, laws and conventions of society that bind the rest of us, yet use their freedom and power for good causes without corruption (until the mid-1980s), or despite their dysfunctions (in later publications). Similarly celebrity conservationists, with their unusual lifestyles, career paths and easy access to other famous and powerful people, stand outside normal society. This appeal is common to celebrity generally, but celebrity conservationists also share with superheroes a devotion to apparently unproblematic good causes, apparently outside the realm of ideology. They are perceived to differ from other celebrities because they are committed to causes and real ideas, not to themselves. Small writes of Jane Goodall that 'what makes her life story so interesting is that she achieved her iconic status not by being a movie star or a politician but by working really hard at issues she believes in' (2007: 498). I suspect many actors and politicians would object to that remark, but the point remains that protecting the environment or endangered wildlife is perceived to be altruistic and this is the mantle that celebrity conservationists take up.

Boorstin would dispute the conflation of heroism and celebrity, arguing that they were by nature quite different.[27] Heroes, he argued, created themselves, scorning publicity. They grew in stature with the stories told about them. They became immortal when they died, but 'the celebrity even in his life time becomes passé', they burn up in the glare of attention.[28] The heroism of celebrity conservationists can give a different tone to the self-satisfaction which so often accompanies celebrity. Whereas the lives of musicians and film stars are unapologetically hedonistic, celebrity conservationists differ because, although many can enjoy all the trappings and privilege of fame, they are devoting their lives to a good cause. This might explain the smugness I perceive in some of the literature and promotional material. Indeed, it would be difficult not to appear smug in such circumstances.

Celebrity conservationists do not have to win their battles to win public acclaim. Muir lost the battle for Hetchy-Hetchy. Rather, like explorers, their tasks are to live the lifestyle, and to be seen to try. Arguably, the least a celebrity conservationist has to do is inspire a generation of new conservationists who will continue to fight the battles after them. Anne LaBastille fought for twenty-five years to save the flightless Atitlán grebe of Guatemala, which was found only on one lake, from extinction. She failed after battling civil wars, population increase, predatory fish introductions and an earthquake that caused the lake to shrink, destroying the bird's habitat; the survivors then began cross-breeding with the more common pied-bill grebe. Despite the failure, LaBastille won acclaim and recognition, with the rich and famous of Guatemala gathering to the swansong of her campaign to lend their support.[29]

Whether they are successful in their conservation aims or not, celebrity conservationists have to be good communicators and publicists, or part of a powerful publicity machine. Leakey showed brilliant panache in burning millions of dollars' worth of ivory in front of the world's press, and earning more millions from taking such a hardline stance. In 2002 a chimpanzee called Frodo, the dominant male of the group Jane Goodall had first worked with, killed and partially ate a young child in Tanzania. The chimp was not euthanized, as would normally be routine. Garland argues that this was partly because Goodall herself intervened to save the chimpanzee's life, and that the intervention arose in part because the bad publicity, which would inevitably surround the chimpanzee's own death, would have been harmful to her cause.[30]

Racial politics

There are some aspects of celebrity conservation that I find disturbing. For example I find the general prominence of Tarzan odd. Paul Theroux analysed the grace and power with which Tarzan masters the jungle in a famous satirical essay.[31] Tarzan, he noted, conquered animals 'with an attitude, an air'; he 'could beat his chest and win respect, [when] others would be laughed at', and he lived in a distinct unassailable white society, untainted by, but dominant in, the jungle.[32] The essay is notorious because Theroux then suggested that Tarzan lives on in Africa, and can be seen every day in the deportment of expatriates and the mores of expatriate society. He observed his expatriate colleagues revelling in the privileges and racist separation that white social circles on the continent so often provided in the 1960s.[33] They were free of the 'anonymity of the industrial setting' and enjoyed both a high standard of living and the glamorous association of being perceived by their friends and relatives overseas of doing something good or difficult in dangerous places.[34] The essay is laced with everyday photographs of expatriate life caustically captioned to invoke a Tarzanesque superiority. Theroux made explicit the many ways in which Tarzan has long been associated with African inferiority and European mastery. It is odd that celebrity conservationists do not want to disassociate themselves from him more.

It is impossible not to notice that celebrity conservationists who work in Africa, and especially Eastern and Southern Africa, are generally white. Think of Fay, Goodall, the Adamsons, Fossey, the Leakeys, David Western, Moss, Schaller, Marker, Joyce Poole, the Douglas-Hamiltons, Jean and Mathieu Laboureur, Bill Webber, Craig Packer, Ian Redmond and Amy Vedder (who these people are is explained on pages 83–9).[35] It is in its public face, where black Africans are relegated to the roles of poachers, game guards and politicians, that wildlife conservation in Africa most clearly demonstrates its colonial legacy and continuing post-colonial domination. As Garland observes, 'Africans are simply not currently a central part of the narrative which renders African wild animals glamorous and valuable in the global scheme of things.'[36] The continent has a number of famous black African musicians, actors, sport stars and politicians, but no black celebrity conservationists. Black African conservationists win international awards, but not the renown that normally accompanies them. How many of us, for example, have heard of Eugène Rutagarama, who fought to protect gorillas in Rwanda and the Democratic Republic of the Congo (DRC), and was a CNN hero for defending the planet in 2007, or Hammer Simwinga (Zambia) who worked with Delia and Mark Owens (US conservationists) around North Luangwa National Park, and who was a *Time* magazine hero of the environment in the same year, or Magqubu Ntombela (Ian Player's mentor; see page 87) or Johnathan Kang (Cameroon) a Disney Wildlife Conservation Fund Conservation Hero in 2007? A rare exception might be Wangari Maathai, the Kenyan winner of the Nobel Peace Prize, but she is known in the first instance as an environmentalist, rather than a conservationist.

Why, in Africa, should this domain be dominated by white people? There are no clear answers. In South Africa, Namibia, Zimbabwe and Kenya conservation was and often still is dominated by the descendants of white settlers who did not, and to some extent do not, admit black Africans easily. These are prejudices that change only slowly. Adrian House noted of the Adamsons 'that neither George nor Joy ever entirely lost the prejudices about Africans that had been prevalent among whites when they each arrived in Kenya'.[37]

More generally, celebrity conservationists in Africa tend to enjoy close affinities with white social groupings in the West. The social circles of actors, politicians and royalty from which celebrities who support conservation in the West arise are more than usually white. So are the intellectual communities. Conservation's academic wings, geography, wildlife science and conservation biology tend to be relatively white disciplines in an already white academe. Few people in the list of presenters of wildlife film in the previous chapter are not white. All the explorers-in-residence who are sponsored by *National Geographic* are white. I have scoured websites of the Explorers' Club (based in New York) and the Royal Geographical Society (based in London) but rarely see people of colour in the photos of their parties and galas.

It is instructive to compare the Indian conservation scene with that of Africa. The former is dominated by its own conservationists: Salim Ali, Valmik Thapar, Billy Arjan Singh, Ullas Karanth, Gerry Martin, Shekar Dattatri, Ravi Chellam, Ashish Kothari, Mahesh Rangarajan and Charu Mishra. Even its celeactor, Mowgli, is Indian. There are some white faces (Belinda Wright, Rom Whitaker) and the Phantom was influential, but in the main the white role models are noticeable by their absence. This probably reflects the vigour and vibrancy of the Indian wildlife science and civil society, and its fierce exclusion of unwanted foreign interference, to the detriment of its tiger science. Foreign NGOs such as the Wildlife Conservation Society or the WWF which are active in India are dominated by Indians. Expatriates such as George Schaller could not sustain their research there.

In contrast, most countries in Africa lack such ready expertise in wildlife science, and in many cases their civil society sectors are younger. Rather, the commonplace acceptance of a whitewashed conservation NGO movement in Africa is visible in the delayed reactions to counter it. The first academic examination of the issue has only just been written.[38] Over thirty years after the independence movement swept Africa Bonner could still suggest that NGOs helped to perpetuate white domination because they were predominantly staffed by whites.[39]

Perhaps the most fundamental forces derive from the place of Africa in the European imagination. Iain Douglas-Hamilton can state without difficulty that as a ten-year-old child he wanted 'to have an airplane ... [and] to fly around Africa and save the animals'.[40] The role models were in place for him, and countless others, to imagine, as a child, doing just that. Thanks to Iain and his kind they still are. However, these European expectations are not always the most nuanced of understandings. The ideas at work have been rather brutally captured in Binyavanga Wainana's short comic essay called *How to Write about Africa*. Writing as a cynical advocate, having clearly encountered too many Western portrayals of the continent, he advises that:

> African characters should be colourful, exotic, larger than life, but empty inside, with no dialogue, no conflicts or resolutions in their stories, no depth or quirks to confuse the cause ... Animals, on the other hand, must be treated as well rounded, complex characters. They ... have names, ambitions and desires. They also have family values: see how lions teach their children? Elephants are caring, and are good feminists or dignified patriarchs. So are gorillas. Never, ever say anything negative about an elephant or a gorilla. Elephants may attack people's property, destroy their crops, and even kill them. Always take the side of the elephant. Big cats have public-school accents. Hyenas are fair game and have vaguely Middle Eastern accents. Any short Africans who live in the jungle or desert may be portrayed with good humour (unless they are in conflict with an elephant or chimpanzee or gorilla, in which case they are pure evil).
>
> After celebrity activists and aid workers, conservationists are Africa's most important people. Do not offend them. You need them to invite you to their 30,000-acre game ranch or 'conservation area', and this is the only way you will get to interview the celebrity activist. Often a book cover with a heroic-looking conservationist on it works magic for sales. Anybody white, tanned and wearing khaki who once had a pet antelope or a farm is a conservationist, one who is preserving Africa's rich heritage. When interviewing him or her, do not ask how much funding they have; do not ask how much money they make off their game. Never ask how much they pay their employees. (Wainana 2006)

In some ways African conservation's most powerful constituency, particularly for some of the conservation NGOs at work there, is the (predominantly white) Westerners, many of whom expect to see prominent roles for white conservationists in Africa. Here we see one of the central paradoxes facing African conservation. The affection Westerners feel for wild Africa is not, indeed cannot be, founded on the the everyday interaction and intimacy that fuels most conservationist sentiment.[41] Western (or northern) knowledge and experience of African wildlife and society is the product of decidedly impersonal, irregular, staged and often vicarious encounters. The West knows Africa from carefully constructed wildlife films, or through heavily filtered experiences of safaris on national parks where we visit places without apparent history ('timeless Africa'), often ignorant of the people who have been moved in order to create these landscapes. At the higher end of the market safari experiences deliberately mirror the colonial privilege, where part of the purpose is to relive a version of the past (popularized in films like *Out of Africa* [1985], or *White Mischief* [1988]) as much as it is to enjoy the present.[42] Otherwise, tourist encounters with African cultures are typically the highly staged 'cultural bomas' or replica villages. My point is not that tourists' encounters and experiences are not authentic. Quite the opposite, they are all too real, but they are often based on a particular idea of Africa, which has been developed and reinforced in the West for decades. Conservation activities sustain, and are sustained by, a vision of African societies which emphasizes roles for Europeans.

Charisma

The social relations and historical encounters between Africa and the West may also explain some of the characteristics of charismatic conservation in Eastern and Southern Africa. Charismatic power differs from celebrity in that it results from face-to-face meetings and encounters; it is not manufactured by the media. There are no parasocial relations involved. However, the line between a conservation celebrity and a charismatic conservationist is a thin one and easily crossed. Some people we now acknowledge as celebrities were just charismatic leaders in the early stages of their careers. The late Edward Abbey (US author) was a charismatic environmentalist before his writings won him fame. Van der Post was influential both personally and publicly. Goodall enjoys celebrity status but devotes three hundred days a year to meeting people face to face to encourage them in their work.

When I sent out requests on email lists for suggestions of names of celebrity and charismatic conservationists I recognized well some of the suggestions for the latter category – individuals like Grazia Borinni-Feyerabend, Taghi Favor, Alan Rodgers and Kent Redford, whose different mixes of lively personality, smart dress, charm, intelligence and energy are part of their leadership style. Many others I did not – such as Phrakhru Pitak, one of the leaders of a band of ecology monks in Thailand who are active in defence of Thailand's environments and have taken to ordaining trees in their efforts to protect nature;[43] Tony Hams, chair of the Peak District National Park Authority in the UK; Aroha Mead, an IUCN councillor from New Zealand; Simone Lovera, director of Global Forest Coalition; Fiu Elisara, executive director of the O Le Siosiomaga Society in Samoa and Muawia Shaddad, the president of the Sudanese Environmental Conservation Society (SECS). I could go on but the point has been made. Charismatic conservationists can be found everywhere. It is hard (and unappealing) to imagine a social network where charisma is not important. It is also plain that in many situations conservationists find themselves, being charismatic, persuasive and generally larger than life is an essential part of the job. Conservationists often have to challenge ideals of growth and development, and cope with the inflated egos of politicians and captains of industry. A healthy dose of self-belief, as well as the strong support of followers, is useful in such circumstances. Richard Leakey has a reasonable amount of self- confidence, and it helped when taking on the machinations of the Kenyan government under President Moi.

Weber observed that charismatic leaders' authority will become institutionalized into bureaucratic structures.[44] This process has an opposite effect. The bureaucratization of conservation fuels the demand for, and supply of, charismatic conservationists. Conservation bureaucracies get mired in red tape, procedures, policy and office work. Many conservationists want to be out there in the field, fighting personally for nature, as do their supporters. Charismatic power becomes domesticated into the routine of conservation bureaucracies, and the presence of bureaucracy empowers new charismatic leaders. Charisma and bureaucracy thus feed off each other in close symbiosis. Part of the allure of some charismatic conservationists is their immediacy, their ability to bypass and evade bureaucracies. Organizations like Tusk Trust, Friends of Conservation and the Wildlife Conservation Network function in part by carefully selecting charismatic individuals for special support, nurturing their activities, and then proclaiming their support to these individuals who personally constitute conservation's frontline as part of their fundraising.[45]

While they may be found everywhere, charismatic conservationists again appear to be more prominent in Eastern and Southern Africa. Historical factors explain this in part. Conservation in Southern Africa, for so long influenced by the white male circles of South Africa and their trappings (toughness, gruffness, machismo, beer, 4WD cars and spartan dress), is still shaking off a propensity to admire individuals who excel in these qualities.[46] Conservation in East Africa is full of stories of the dramatic and charismatic. Steinhart notes the importance of charismatic white hunters for the safari business, like Baron Bror von Blixen, Beryl Markham, Karen Blixen and Denys Finch-Hatton, who combined sophisticated social skills with the knowledge of how to track and hunt.[47] As safaris grew in popularity so the demand for guides and white hunters grew too, and they were cast in the mould of these early entrepreneurs who had so personally entertained royalty and rich elites. As Steinhart observes, '[i]t is difficult to know how many white hunters were not gentle-men but simply brash young men, who took to hunting and guiding others as part of a life of outdoor adventure.'[48] Their prototype can still be adopted by conservationists, who live lives on the frontline between wealthy Western civilization and exotic African wildlife, just as the first white hunters did.

Another significant factor is the poverty of the region. The inequal-ities between the poor countries of Africa and the wealth of the West make it easier to sustain charismatic conservationists. With the cost of living and labour so cheap, conservationists can pursue their dreams relatively cheaply.[49] They require no media spotlight to carry out their work; an informal network of wealthy friends and contacts will bring renown sufficient for their cause. Society in the West is ever ready to listen to exotic tales of exploration, discovery and derring-do from Africa, especially if they involve its wonderful wildlife. The region remains, for most Westerners, a difficult place to understand, full of dangers and difficulties. Few audiences of charismatic conservationists will have the knowledge or experience to test the stories they hear. Charisma, as Weber emphasized, is a *recognized* authority. It is a property bestowed by audi-ences as much as it is claimed by personalities.

Consider Mark and Delia Owens who run the Owens Foundation for Wildlife Conservation.[50] They have worked with hyenas and lions in Bots-wana, a national park in Zambia and now work with grizzly bears in the US. Their website constructs a narrative of a smoothly evolving career, moving from Botswana to Zambia to the USA driven by their mutual passion for wildlife, and reports a string of awards, favourable publicity and scientific honours.[51] However there has also been strong criticism of their activities. Ward argues that they were about to be thrown out of the country in 1997 by a Zambian government tired of their high-handed and excessive behaviour.[52] Adams and McShane report that earlier they were denied permission to continue working in Botswana. They were expelled because of their confrontational campaign against livestock dis-ease fences which killed thousands of wildebeest.[53] However the website makes no mention of these difficulties. They exist in a world which is so secure from criticism that they do not even need to counter these attacks. The people that they rely on for support are simply unlikely ever to meet, much less believe, the ideas of Ward, Adams and McShane. There can be relatively few limitations to the self-portraits charismatic conservationists wish to paint. They can miss out what they want, and embellish as they please, playing on their audiences' fears and romanticism.

Without the taming, dampening influence of bureaucracies, charismatic conservationists, as an aspect of their charisma and dynamism, can get drawn into violent excesses, particularly where state supervision is weak. After the Owens' favourite elephant was attacked by poachers in Zambia, Mark Owens retaliated by shooting up suspected poaching camps with 'cherry bombs' (firecrackers) which were fired from a shotgun out of the door of their light aircraft. Cherry bombs explode with great effect, but are 'virtually harmless' (Owens and Owens 1992: 235). He describes one such event like this:

Even with her lights switched off, to the poachers on the ground Zulu Sierra [the plane] must look like a huge bat flitting about the moonlight sky – a nice fat target. And after about two passes, they must be getting the hang of tracking us with rifles. I circle to the side of the camp away from the moon so we won't present quite such a strong silhouette. Then I drop to minimum safety height that will keep us clear of the trees, hoping to pass over the camp so quickly they won't have time to get off a shot, at least not an accurate one. The dim shadow of trees are skimming by just under the plane's wheels, and then the meat fires are below us. I throttle back, kick right rudder and corkscrew the plane above the poachers' camp. A tracer streaks past, and another, much closer.

'Fire!'

And Kasokola answers: pfsst-pfsst-pfsst-pfsst-pfsst! From its barrel the twelve-gauge issues a trail of red and orange sparks as each cherry bomb arcs into the night.

BOOM-BOOM-BOOM-BOOM! Great thunderflashes of light and sound rock the poachers' camp. Kasokola's face is strobe lit as he cackles with laughter, unable to believe that he has caused all this ruckus. BOOM! The last cherry bomb lands in the campfire. Sparks and fiery traces of burning wood rocket through the camp and into the trees like Roman candles going off. One of Chikilinti's tents starts to burn, set alight by the scattered embers of the campfire.

'Happy Fourth of July, bastards!' I shout. Then, 'Reload!' I yell to Kasokola as I haul Zulu Sierra through a tight turn. This time we come in fifty feet higher, spreading our cherry bombs over a broader area, hoping to catch the scattering poachers. I jink and sideslip the plane, avoiding their tracers. Kasokola reloads four more times, shooting up the camp again and again until there is no more return fire. (Owens and Owens 1992: 237)

Such actions can be part of the charisma and appeal of ardent conservationists, as we shall see in Chapter 7.[54] Fortunately, however, it is unusual.

This sort of conduct does not necessarily reduce the conservation achievements of these individuals' work. Precisely because they are free of bureaucracy they may be able to offer better value for money than larger conservation organizations. Little of their expenditure goes on overheads, offices or salaries for secretariats. Many are not interested in high salaries and genuinely offer their supporters a chance directly to support conservation work. Furthermore, the outcomes of their activities can be beneficial for conservation's cause, even where, or because, it involves violence or other dubious procedures. The Owens' work in Zambia did help to reduce poaching. This may not be the 'just world which values nature' that the IUCN strives to achieve, but a conservation venture can be highly successful without being fair or just, as I have argued elsewhere.[55]

Conclusion

Heroic white conservationists in East Africa are clearly produced by forces other than their own personality. Otherwise far fewer would be white, and they would not be able to portray their privileged lifestyles as heroic with such ease. They would represent the environmentalisms of poor natural resource users, not the colonially forged dreams of their forefathers.

Wilde's words, with which this chapter began, bear repeating: '[m]ost people are other people, their thoughts are someone else's opinions, their life a mimicry, their passions a quotation'. Behind their dismissive arrogance is a dictum which applies as much to the celebrities themselves as it does to their followers and consumers. Celebrity conservationists, and their lesser, charismatic cousins, are fulfilling the expectations of Western publics. They are a creation of society, a group of individuals' varyingly similar responses to market forces which demand they perform particular roles. The products they create, and the stances they adopt, are demanded of them, as much as they arise from their own breasts. They quote and mimic the dreams of their audiences. It takes much more than heroic individualism to break the traditions of collective experience.

This is not the popular image of celebrity conservationists. They are generally portrayed as independent individuals who have broken the mould, and set out to do their own thing, while the rest of us watch. As Wilde put it: 'the world is simply divided into two classes, those who believe the incredible ... and those who do the improbable'.[56] Believing the incredible, however, is a more influential role than it might at first appear; it determines what can be considered improbable in the first place. The projects for which celebrity conservationists can raise money will be constrained by the collective imagination of their friends and countrymen. They are also restricted by the collective and institutional imagination of the journalists and media who represent them and who are unlikely to get the air time unless they provide a suitably recognizable story. Pierre Bourdieu complains that news on television is produced to 'suit everybody because it confirms what they already know' and deliberately fails to 'change the ways we see and think'.[57] In some senses Belaney had to become Grey Owl, for '[i]f he wrote as a North American Indian he knew that his public would credit him with an insight into nature denied non-native writers.'[58]

The authenticity of celebrity conservationists is bolstered by its accordance to well-established myths of heroic behaviour, and the roles exotic places enjoy in the Western imagination. To use Wilde's language (at the beginning of Chapter 2), the skeletons of these people's legends are already laid out; all they need do is put flesh on to the bones. This constrains the freedoms that celebrity conservationists have in some ways, while making the networks they need to function easier to service in others.

It is time now to take a more analytical stance and consider the forces driving the growth of celebrity in conservation, and its consequences. Chapter 6 begins this task by examining changes in conservation networks, and in the work of celebrity, which have led both to produce, and require, celebrity within the conservation movement.

An abbreviated list of famous or charismatic conservationists and environmentalists

Edward Abbey A gun-toting, anarchic author who loved the landscapes of the American West and championed the fight for them in his fictional book *The Monkey Wrench Gang* (1975) which inspired groups like Earth First!.

George and Joy Adamson George was a game warden in Kenya, Joy an artist. Their marriage was tempestuous and unhappy. Both won international acclaim following the publication of Joy's book about their remarkable life with an adopted lioness named Elsa.

Anil Agrawal Promient Indian environmentalist journalist and activist.

Salim Ali Indian ornithologist whose writings remain standard works.

Karl Ammann Photographer and campainer agains the bushmeat trade in central Africa.

Lawrence Anthony South African conservationist and explorer who founded the Earth Organisation, rescued animals from Baghdad Zoo in the second Gulf War and negotiated with the rebels in Uganda to safeguard the northern white rhino in the DRC.

Edgar Bauer Staunch supporter of Anne LaBastille's work in Guatemala and eventually killed during disturbances in that country. Elected to the WWF roll of honour.

William Beebe Popular and scholarly explorer and naturalist with the New York Zoological Society. He excelled as an ornithologist, ocean explorer and in publicity stunts.

Archibald Belaney Englishman who emigrated to Canada and won fame speaking for conservation as an Ojibwa elder known as Grey Owl.

Peter Blinston Manager of the Painted Dog Conservation Project in Zimbabwe.

David Brower An accomplished mountaineer, he was executive director of the Sierra Club in 1952, but founded Friends of the Earth in 1969 after splitting with the Sierra Club.

Elena Bykova Uzbeki founder of the Saiga Conservation Alliance and leading conservationist of the Saiga antelope in her country.

Rachel Carson A marine biologist and author of popular books about the environment whose work *Silent Spring* marked a turning point in the environmental movement as a whole. A courageous opponent of industrial degradation.

Eugenie Clark   The 'shark lady'. Innovative researcher on shark behaviour and fishes who pioneered new ways of repelling sharks. One of North America's leading icthyologists.

Jim Corbett White naturalist and conservationist resident in India for most of his life who is famous for his accounts of hunting man-eating tigers and leopards (he only shot man-eaters). A large national park in the Kumaon Hills in northern India is named after him.

Iain Douglas-Hamilton Scottish elephant researcher of aristocratic stock. Based in Kenya and founder of Save the Elephants.

Rene Dubos   Credited with 'Think global, act local' and author of books like *Only One Earth* (1972) (with Barbara Ward) and *So Human an Animal* (1968) which won a Pulitzer Prize.

Gerald Durrell A wildlife collector, became famous for his writings about his work and went on to establish his own zoo and conservation foundation.

Five

Paul Ehrlich Entomologist and uncompromising environmentalist, author of *The Population Bomb* (1968).

Mike Fay National Geographic explorer-in-residence whose mega-transect across forests in central Africa is credited with facilitating the expansion of protected areas in Gabon. Has since worked on a mega-flyover of Africa. Works for the Wildlife Conservation Society.

Tony Fitzjohn Once George Adamson's assistant, now working in Tanzania.

Tim Flannery Scholarly and populist Australian scientist with independent views on whaling and an advocate of action on climate change.

Dian Fossey A pioneering, passionate and controversial researcher of mountain gorillas. She opposed expensive tourist trips to visit mountain gorillas which are now substantial revenue earners. She was killed while pursuing her research.

Dhrubajyoti Ghosh Indian ecologist and activist.

Jane Goodall Primatologist who won fame first for her ground-breaking work among chimpanzees and subsequently for her environmental activism, incuding founding the Roots and Shoots organization. She is widely acclaimed and has been awarded a number of international awards from a variety of institutions.

Rosamira Guillen Former zoo-keeper who campaigns for the cotton-top tamarin in South America.

Daniel Hooper Road protester in the UK, popularly known as Swampy.

William Hornaday A pugnacious defender of wildlife from over-hunting who worked for the New York Zoological Society.

Julian Huxley Eminent and popular scientist who co-founded the WWF. Also collaborated in the Oscar-winning film *The Private Life of Gannets* (1934).

David Icke One time environmental spokesman, now a conspiracy theorist with extraordinary ideas.

Rodney Jackson Expert on snow leopards and pioneered radio-collared tracking of them.

Yolanda Kakabadse Served as President of the IUCN for two terms, and Minister for the Environment in her home country (Ecuador). An internationally recognized leader in reconciling industrial and environmental interests.

Petra Kelly Prominent German Green politician.

Maria Khosa The 'Lion Queen' of Timbavati in South Africa. Spiritual guide to Linda Tucker (see below).

Rebecca Klein Works for cheetah conservation with the NGO Cheetah Conservation Botswana.

Jean and Mathieu Laboureur A father-and-son team of French conservationists and safari operators in the Central African Republic who fought violently with elephant poachers.

Anne LaBastille An ecologist and free spirit who campaigned for the survival of an endemic grebe in Guatemala, when not living simply in North America.

Richard Leakey Son of the pioneering palaeontologist Louis Leakey, Richard was an enterprising archaeologist when he was unexpectedly made the head of the newly formed Kenyan Wildlife Service. He was a powerful and effective advocate of the ban on the ivory trade and famously burnt millions of dollars' worth of tusks in a staged event in Kenya.

Boonsong Lekagul Leading Thai conservationist and ornithologist.

Aldo Leopold Founded the Wilderness Society and taught for many years in Madison from which he commuted to the second home which inspired so much of *A Sand County Almanac*. His revolutionary ideas on system and connection in nature are still inspirational.

Blythe Loutit A South African who founded the Save the Rhino Trust in 1982 in Namibia which played a leading role in saving the black rhino. Described by Saba Douglas-Hamilton, who served with her, as 'a real eco-warrior who lived on absolutely nothing'.

John Lukas Founder of the Okapi Conservation Project in the DRC.

Wangari Maathai A Kenyan environmentalist, has won the Nobel Peace Prize for, among other achievements, standing up to the environmental abuses that characterized the last years of President Moi's reign.

Laurie Marker Expert on cheetahs and advocate for their conservation. Co-founded the Cheetah Conservation Fund and is based in Namibia.

Gavin Maxwell A famous author and son of Scottish nobility who opted for a simple life in Scotland. He is most well known for his book *Ring of Bright Water* about how he raised an otter, which he acquired while visiting the explorer Wilfred Thesiger in Iraq. The book was made into a film by Bill Travers and Virginia McKenna.

Chico Mendes Campaigned successfully for rubber-tappers' livelihoods against the encroachment of cattle ranching in the Amazon. Was eventually killed by one of the ranchers he opposed.

Charudutt Mishra Whitley award winner for his work on high altitude conservation and leading light of India's Project Snow Leopard. Founding member of the Nature Conservation Foundation, Mysore.

George Monbiot Radical journalist and campaigner for socially just environmental policies and action on climate change.

Mohammed Valli Moosa Former South African politician who is now President of the IUCN.

Cynthia Moss American elephant researcher famous for her work on elephant families and relationships in and around the Amboseli National Park in Kenya. Former research assistant to Iain Douglas-Hamilton.

Guy Mountford Co-founder of the WWF and effective campaigner for tiger conservation. Published *A Field Guide to the Birds of Britain and Europe* and several travel and conservation books.

John Muir Scottish-born naturalist whose defence of wild places in the American west lead to the founding of the Sierra Club. Probably the most famous of all US conservationists.

Credo Mutwa South African 'Zulu shaman', mystic and healer with links to David Icke.

Norman Myers Ecologist who drew attention to mass extinction and invented 'hotspots'.

Abi Kusno Nachran An Indonesian journalist and activist who was nearly killed for his effective opposition to illegal forestry.

Magqubu Ntombela A game guard who was guide and mentor to Ian Player.

Delia and Mark Owens Controversial wildlife researchers who have worked in Botswana, Zambia and the USA.

Craig Packer An expert on lions and founder of the NGO Savannas Forever.

Rocio Palacios General Co-ordinator of the Anden Cat Alliance.

Roger Payne An expert on whales who discovered whale song, and released a commercial recording of it as well as working on films about whales. He founded the Ocean Alliance and campaigned against commercial whaling.

Ian Player South African who founded the Wilderness Leadership School, and prominent in the Wilderness Movement and played a prominent role saving the southern white rhino in the 1950s.

Joyce Poole American elephant researcher and associate of Cynthia Moss.

David Quammen Journalist and popular author on diverse conservation topics. Writes for *National Geographic* and *Outside*.

Martin Rapley Known as the Bug Man and presents science shows to schoolchildren in the UK.

Gregory Rasmussen Founder of the Painted Dog Conservation Project in Zimbabwe.

Ian Redmond An independent biologist and conservationist who espouses conservation causes generally but especially the cause of great apes in Africa. He worked with Dian Fossey and set up the African Ele-Fund.

Bittu Sahgal Editor of *Sanctuary Magazine* and active campaigner on diverse causes in India.

Jim Sanderson Former mathematician who campaigns for the welfare of small wild cats globally.

Ken Saro-Wiwa Nigerian environmentalist and activist who was executed for his resistance to oil pollution in the Ogoni people's lands.

George Schaller Known as the world's greatest field biologist, who began ground-breaking work with gorillas in 1959 and went on to work with tigers, lions, pandas and snow leopards. He has discovered and rediscovered several new and lost species of mammal and promoted the establishment of large protected areas.

Ernst Schumacher Wrote *Small is Beautiful*, one of the most influential books of the last century, and championed small-scale technologies.

Vandana Shiva An Indian writer and leading eco-feminist who has championed the Chipko movement, in which villagers resisted loggers by hugging the trees.

Claudio Sillero Argentinian scientist based in Oxford who is an expert on the critically endangered Ethiopian Wolf, and founder of the Ethiopian Wolf Conservation Programme.

Achim Steiner Formerly the Director General of the IUCN and now Director General of UNEP.

Valmik Thapar Fiery Indian conservationist and tiger advocate. Politically well connected.

Henry Thoreau Eccentric anarchic individualist with radical views on slavery, the state and nature. He lived simply at Walden Pond on land belonging to his friend Ralph Emerson. The book from that experience won him posthumous fame.

Russel E. Train US judge and a former big game hunter who established the African Wildlife Leadership Foundation in 1961 (later the African Wildlife Foundation) and later president of the WWF (US).

Linda Tucker Campaigner for the survival of, and respect for, white lions in South Africa.

Amy Vedder Partner of Bill Webber with whom she co-wrote the highly influential book *In the Kingdom of Gorillas*, works with the Wildlife Conservation Society.

Barbara Ward An economist whose concerns for international economic equity lead also to environmental awareness. She was a pioneer of sustainable development and wrote *Only One Earth* (1972) with Rene Dubos.

Bill Webber Partner of Amy Vedder (see above), works with the Wildlife Conservation Society.

David Western Former head of the Kenyan Wildlife Service who pioneered new community conservation schemes around the Amboseli National Park.

Edward Wilson A professor at Harvard University, who has won international recognition for diverse scientific work but is most well known for his writings about biodiversity.

David Wingate Bermudan ornithologist who helped to rediscover the Bermudan petrel and devoted his life to its restoration.

6 | Concentrations of wealth and power

[H]e led me through his wonderful picture galleries, showed me his
tapestries, his enamels, his jewels, his carved ivories, made me wonder
at the strange loveliness of the luxury in which he lived; and then he told
me that luxury was nothing but background, a painted scene in a play,
and that power, power over other men, power over the world, was the one
thing worth having, the one supreme pleasure worth knowing, the one
joy one never tired of, and that in our century only the rich possessed it.
(Oscar Wilde: *An Ideal Husband*)

The International Conservation Caucus Foundation combines the forces
of over 100 members of congress in Washington DC and enjoys the support of a special advisory council made up of the four largest conservation
NGOs in the world – the Nature Conservancy, the WWF, Conservation
International and Wildlife Conservation Society. The Foundation is committed to incorporating sound conservation principles into US foreign and
aid policy, believing that 'as America has exported freedom, democracy,
and free enterprise, we have the ability and the interest to see that America
also exports good natural resource management'.[1] As part of its activities
it holds galas and balls in Washington to honour the rich and famous
for their support for conservation. Its inaugural gala in September 2006,
with levels of sponsorship varying from US$1,000 to US$50,000, enjoyed
substantial corporate support from its partners in conservation, including
ExxonMobil, International Paper, BP and Wal-Mart, among others. The
gala honoured Harrison Ford with a newly created 'Good Steward' award.
The 2007 gala gave the same honour to millionaires Kris and Doug Tompkins for their work in Patagonia, bestowed the 'Teddy Roosevelt International Conservation Award' on Tony Blair and fêted Festus Mogae and
Jakaya Kikwete, the presidents of Botswana and Tanzania respectively,
whose countries have both set aside more than 30 per cent of their land
mass to conservation areas which prohibit human use and habitation.[2]
The chief executive officer (CEO) of DuPont presented the Conservation
Leadership in Business Award to the National Geographic Society at the
same event. At these galas corporate wealth, political power, conservation
NGOs and celebrity merge in a faultless demonstration of the powerful
networks that lie behind the rise of celebrity in conservation.

I have argued in the previous chapter that the power of celebrity in conservation can only properly be appreciated by understanding the networks of which celebrities are part. This chapter examines the four main elements of these networks. These are conservation NGOs, the foundations and companies that support them, and the wealthy individuals who support all the previous three. The latter are also interesting for their independent contributions to conservation work. I shall argue that the interactions of NGOs, foundations, business and the wealthy with celebrity have been shaped by a series of developments affecting each separately within the last thirty years. The spaces and opportunities for celebrity have multiplied at the same time as NGOs, which are central players in the integration of celebrity into conservation, have expanded in size and number. Foundations similarly have grown more powerful and numerous; businesses have found it increasingly valuable to be perceived to be 'green', and levels of inequality, and hence the philanthropic resources of wealthy individuals, have grown. These developments are not directly related, although some share similar causes. However, they have combined to produce a host of new interactions, and new possibilities for interaction, between celebrity and conservation.

I shall suggest in this chapter that the recent trends in the networks that have produced celebrity conservation have important implications for the democratic character of the environmental movement. Simply put, the trends reveal a decided turn towards a few wealthy organizations and individuals having a disproportionate influence over conservation affairs. I shall first examine recent changes in the world of celebrity and second, change in the number and variety of NGOs and the way that they interact with celebrity. Then I shall explore changes to NGO funding, considering the role of foundations and companies. Finally, I shall look at the work of the rich and its influence on conservation.

Changes in celebrity and conservation NGOs

The principal recent development in celebrity affairs has been the proliferation of media attention on famous people. We have seen the creation of celebrity magazines (*Hello!* began in 1989, *OK!* in 1993), lifestyle magazines aimed at men and women, the birth and expansion of the Internet, and cable and satellite TV. New forms of entertainment are being aired, with a multitude of reality TV shows, and televised quests for new talents and stars. There are more celebrities and opportunities to be famous than ever before.

We must not extend this argument too far. There has not been a qualitative change in the way celebrity works in recent years. People are still just as 'well-known for their well-knownness' as they were when Boorstin so aptly made that observation in 1961, and he was commenting on the developments in the nature of fame over the previous few decades. There has been, as Turner and colleagues have shown, some alteration in the structure of the industries producing fame.[3] By and large, this is mainly a change in quantity. There are more opportunities to shine in the public eye, more stages in the limelight. The reality television shows that make people famous are arguably just more intensive, deliberate and staged versions of what television has been doing for many decades.

More celebrities means more people who need to be seen to support good causes. The increase in the amount of celebrity activity and publicity has been accompanied by an increase in the scale of celebrity involvement in charitable activities, and some change too in its nature. Famous people have been sponsoring good causes publicly for a long time, but coverage in *Hello!* magazine of their heart-warming trips to help needy children is relatively new, as are mass international concerts to save the Earth, or Africa from famine.[4] The importance of their work has led the journal *Third Sector*, since 2005, to publish a weekly column on celebrities' activities for charity.

Celebrities are also continuing a long established practice of the wealthy by setting up charitable foundations to pursue good causes. They are exploiting the political leverage their media attention provides to set up pressure groups. *Forbes* magazine found that there had been a steady increase in celebrities' personal foundations (25 per cent of celebrities on their list had them), partly because foundations build up a celebrity image more than mere giving, since the foundations become part of each celebrity's personal brand.[5]

Celebrities' charitable work itself is increasingly professional and organized. One company, Celebrity Outreach, earns its money partly by linking up celebrities (from a database of over 2,500) to appropriate good causes.[6] Others, like Cision, offer a range of services in 'reputation management' and also 'media communications management solutions' including media monitoring and media contacts. The market has expanded to meet the opportunities created by celebrities' increased activities.

In this context, therefore, we should expect to see more celebrities around, and more of them taking an interest in, or even being produced by, conservation activities. Conservation and the environment are perceived to be good causes and will receive due attention from the great and the good. Unfortunately it is not quite so simple or straightforward for celebrities to connect with good causes. Many causes involve complex issues. As we saw in Chapter 3, the politics of environmental debates can be dangerously contested terrain carrying the risk of bad publicity and criticism. While more distant issues overseas may well appear to be simple and straightforward, and thus less of a risk for celebrities' images, they are also much harder to intervene in credibly. The foreign exotic countries in which dwell the most exciting wildlife also speak strange languages, practise unusual customs and may have governments that are difficult to work with. The science of environmental change can be hard to understand. It requires good advice to do the right thing.

All the new opportunities for celebrity intervention will require a special set of brokers who are needed to mediate between celebrity and environmental issues. This is one of the key roles that environmental and conservation NGOs perform. NGOs combine scientific skill and understanding with a desire to communicate with the public. Ideally they have a good network of employees, volunteers or contacts on the ground who know the places and issues well and who can guide famous guests around and advise them with regard to what to say and how to respond to the needs they see. Some of these, moreover, are also trusted household names whose logo and support act as guarantees of the authenticity and effectiveness of the work supported by celebrities.

NGOs need celebrity support.[7] The Natural Resources Defence Council Action Fund, a US organization, claimed that in one week in 2006 more than 50,000 people downloaded a video by Robert Redford about threats to the Arctic Refuge (a US protected area), making it one of the most popular Internet videos of that week.[8] The WWF reported that its collaboration with the Benfica football team (see page 27) resulted in free publicity worth €2 million.[9]

Just as the conservation work of celebrity has increased of late, so also has the scale of NGO activity. NGOs have flourished in the last thirty years. Data from the Charity Commission report a steady rise in charities registered in the UK from a few thousand in the 1960s to nearly 200,000 today. One of the major areas of growth has been in NGOs associated with development and conservation overseas. Since the 1980s, faith in the ability of states to promote development has declined. Governments, especially those of poorer countries, have often been seen as inefficient and undemocratic, with a poor track record in sponsoring effective development programmes. They can impede the function of the market. Instead, hope and resources have been increasingly vested in the third sector, i.e. in the development and conservation NGOs, which were thought to be staffed with ardent professionals keenly committed to their causes, and offer efficiencies that bureaucrats cannot match. A healthy civil society has been considered good for democracy, for it provides a body of well-informed pressure groups lobbying government and warning of the impact of bad policies. Accordingly, since the 1980s, multilateral and bilateral aid has been increasingly channelled into NGOs and away from states. Large international NGOs based in the West have grown in reach and influence. Individual countries have also relaxed restrictions on the establishment of NGOs, resulting in explosions of smaller, new organizations. Igoe and Kelsall state that India has over 1 million NGOs, and that whereas Africa was once reported to have just 9,000 NGOs in 1988, now there are nearly 100,000 in South Africa alone. Registered NGOs grew from 80 to 1,300 in Ghana between 1980 and 2001.[10]

The role, independence and benefits of the third sector have been increasingly questioned since the 1990s.[11] NGOs are no longer seen to be the 'magic bullet' of development that they once were. There are problems with their accountability and transparency, and they can be undemocratic. There are also all sorts of criticisms surrounding their work and its consequences, including conservation NGOs, as we shall discuss in Chapter 7. Multilateral and bilateral funders are now looking to support sectoral funding (government department budgets) rather than individual projects run by NGOs. Nevertheless, recent changes notwithstanding, the point is that over the last thirty years their presence, prominence and influence have been transformed.

Conservation NGOs have expanded and multiplied since the 1980s to meet demand for them. Scholfield and Brockington recently undertook a comprehensive survey of conservation NGOs working in sub-Saharan Africa, recording over 280 organizations.[12] The establishment dates of these organizations illustrate the trends described above, with the number of NGOs being formed increasing in the 1980s and peaking dramatically in the 1990s (Figure 6.1). Moreover, nearly 50 per cent of the organizations in the survey were based in the global north, with nearly half of these based in the USA. Such NGOs will be particularly suitable bridges across which Western-based celebrities can cross to serve remote and exotic places while at the same time communicating their work to the Western audiences so keen to hear about it.

The structure revealed by this survey is also important, for it shows an inequality (Table 6.1). One organization, the WWF, dominates, being greater than the next two largest organizations combined; it also works in more than twice as many countries in Africa as any other. The survey

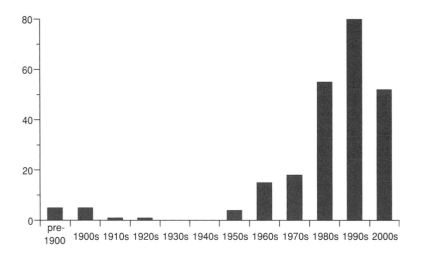

FIGURE 6.1 The development of conservation NGOs working in sub-Saharan Africa (*Source*: Scholfield and Brockington 2009)

predicts that the top ten organizations control 66 per cent of expenditure in the sector. Smaller, poorer and more numerous conservation organizations (74 per cent of those in the survey) controlled just 11 per cent of expenditure. There will be many small organizations which the survey missed, but these will not alter the basic findings. Nor does the fundamental pattern vary in other parts of the world. The WWF is also strong in the Americas, while Conservation International, the Nature Conservancy and the Wildlife Conservation Society are stronger there than in Africa.

These findings match structures elsewhere. The Charities Commission in the UK reports an even more unequal situation with 0.4 per cent of the country's 170,000 charities controlling 50 per cent of total charitable income (£46 billion), and 85 per cent of the smaller charities controlling just 4 per cent of that income.[13] There also appears to have been a concentration of resources within the conservation sector recently. The growth of the conservation NGO sector as a whole has been accompanied by a rise to dominance of the 'big four' – the WWF, Conservation International, Wildlife Conservation Society and the Nature Conservancy.[14] These organizations have managed to command an increasing share of the diminishing resources available generally to conservation organizations.

The growth and changing nature of the conservation NGO sector have

TABLE 6.1 The structure of the conservation NGO sector in sub-Saharan Africa

Size class	Range of expenditure inc. overheads ($ million)	Counted NGOs	Average expenditure inc. overheads ($)	Predicted NGOs	Predicted total expenditure inc. overheads ($)	Predicted structure (%)
7	Over 40	1	42,708,026	1	42,708,026	21
6	10–21	4	15,559,663	4	62,238,654	31
5	4.2–6.2	5	5,467,690	5	27,338,451	14
4	0.8–1.9	10	1,351,520	18	24,026,500	12
3	0.3–0.72	14	479,142	46	21,913,962	11
2	0.1–0.3	26	200,090	90	18,095,153	9
1	Up to 0.1	27	54,927	102	5,605,369	3
Total		87		266	201,926,115	

Source: Scholfield and Brockington 2009

important implications for the work of celebrity in this arena, particularly the presence of a few household names vying with each other for public recognition. The larger organizations have become increasingly professional. The WWF uses SAS software that, combined with detailed databases of supporters' preferences, allows it to tailor appeals to declared interests, making them much more effective.[15] The large NGOs have sophisticated marketing and publicity departments, and bigger budgets with which to work. They carefully forge deliberate relationships with particular celebrities. Mark Dowie, a prominent environmentalist author and critic, observes that 'American environmental NGOs thrive on celebrity and they are very territorial about their "indentured" celebs'.[16] The bigger NGOs are guarantors of authenticity and credible conservation effort. They provide potential opportunities for good publicity and will have databases of celebrities who support them in different ways and will cultivate these relationships carefully, much as businesses do with valuable clients. This means that celebrities will rarely get paid for their work, but the organizations would want to ensure that celebrities do not suffer any expense while promoting them, and that they are given sufficient time to appreciate the significance of the work NGOs are undertaking in beautiful and important parts of the world.

While these large NGOs are vital, both for their sheer size and the magnitude of their effects, and for their professional relationship with celebrity, there are more players whom we need to consider. There are a small group of conservation NGOs that feature frequently in celebrity social activities in part because the celebrities and the conservation NGOs move in similar circles. NGOs like Tusk Trust, Friends of Conservation, Elephant Family or the David Shepherd Wildlife Foundation have strong links with wealthy establishment figures in Britain for whom safaris (hunting or photographic) are an important part of their lifestyle. These organizations enjoy few, if any, degrees of separation from influential public figures, not the normal six. Moreover their success can breed success. Prince William's patronage of Tusk Trust boosts their prospects of capturing more celebrity support, for his star is much on the rise, and other celebrities want to meet him.[17] Fauna and Flora International, which started out as the aristocratic Society for the Preservation of the Fauna of the Empire, is awash with celebrity talent, with fourteen vice-presidents ranging from Princess Laurentian (Dutch royalty) to Charlotte Uhlenbroek. David Attenborough (another vice-president) is used in some membership advertisements stating that he is 'proud to be associated with what I regard as the doyen of all conservation societies'.[18] Similarly, the William Holden Foundation and the Wildlife Conservation Network have strong links with the glitterati of California whose social habitat includes wild Kenya or Botswana. Celebrity support is easily forthcoming because these are enjoyable locations to visit, as well as worthy sites to be seen to promote. Moreover the fundraising events can be lavish, or lively or well covered in the press, maybe all of these. Saving wildlife with conservation NGOs can bring people, wildlife and landscapes together in thoroughly pleasurable and worthwhile ways.

A substantial number of NGOs support the work of individual conservationists. These NGOs are integral to the work of celebrity conservationists because they give them an independent means to pursue their work and are dedicated to keeping these individuals in the public limelight. They can tap into ready markets and audience expectations that good conservation work should be peopled with heroes, individuals battling to save the planet. The Wildlife Conservation Network deliberately pursues this strategy, naming one of its fundraising galas 'A celebration of wildlife heroes'.[19] The NGOs are vehicles of fame.

All the Leakey's Angels have their own NGO. The Jane Goodall Institute is the sixth largest conservation NGO (by budget) at work in Africa. The Dian Fossey Gorilla Fund is the tenth largest in Africa. Biruté Galdikas's orang-utan foundation is smaller but still regularly raises about US$800,000 per year to support her work. There are many more. Laurie Marker, Iain Douglas-Hamilton and Cynthia Moss have all established NGOs as means of sustaining and prospering their work. Gerald Durrell established three.

Curiously, relatively few wildlife and nature film presenters have had the cachet to establish their own conservation organizations. There is Steve Irwin's Wildlife Warriors Worldwide (a company); David Bellamy co-founded the Conservation Foundation, David Suzuki the David Suzuki Foundation and Jacques Cousteau established the Cousteau Society for the Protection of Ocean Life. On a smaller financial scale Mike Pandey has used the populist reach of his *Earth Matters* series in rural India to set up the Earth Matters Foundation, but otherwise few names appear to be sufficiently well known to justify independent foundations. The one man whose image and brand could realize millions of dollars of funding for conservation causes, David Attenborough, appears not to want to exploit those directly, preferring instead to support other organizations.

There is a group of fundraising NGOs generally based in the West, yet to become household names, who are competing vigorously for publicity and for celebrity attention in order to raise their public profiles. Of the ones that I spoke to in my research some rely on personal contacts and friendships, or well-crafted invitations to celebrities whom they have spotted as potential supporters.[20] These NGOs face the problem of being but one good cause among many. They are not attached to particular charismatic or celebrity conservationists, and might have to encourage celebrities to come on board by enabling them to visit particular projects and see for themselves the work that they are doing and its importance. Others solve the problem by specifically seeking associations with known conservation personalities. They then raise funds by allowing the public to get access to these people at special events.

Some NGOs in fact shy away from celebrity. Celebrities are a relatively minor feature of Greenpeace campaigns, for example. Employees of some organizations find the celebrity world difficult to work with, and not a good authority on environmental matters.[21] They prefer to invest resources in less visible behind-the-scenes campaigning. Others have worked with them to good effect but are wary of too much involvement. Celebrities can easily go 'off message', and many can be 'very bunny hugger', i.e. concerned about individual animals rather than species' viability as a whole.[22]

Changing conservation resources

Behind the rise in conservation NGOs in recent decades and the proliferation of celebrity support lie some important changes to the configuration, origins and scale of funding available to conservation and environmental NGOs. Before the economic crisis, funding for conservation organizations had been increasing steadily. In Africa observed expenditure increased from US$113 million in 2004 to US$143 million in 2006.[23] While the crisis has derailed many plans, the long-term trend is that philanthropic foundations and companies are becoming more important. Associated with that, a number of wealthy individuals are making either significant individual donations or their own independent contributions to conservation causes.

The scale and nature of philanthropic funding for conservation NGOs is changing quite dramatically. The arrival of new celebrity-sponsored NGOs is part of the story. Leonardo DiCaprio's foundation is devoted to environmental issues and publicizes the work of select charities such as the International Fund for Animal Welfare.[24] The musician Sting set up the Rainforest Foundation, which he supports with annual concerts. Perhaps the most powerful conservation foundation was that set up by Ted Turner; the Turner Foundation gave away nearly US$70 million in 2001 to conservation causes.[25] The Disney Wildlife Conservation Foundation distributed more than US$8.5 million between 1998 (when it started) and 2005.

More importantly, the size and scale of philanthropic foundations has been increasing. In 2005 US foundations gave away US$3.8 billion, a 12 per cent increase from 2004. One-third of that came from the Bill and Melinda Gates Foundation, which has been boosted by a pledge from Warren Buffet that will be worth about US$30 billion. Despite financial crises Sachedina predicts that the Gates Foundation could rival, if not exceed, the work of USAID (the US government's department for development aid).[26] Edwards predicts that foundations will create US$55 trillion in the US in the next forty years.[27]

However not all organizations will follow this model.[28] A reliance on grants can make NGOs less responsible to their members. Organizations like Greenpeace, Friends of the Earth and the Royal Society for the Protection of Birds remain deliberately membership-based. Others try to grow to meet the immense conservation needs they perceive but are wary of the dangers of expanding too far. As one member of a prominent conservation NGO working in Africa explained to me:

> We try not to grow above a certain level as we believe that conservation NGOs that grow too fast are losing their grassroots and their ability to work efficiently. We have tried to keep the HQ staff at ten people and only slowly increase our third party funding capability. But we also found out that not growing means shrinking – with increasing salary levels, and fuel prices out of control. (Source 11, January 2008)

If conservation NGOs access more philanthropic foundations' resources, the increased scale of philanthropy does not just mean that more money is given. It also means that it is given away in larger chunks. The Gordon and Betty Moore Foundation, a product, like the Gates Foundation, of the information technology revolution, donated US$261 million to Conservation International, the largest grant in conservation history. Foundations giving away tens of millions of dollars every year cannot afford to give in small quantities. This means that they favour large organizations that have the capacity to spend abundantly, or to intermediaries that can pass it on to these organizations. The unequal structure of the conservation sector we observed in Africa is, if anything, only likely to increase. Indeed, two of the top five players are relatively recent arrivals on the scene (Conservation International was created in 1987; the Peace Parks Foundation in 1997). Thus the corporate-style marketing, image management and associated celebrity endorsements, which larger conservation NGOs are so good at, look set to continue.

The second source of increased income for conservation organizations comes from developing closer ties with industry and business. This is partly because they need their money and partly because they have to engage with business in all sorts of issues if they are to effect change. It also reflects the increasing needs of many companies, particularly the larger ones, that want to be seen to be green through sponsoring environmental causes.

This is not a new development. The first national parks in the USA were established with the support of railroad companies who were quick to appreciate their importance in promoting tourism to wealthy families on the East Coast. When the WWF launched one of its first appeals in 1961 they were able to raise £30,000 from general public donations, and two individual donations of £10,000 each from one wealthy property developer and Shell International.[29] Nevertheless, many organizations in the environmental sector have lost the confrontational edge that characterized their work in the 1960s.

The strength of the links between conservation NGOs and large companies these days is undeniable. Dorsey has noted that three-quarters of Conservation International's board were corporate representatives, half of the board of the Nature Conservancy, and one-third of the WWF's board of directors were affiliated with corporations, including a number of CEOs. The links are becoming increasingly well marketed and ingenious. Conservation International and the Ford Motor Company have established the Centre for Environmental Leadership in Business 'to engage the private sector worldwide in creating solutions to critical global environmental problems in which industry plays a defining role'.[30] The film *Kung Fu Panda* (2008) promoted Conservation International's conservation work with pandas in China in conjunction with McDonald's. Mitigation is an increasingly standard practice by which conservationists, miners and engineers can find common purpose (as we saw in Chapter 2). The US$50 billion project to dam the Mekong River in Laos is supported by the IUCN and WWF because it comes with the establishment of new protected areas in the highlands around the new dams' watersheds.[31] Conservation International and Newmont are collaborating in a mitigation deal in Ghana where Newmont's mining activity in one forest reserve is being offset by its funding of conservation and rehabilitation work in a larger forest reserve elsewhere in the country.[32]

As with the larger foundations, size matters when dealing with large corporations. When greening their image and practices, large companies want to deal with conservation groups whose brand and presence will have global recognition, and who have the capacity to cope with the scale of their needs. This will inevitably result in the emergence and growth of a set of large conservation NGOs that are able to cater for the needs of big business.

Finally, the larger NGOs are also the best vehicles for those extremely wealthy individuals who want to make significant donations to charity but who do not want the expense, cost and time of setting up their own organization. These large organizations matter because they alone have the capacity to spend the resources that the super-rich wish to give them. For example the Wildlife Conservation Society has received the Steeple and Grand Jason islands in the Falklands from Michael Steinhardt and 275,000 hectares in Tierra del Fuego from the firm Goldman Sachs. It also received a US$20 million challenge grant from Robert Wilson in 2002 to manage wild areas of the world. In 2006 their 'Tigers Forever' programme attracted US$10 million from venture capitalist Michael Cline and Wall Street financier Thomas Kaplan.

The change in conservation NGO funding could have significant implications for the responsiveness of conservation NGOs to grassroots concerns. It is possible to imagine some international conservation organizations springing up which are funded by a few wealthy people, companies and foundations, and which market their ideas and policies vigorously with the use of a few select celebrities. They would undoubtedly be effective, and would certainly change the world, but whether we could call them part of a broader environmental movement is not clear. This would be elite-led and elite-driven conservation. The abilities of such organizations to hear, represent and act effectively on grassroots agendas would be questionable.

The rich list

All over the world, like lords of creation, are those who, by travel, command the seasons and, by many houses, the very landscape they will see each morning or afternoon they are awakened. (C. Wright Mills: *The Power Elite*)

Since Mills wrote these words in 1959, the rise in philanthropic wealth and green corporate power has been accompanied by increasing levels of wealth and inequality, both globally and within key wealthy countries which are the source of much charitable giving. Rothkopf observes that it is not just the broad trends of persistent inequality in the world's wealthiest countries that are important. Rather it is the levels of inequality within the wealthiest portion of these societies.[33] Just 95,000 people control over 25 per cent of the world's wealth, and the richest thousand of these are more than twice as rich as the poorest 2.5 billion people. Moreover, this trend is becoming more pronounced. Within the USA between 1990 and 2004 real household income increased by about 2 per cent. It increased by over 50 per cent for the top 1 per cent of earners, and by 112 per cent for the top 0.1 per cent.[34] Privately wealthy individuals are increasingly able to pursue their own conservation agendas.[35]

For most of history, political power and economic power have coincided. Wealthy individuals who wanted to set aside land for conservation purposes (typically for hunting) were often the rulers with the authority and means to do so, or were closely related or socially connected to those who did. The antecedents of modern conservation policy today can be found in the practices of princely India, with their hunting reserves, on occasion stocked with imported wildlife.[36] Some princes even introduced African lions to cope with the disappearance from their lands of Indian specimens. Or consider William the Conqueror, a Norman king who invaded England, and claimed one-third of the land for his hunting estates. Indeed, what is unusual about wealth today is that, despite its influence, it is so often disassociated from direct political power.

This disassociation does not matter so much in conservation affairs, for the wealthy still retain direct control over practical conservation outcomes through their great, and growing, land holdings. The lands of the wealthy already have substantial effects on the use of significant portions of the planet, and their potential in this area is increasing. Wealthy conservationists can function in much the same way as charismatic conservationists. They are independent individuals who set out to pursue their own agenda because they believe it to be right, or because it makes good business sense as part of tourism ventures. The difference is that the rich do not even need backing from a close network of friends (although they often enjoy it). It is vital that consideration is given to the rich because they have the scope to do what they want in many countries, and the resources to quell or dissuade most opposition. They are a central element of what George Holmes calls 'the transnational conservationist class'.[37]

Perhaps the most prominent contemporary super-rich conservationist is Ted Turner. As vice-president of Time-Warner (a media and communications company) and founder of CNN, he already has considerable influence over the careers, and use, of many celebrities. His Captain Planet cartoon show features a superhero who helps five young activists tackle environmental problems. However, his independent actions as a wealthy individual are also important and perhaps his most direct personal influence on conservation. Turner is a major landowner. He has purchased hundreds of thousands of hectares of rangelands in the American West. On them he has reintroduced wolves and prairie dogs and given protection to threatened species. He even has the largest private herd of bison in the world, numbering some 40,000 animals, which he manages partly as a commercial venture.

Turner's extensive property along the east of the Rocky Mountains demonstrates how the influence of wealthy landowners can be enhanced simply by the size of land parcels available for sale. Former settler societies who made available large areas of land for public purchase and development by alienating it from former owners (such as in Australia, New Zealand, Canada, South Africa and the USA) are often able to offer individual plots which make a substantial difference to the conservation estate if managed appropriately. Eileen Lange (musician popularly known as Shania Twain) has been able to buy two large hill sheep farming stations in southern New Zealand covering nearly 25,000 hectares. The New Zealand government was able to negotiate conservation and public access concessions on the properties before allowing the sale to go ahead. Ian Koblick (diver) similarly purchased a stake in the popular 26,000 hectare Walter Peak Station near Queenstown in the same country.

By spending their wealth in relatively poor regions, the world's richest people can purchase even larger estates. Recently, they have been particularly visible in Africa and Latin America. In the latter, Johan Eliasch (Swedish businessman) bought 162,000 hectares of rainforest in Brazil. Doug and Kris Tompkins have spent millions of dollars securing hundreds of thousands of hectares of land in Patagonia and establishing the Pumalin Park. Their neighbouring landowners include Ted Turner and George Soros (billionaire financier).

In Africa, Brian Tudor Jones, an American who made billions as a futures trader, is managing a large area of land near the Serengeti National Park in Tanzania. He has set up Grumeti Reserves, a private company which will market holidays in the Reserve to 'high-end' tourists at US$1,500 per night and has offered diverse forms of local development support while trying to persuade some nearby villagers to move.[38] Rick Carr, a US entrepreneur, has committed US$40 million in a bid to reopen the Gorongoza National Park in Mozambique; Halvor Astrup, a multimillionaire Norwegian businessman and supporter of numerous conservation projects, is funding substantially the redevelopment of the Niassa Reserve in the north of the same country.

One of the most prominent and wealthiest investors in Africa was the late Paul van Vlissingen (Dutch billionaire) who founded the African Parks Foundation. His foundation manages parks in Sudan, Ethiopia, Malawi, DRC, Zambia and South Africa. Van Vlissingen believed that parks could and should become independent income earners in their own right.[39] This approach is similar to that of Tudor Jones: a mixture of investment in tourism and attempts to win local support.

Van Vlissingen displayed another characteristic of the work of the rich: he enjoyed a close association with another rich individual, Sam Robson Walton (the world's richest man in 2001). The rich work through inter-connected networks of friendship and mutual support. Consider Elephant Family. Its founder, Mark Shand, is the brother of Camilla Parker-Bowles (consort to the Prince of Wales) and married to Clio Goldsmith (former actress) who is the niece of the late billionaire Sir James Goldsmith. Elephant Family patrons include a member of the Rothschild family (bankers) and royalty from the UK and India. Small wonder then that reports on its fundraising events and expensive charitable auctions are reported in the upmarket magazine *Tatler*.

Perhaps the most notorious example of this network is the 1001 Club which was run by the WWF. This was a group of wealthy individuals and corporate donors to the WWF initiated by the late Prince Bernhard of the Netherlands and the late Anton Rupert, a billionaire South African tobacco and alcohol magnate, who founded the South African branch of the WWF. One of the additional benefits it offered to its members, many of whom were South African, was a chance to bypass the economic sanctions being applied to South Africa under apartheid because it made it easier for its members to meet and conduct business.[40] Rupert went on to found the Peace Parks Foundation, which is seeking to expand and consolidate protected areas along the borders of African nations. He, Prince Bernhard and Nelson Mandela gave the foundation stability through Club 21, composed of twenty-one companies that have made substantial donations.[41] The club is a roll-call of some of the most wealthy businesses, people and foundations in Africa.

In many respects the work of these wealthy landowners is no different from that of numerous land trusts and conservation groups set up to preserve private land from development. There are hundreds of these organizations in the United States, protecting hundreds of thousands of hectares of land every year. The wealthier individuals stand out for the stamp of their personality which they bring to their diverse schemes.

Consider the independently acting conservationist Li Quan who founded and runs the charity Save China's Tigers. Quan is a wealthy Chinese businesswoman who, with her Wall Street financier husband, Stuart Bray, has spent more than US$8 million (with more support from other organizations) rehabilitating the rare South China tiger back into the wild. Three are now running free in a private game ranch in South Africa. Quan is an unusual figure, even for African conservation. She was once the licensing director of a fashion company, Gucci International. Her enthusiasm for cats means she wears paw-print glasses, a cat necklace, cheetah charm and a tiger-print jacket. Save China's Tigers also has notable celebrity support including a recent endorsement by Jackie Chan (actor), Chen Kaige (film director) and David Tang (socialite).[42] Tigers in Africa tend to ring alarm bells, as Monty Python (British comedy group) has shown, and some conservationists feel this is gimmicky. Quan, however, is a pragmatist. There are between ten and thirty of these tigers in the wild, and about sixty in zoos. Quan hopes to use the space available in South Africa, and the tigers' well-known breeding ability, to build up a group of animals who are able to fend for themselves, so that they will be capable of thriving in their home territory. Quan is working with others to create the reserves in China to which the animals can return.[43]

Similarly independently minded was the late John Aspinall.[44] Having built a fortune on gambling Aspinall established his own zoos and advocated 'going in', crossing the boundaries with dangerous animals. His zoos also had strong conservation missions and he was commended by some scientists for his 'uncanny knack' with animals. He idealized the Zulu people in South Africa and was initiated into the Zulu nation in 1990. He held singular opinions about the dangers of overpopulation. When told by Richard Nixon that a nuclear war would kill 200 million people Aspinall responded that this was not enough. He wanted 3.5 billion fewer people, and was prepared to be among those who would have to go. These are not, however, the harmless dreams of an individual; they had reach and influence through his wealth and connections. He was a friend of the Goldsmiths (both Sir James and Edward who established *The Ecologist* magazine).[45] His friendships with Ian Player, Magqubu Ntombela and Laurens van der Post saw him sponsor the first World Wilderness Congress in 1977 which helped to drive the movement and wilderness network so instrumental in spreading Player's ideas.

Conservation on private land can make substantial contributions to conservation goals. State protected areas conserve 6 per cent of South Africa's land mass, but private game reserves cover 13 per cent of the land. In Scotland and Patagonia private landownership makes valuable additions to the protected area estate. Pasquini's study of private wildlife farms in the Eastern Cape of South Africa showed that they made significant contributions to the diversity of habitats protected in the Province.[46] She also showed that these wildlife reserves were not necessarily tied to tourism. Many landowners were simply wealthy people who enjoyed restoring what they perceived to be the proper condition of the landscape.

The presence of private money, and the absolute ownership title confers, do not prevent conflict over landowners' conservation ambitions. From the earliest days of modern conservation rural people have contested its goals, and restrictions on use of resources placed by their wealthy neighbours. Jacoby reports that in 1893, 60 privately owned hunting estates covered over 380,000 hectares in the Adirondacks, where state Forest Preserves protected only 295,000 hectares.[47] The restrictions these private landowners imposed on access to fishing and game were unpopular. One, Orlando Dexter, was shot dead in 1903, in all probability by a local resident who resented such restrictions. Another was William Rockefeller (super-rich oil magnate) who bought up large areas of land, tearing down the houses built upon them. His actions were unpopular locally: he was labelled 'the Maker of Wilderness', and his guards had to cope with arson, theft, poaching and being shot at. When Rockefeller took one poacher to court, the legal wrangling went on for four years as locally raised juries quickly found him innocent.[48]

The African Parks Foundation's work in Ethiopia has been dogged by controversy because of evictions from the Nechisar National Park in which the Foundation was working. Van Vlissingen did not help the controversy by admitting: 'We didn't want to be involved in the resettlement, so I put a clause in the contract that said we wouldn't take over the park until the resettlement was completed.'[49] In other words, the Ethiopian government would have to ensure the park was clear before the Foundation would act. Van Vlissingen did not specify whether or not the contract insisted that the resettlement was carried out in accordance with internationally recognized best practice.

Park expansion in South Africa, also fuelled by private money, is meeting similar problems. Here the lands destined for conservation are often former white-owned farms with substantial populations of resident labourers.[50] Turning agricultural land into private wildlife reserves can substantially reduce labour requirements, or it can impinge on the keeping of livestock and use of resources labourers have been accustomed to.[51] Although these are employees, who could in theory, under a capitalist system, merely be laid off and asked to leave, many are families who have lived, worked and served in the area for generations. They have ties to the land which are little different from those of the smallholders and rural dwellers displaced from their own lands elsewhere on the continent.[52] Conversely, when private wildlife reserves become lucrative tourism destinations, there have been substantial increases in the number of people employed and in their average incomes, although it is not clear whether these are jobs former labourers can easily take on.[53]

Conclusion

The celebrification of conservation has arisen through the convergence of four trends. Conservation NGOs and philanthropic foundations have grown in size and power; corporate wealth has become more important to both, and expectations of good corporate social responsibility have made them important to industry; private wealth and landownership are also being enrolled to conservation causes. Celebrity, which itself has grown in prominence over the same period, has emerged with a need to serve good causes, just as conservation has become more media conscious and professional in its use of new-found resources. Access to celebrity has become one of the additional inducements that conservation can offer its wealthy donors.

It is undeniable that these forces benefit elites. Membership of the privileged circle of decision-makers depends on great wealth, fame or connections, but I do not think that it makes things that much more unequal than in the past. In general our world is not more unequal now than 200 years ago; it is more equal, and more democratic. Rothkopf observes that Carnegie's (a steel magnate) and Rockefeller's wealth was as spectacular as Bill Gates's (co-founder of Microsoft and the Gates Foundation) is now.[54] Indeed theirs was greater, when expressed as a proportion of GDP, or compared with the US federal budget.

The magnitude of inequality between rich and poor is not substantially different now from previous eras. The lives at the top have long appeared unimaginably wonderful when viewed from the bottom. What has changed over the decades is that the elites are better connected and more cohesive; they behave as a class.[55] If Wilde is right and wealth is but the means to power then it is now wielded in groups, not individually. The networks of celebrity and conservation are part of the glue that binds these new allegiances of the rich and powerful together, providing the good causes and pageantry of philanthropy.

In this context the role of celebrity in conservation becomes particularly interesting. It could compound the problem of elitism in conservation, in that celebrities are part of the global elite who are chosen undemocratically to speak for us on matters environmental. This would be the case where celebrity merely works within a sealed circle of influence which gives the illusion of representativeness, but without the interactions democracy requires. Alternatively, celebrities could challenge this status quo, for with their legitimacy to speak out comes an ability to connect with, and represent, the ideas of all the rest of us. Viewed thus celebrity could bring the rich and powerful to heel. It subjects their actions to the direct inspection by everyday citizens who can access their leaders through the likes of Bono and Geldof (both musicians now famous for their campaigns against poverty) and who can lobby business leaders through these celebrity leaders for the first time.

It is time to examine more closely the consequences of celebrity's interaction with conservation. We shall begin by examining the discontent that arises from the lack of integrity which is perceived to pervade celebrities' environmental activism, and the mistakes and violence that it can entail. Then, in the final chapter, we shall consider in more depth the relationships between democracy, conservation and capitalism.

7 | Criticisms

Discontent is the first step in the progress of a man or a nation. (Oscar
Wilde: *A Woman of No Importance*)

In 2007 the actress Sienna Miller was interviewed on the *Today* programme for BBC Radio 4 about her work with Global Cool. The presenters
were concerned about the possible hypocrisy of Global Cool's message:
wealthy celebrities were asking everybody else to curtail their consumption in the name of the environment, when the celebrities' own luxurious,
hedonistic lifestyles made them the most voracious consumers of all.
Miller put up a brave fight but there was not much she could say about
this contradiction. In the end she admitted she could do little about her
own extensive jet travel, but she could take fewer hot baths in order to
promote good planetary stewardship.

Critics complain that the celebrities supporting conservation are too
ignorant or hypocritical to be taken seriously, or they are incompetent,
even criminal. This chapter examines the problems that celebrities' involvement in environmental and conservation causes have produced. I
argue that these issues need to be taken seriously; there are elements of
the celebrification of conservation which could detract from conservation's message, or compromise it in other ways. However, my principal
discontent is with these criticisms themselves; they do not result in
much progress at all. I do not believe that these issues are a problem of
celebrity conservation per se; rather they illustrate more general problems with the environmental and conservation movements. The work of
celebrity may compound them, but celebrity is not the cause of them. I
shall further suggest that all these complaints fail to comprehend how
celebrity conservation works, and thus underestimate its reach and trans-
formations.

I shall consider first the problems which celebrities' actions and
interventions have given the movements they support and argue that
those associated with celebrities' conservation NGOs are generic to
the NGO sector. Second, I shall examine the violence of conservation
to people and animals (in debates about hunting), arguing that anti-
poaching violence and hunting are both integral to conservation practice,

and not substantially altered by celebrity. Finally, I shall examine the charge of hypocrisy, and suggest that this stems from larger compromises which the sustainable development movement has already made. Radical critiques, if offered in celebrity mode, provide no escape from these dilemmas.

Problematic interventions

David Icke has had a rich, multifaceted career. He began playing professional soccer in English leagues, and later became a journalist and sports presenter, then national spokesperson for the Green Party (UK). However things became particularly interesting when, in 1991, he proclaimed himself to be the son of God with a mission to call everyone to wear turquoise to heal the world. He declared, *inter alia*, that Stonehenge was a global powerpoint which Merlin had switched off when leaving the planet. Icke failed to win many converts. He went on to become a conspiracy theory lecturer in North America.[1]

There is a wonderful, barmy Monty Pythonesque character to the liberties that some of the rich and famous elites take with their conservation activity. Few have the imagination of David Icke, but the examples of relatively harmless eccentricity I encountered while researching for this book gave the work the odd moment of joy. Where else might one encounter tigers in Africa (see page 106)? Or consider Linda Tucker, CEO and Founder of the Global White Lion Project Trust,[2] who campaigns to restore white lions to their natural habitat in South Africa, and prevent them from being hunted. She enthuses that:

> There is not time to take you deep into the mystery of the White Lions, but I want to leave you with one thought: Timbavati, the birthplace of the White Lions, aligns exactly with Giza, the resting place of the Great Sphinx, humankind's greatest riddle. This is the exact meridian with the ancient Egyptians called ZEP TEPI, the most sacred leyline on earth – the birth canal of the human species. (Tucker 2003)

The freedoms of the wealthy and famous include the ability just to act on their beliefs, without having to justify their work to tiresome sceptics, scientists or bureaucracies.

Every now and then the liaisons between celebrities and the conservation movement can produce embarrassing errors. In 1961 Prince Philip provoked public protests in Britain for shooting a tiger, just a few months before he helped to found the WWF.[3] The Bollywood film actor Salman Khan was caught poaching the rare black buck in India in 1996. This was

111

awkward for the WWF, which had recently produced a calendar featuring photographs of various celebrities, including Khan, in support of the organization's work. Sometimes rumours about environmental work are used to embarrass celebrities. Paris Hilton (model and actress) is alleged to have said that she was going to take up the cause of inebriated Indian elephants which steal home-produced liquor in Indian villages, get drunk, and then electrocute themselves. Commentators welcomed the initiative, arguing she was a suitable authority. Hilton's representatives later denied the story.

More substantial charges were laid against Sting and his wife Trudie Styler, who founded the Rainforest Foundation together in 1988. The Rainforest Foundation quickly became prominent because of its celebrity-ridden benefit concerts arranged by Sting. However, allegations of inefficiency and ineffectiveness soon arose, particularly over the work of Jean-Pierre Dutilleux, who helped establish the Foundation. The Foundation was alleged to have spent too much money on the music concerts and too little, often ineffectively, on actual conservation. This was the subject of an exposé in the British current affairs TV programme *World in Action* in 1990, as well as critical articles in *Rolling Stone* magazine.[4]

It is not clear how much substance there was to these allegations. The Rainforest Foundation severed ties with Dutilleux after the exposé, and took professional advice that led to its restructuring to make its work more effective and accountable.[5] It is now a successful conservation organization. It has continued to thrive and grow, expanding its operations from Brazil to several other continents and with benefit concerts generating millions of dollars. Nevertheless in 2004–06 it received low ratings from the US NGO monitor, Charity Navigator, because it had spent only 43 per cent of its income on programmes on the ground.[6]

The danger here (so common with celebrity) is that one can get caught focusing on the antics of the individual, and miss the implications for the larger systems of which they are part. The problems of fundraising costs and efficient expenditure of resources are not peculiar to the Rainforest Foundation but pervasive to the conservation movement as a whole. The question of how much money gets spent on administration costs is a sensitive one in the charitable sector. In some instances it is not appropriate to minimize overheads. If the organization gives out grants then it will be necessary to research their grantees thoroughly and follow up on their gifts to ensure the money is being well spent. This will not be cheap. In others, performance varies according to the audiences targeted. For example, in 2006 the charity Save the Rhino undertook a plethora of activities, all carefully targeted to particular audiences, which cost over US$383,000 and raised US$1,037,000. In contrast Conservation International reported that just four annual fundraising dinners in the US cost more than US$780,000 in 2004–05 but returned revenues of over US$3,840,000. Conservation International has the good fortune to raise money from the rich, which always yields a better return on their efforts. Save the Rhino, on the other hand, fundraises from a much poorer constituency. It is particularly well known for its marathon running (it spent nearly US$46,000 on marathons in 2005–06), in which runners compete wearing heavy rhinoceros costumes. This activity is a particular favourite among single young to middle-aged men, but they do not always have wealthy friends to sponsor them.

Is the ledger book the best place to evaluate all the consequences of conservation fundraising? The money is important, but these activities are also designed to raise profile and consciousness. The sight of runners dressed as rhinoceroses completing the London Marathon raises awareness of conservation much more broadly. Furthermore, conservation fundraising is part of the pageantry of everyday life. It is one of the means by which people express their love for, and commitment to, nature and its conservation. It is how they 'make a difference'. Surely people who are relatively less prosperous should still have the opportunity of giving to charities, even if it is expensive for the charities to solicit their support. Considering financial returns alone is a mean-spirited way of evaluating this fundraising.

The second aspect of the criticism against the Rainforest Foundation – that its money was not spent wisely on addressing conservation problems – is also a much more general problem. Some studies have found that, at large scales, conservation expenditure is not well correlated with conservation priorities.[7] More telling still is the fact that these studies are few and relatively recent. Conservation has rarely attempted to audit its own effectiveness. The attempt to trace the connections between conservation investment and outcomes is only just emerging, as is the literature exploring how to spend conservation funds in the most cost-effective fashion.[8] With hindsight it is surprising that donations to conservation have not come with more stringent demands for assessment of performance or effectiveness of conservation measures. The trouble with conservation organizations is that it is hard to know what good they are doing, or how well and efficiently they are achieving it. Critical evaluation of their work is just beginning. This underlines the fact that conservation is widely perceived as simply a good cause to which one should give as much as possible, safe in the knowledge that activists' passion would put the money to the best possible use.

There are signs that the presumption of good behaviour is wearing thin. In his book *Losing Ground*[9] Mark Dowie lamented the loss of distinction and voice in the American movement which resulted from excessively close ties to government and industry. MacDonald voiced similar concerns in *Green, Inc.*[10] In 2003 the *Washington Post* published a scathing series attacking the Nature Conservancy for becoming too close to industry and failing to take a stand against the interests of its corporate donors in the US.[11] Rothkopf has suggested that the failure of the WWF US to join the WWF International's opposition to a dam built by the US company Alcoa may be because the WWF US's former CEO, Kathryn Fuller, also served on the Alcoa board.[12] In 2004 Mac Chapin attacked the Nature Conservancy, Conservation International and the WWF for becoming too close to corporate interests, so that they were working against the needs of local environmental groups and indigenous communities.[13] For example, instead of opposing mining or logging, conservation organizations are accepting environmental offsets to mitigate the damage caused, or taking over logging concessions and running them as reserves after they have been logged. Chapin is not alone in his concerns. Romero and Andrade have made similar criticisms and Dowie added the Wildlife Conservation Society to the list of big international NGOs who risk ignoring local environmentalists.[14]

These problems reflect a much more general issue within the NGO movement as a whole – that of accountability, of using funds effectively and transparently so that their use can be scrutinized, and the rigorous assessment of the influence of large donors over the organizations' work. As these organizations become larger they find themselves controlling millions of dollars and wielding considerable influence. But to whom are they accountable, and how can they be transparent? These problems are compounded when the organizations are working across borders, with their funding base in some (rich) countries, demanding action to save the environment in other countries where the consequences of these actions are felt. NGOs may be working with people from whom they have no electoral mandate to act, and who have no representatives on their board or staff. It can be difficult for NGOs to avoid charges of neo-imperialism on the one hand (if they listen too closely to their funders) or disingenuity (if they take the money but listen too closely to local objections) on the other. In some senses the problems with the Nature Conservancy which the *Washington Post* highlighted are unusual – all the allegations of malpractice took place in one country, the USA, by an NGO registered and raising money in that country. This made it easier for the US press and government to call them to account.

Where NGOs are working across borders a host of other problems have been identified. Hassan Sachedina's doctoral thesis offers a compelling analysis of the work of the African Wildlife Foundation, one of the Conservancy's partners in Africa and the fourth largest conservation NGO on the continent.[15] Based on several years' work in the organization as a fundraiser and more in the villages of the Maasai Steppe in Tanzania (one of African Wildlife Foundation's key heartlands), Sachedina tracks in detail how the organization successfully scaled up, doubling its income, by pursuing a close relationship with USAID, as well as wooing celebrities like Ted Turner and courting prominent politicians. At the same time, and as a result of this success, Sachedina shows that the organization became too focused on its own need to grow, and lost its grip on its fundamental mission – promoting wildlife conservation and local prosperity. Sachedina shows with devastating effect how the important ecological and political problems in the Maasai Steppe heartland were being ignored, or worse, aggravated, by the African Wildlife Foundation's actions. He is also clear that the fault did not lie with the organization alone, but arose too from the way that donors handle their relationship with their grantees.

More generally, there are a number of studies of the negative impacts of conservation policies, supported by NGOs, on rural lives and livelihoods due to eviction and, more commonly, exclusion from conservation areas.[16] There are also concerns that conservation policies marginalize or disempower local groups.[17] Some writers have observed that international NGOs can displace local NGOs and compete with them for funds. Where they register national chapters they then become competitors for the same sources of money, and tend to be much better at presenting funding cases.[18] A study in Fiji has found that the presence of international conservation NGOs detracts from the capacity of government departments to deal with conservation, or at least fails to enhance them, and may not necessarily enhance national conservation strategies, or tackle the root causes threatening biodiversity.[19] When international NGOs do work with local NGOs this is no simple empowerment process. Rather they can transform the activities and structure of locally based NGOs. Igoe has argued that international support for pastoralist NGOs in East Africa vitiated their accountability.[20]

Thus it should not be surprising if celebrity-led and -founded NGOs like Sting's Rainforest Foundation experience problems with respect to the governance and use of their resources. These are but manifestations of problems common to the entire sector. It would be more surprising if well-meaning amateurs like Sting could just walk in and get it right. Indeed, given the general doubts and disquiet surrounding the work of NGOs as a whole, the articles in the *Washington Post* were probably most interesting because of the furore they generated. The sensation they caused was considerable, because the Nature Conservancy was (and is) a venerable institution in the US. The critiques against them were a major scoop for the *Post*, but it would surely have been more reasonable to expect the organization to display problems that are characteristic of the sector. The Nature Conservancy could be exposed so sensationally because it was placed, like the environmental causes it championed, on a pedestal.

Violence and hunting

There is an ambivalent attitude towards violence in conservation debates. Violence against (certain types of) people is strangely tolerated, whereas violence against (certain types of) wildlife is not. In fact, it is remarkable, given the levels of violence that some conservation policies can involve, how few people win notoriety as a result of their conservation work. In the course of writing this book I have come across very few examples. Wilde's ridiculous claim that 'Society, civilised society at least, is never very ready to believe anything to the detriment of those who are both rich and fascinating' again seems oddly true when celebrity and conservation interact.[21]

There are exceptions. Dian Fossey attracted some criticism in her lifetime for taking her personal crusade against poachers too far, inflicting some cruelties in the process (such as orchestrating mock executions on suspected poachers).[22] This aspect of her legacy is not widely remembered. Prince Bernhard donated money to the WWF which was ring-fenced for use in hiring paramilitary support against rhino and elephant poachers.[23] This was kept secret at the time presumably because it could have brought adverse publicity.

Among the most infamous conservationists I have encountered while working on this book are the Laboureurs. Jean and Matthieu Laboureur (father and son) were French conservationists working in the Central African Republic who won considerable acclaim in France for their hardline methods against elephant poachers. Matthieu is another of those conservationists who has been compared to Tarzan. There is no doubt their methods of protecting national parks were extreme. Michael Fay recalls that Matthieu 'was 20 years old then, a crazy bad-ass. He and the old man would go out with a few guys and some old single-shot guns, and they'd take on 50 guys with machine guns and scatter them'.[24] However, when one of them killed an innocent man whom they suspected of poaching but, it turned out, had had every right to be in the park, they were forced to leave the country, and some of the press turned against them.[25]

In the US, Earth First! activists won some notoriety for their direct approach to preventing development. They sat in trees marked for felling, buried salt in dirt runways so that deer and elk would grub up and disturb the surfaces, destroyed bulldozers, cut power lines and spiked lumber trees with lumps of metal which could be highly dangerous for lumberjacks. The Sea Shepherds, an activist NGO which fought whaling by scuttling whaling boats with limpet mines, have also attracted criticism.[26]

One of the founders of Earth First!, Bruce Hayse, later followed in the Laboureurs' footsteps, hiring mercenaries to take on poachers in a massive area of the Central African Republic, insisting that 'if we were going to save this place people would have to be killed'.[27] Conservation organizations have been quick to distance themselves from Hayse's policy and the actions of his African Rainforest and River Conservation organization. However, Shanahan argues that this rhetoric may mask a deeper complicity.[28] He suggests that Hayse's bid to take the battle to the poachers may be the only way some protected areas can survive and that 'leaders in the international community must share in this sentiment and, thus, have refrained from interfering with Hayse's cause'.[29] Rhetorical condemnation of Hayse, according to Shanahan, still amounts to implicit approval if it is not accompanied by stronger action.

These incidents, however, stand out as exceptional because of the disapproval associated with them. More often than not, violent conservationists are celebrated as heroes. As we have already seen the Owens were quite candid in the descriptions of the violence they used against poachers in Zambia. Where violence against poachers prevents violence against animals it accords with a current of Western opinion. A strong stance against nature's destruction is often a popular one, particularly in faraway countries. There is a good public demand in the West for heroic (white) poacher-hunters who go out to save wildlife the hard way. Conservation extremists can win considerable public sympathy.

Any discussion of wealth and celebrity in conservation must consider hunting because the rich and famous have been central to the evolution of the hunt, and their money sustains it. Hunters see themselves as stewards of nature, whose behaviour, when regulated, is beneficial for conservation because they only take individual animals and their total take can never endanger the species as a whole. They insist that they enjoy an intimate understanding of their prey and celebrate the proximity to nature hunting allows them to enjoy, as Cartmill has observed: 'Many hunters say that killing their own food gives them a feeling of cutting through the trivia and hypocrisy of civilization and getting in touch with life's elemental realities' (Cartmill 1993: 236).

Hunting is no simple act of killing. It involves a series of ritualized behaviours and attitudes towards the hunt and prey formed over centuries in the royal courts of Europe and India. Cartmill charts the development of the hunt in medieval Europe, and the introduction of an ornate vocabulary to describe different species' dung and body parts.[30] MacKenzie has shown how the imperial hunters in India adopted rituals developed by the Mughals and princely states.[31] He argues that later Victorian hunters 'extoll[ed] … the valour and violence involved in vanquishing foes animal'[32] and that these attitudes became part of a universal experience of expatriates in the Empire, and a popular theme of stories and education for British children. These traditions have not died, but have been reinvented anew in contemporary African hunting safaris. Hurt and Ravan quote the Spanish philosopher José Gasset, insisting that hunting constitutes an experience and practice in which killing is just the last regretful necessity: 'one does not hunt in order to kill: on the contrary one kills in order to have hunted'.[33] Mark Sullivan, who runs hunting safaris in Tanzania, specializes in shooting animals at extremely close range on foot and encouraging them to charge at him and his clients. When he claims that '[r]ather than shooting the great and noble beast into oblivion from a safe distance, my clients and I choose instead to walk up and give the animal a choice of how he is to die in battle' he is following in the tradition of codifying some forms of hunting as honourable and brave. The act of killing is enobled, the wildlife are given the chance to 'die with honour', and the bravery of the hunters confirmed in the process.[34]

Hunting is a socially exclusive activity in two ways. First, the codes that evolved around it were ways of privileging some forms of killing, while delegitimizing others. Rod Neumann provides an analysis of legitimization and delegitimization at work in pictures of an African poacher with a European hunter in an article in *National Geographic*.[35] He observed that the poacher was nameless, loincloth-clad, and photographed against a rotting elephant carcass with its tusks hacked from its face. He is not looking at the camera, or smiling, and the caption to the photograph portrayed him as a morally vacuous individual who did this to an elephant in return for a few base material goods. The European hunter is shown next to an elephant she has just killed on a hunting safari. She is named, portrayed with her family, and all, wearing pressed clothes, are smiling at the camera. The dead elephant appears calm, 'almost in repose'. The photograph caption emphasizes the hunter's compassion, for killing the elephant is 'less painful than starving'. Thus the white hunter is humanized, while the black poacher's ties with recognizable society and values are diminished.

The second exclusivity of hunting is its expense. Steinhart shows that originally the costs of hunting safaris in Africa were so great that they were the exclusive preserve of the extremely wealthy.[36] President Theodore Roosevelt popularized them with a massive slaughter of big game in East and Southern Africa in 1909. The idea of the safari subsequently 'became a symbol of elite life in Kenya, and Kenya itself became the beacon for those seeking the return to the lost era of aristocracy and opulence'.[37] While somewhat less costly now, hunting remains the preserve of the rich. Prize trophies of some beasts will cost tens of thousands, even hundreds of thousands of dollars. Standard hunting safaris in Africa cost between US$25,000 and US$53,000, not including air fares.[38] Ritualized hunts continue because there is a large body of wealthy individuals who are prepared to pay so much for the privilege.

Hunting divides conservationists. Some welcome the resources it brings in. One estimate suggests that the hunting industry is worth as much as US$200 million dollars per year in Africa, which is as much as conservation NGOs spend on the continent annually, and US$723 million per year in state licence fees in the USA.[39] Hunting has been central to the community-based conservation strategies such as CAMPFIRE, which try to make wildlife valuable to rural groups and thus reduce poaching and pressure to change habitat.[40] These schemes hinge on devolving the power over hunting revenues to the lowest level possible so that those people who have to live with large dangerous wildlife are also those who benefit most from them. In North America hunting is also part of a larger debate about the freedom to bear arms and the pursuit of an outdoor way of life, even as the number of people participating in hunting continues to diminish.

Opponents of hunting decry the act of killing and the pleasure it appears to give hunters. John Muir famously rebuked Theodore Roosevelt over the campfire for his eagerness to kill wildlife, asking him, 'Mr President, when are you going to get beyond the boyishness of killing things?'[41] Grey Owl spoke against the vanity of hunters who were prepared to take the lives of animals just to adorn their walls. Hunting has been banned in Kenya, much to the chagrin of the sustainable use and community management lobby in the rest of the continent.[42] It is also banned in India, where many people are vegetarian. Cartmill observed that, at bottom, hunting debates are about what is natural, and what is human. Hunting presumes that there is 'a qualitative moral difference between people and beasts', which he finds increasingly hard to accept.[43]

The hunting debate thus captures many of the compromises that the alliance of conservation with the rich and famous entails. If you want their money and power you have to accept the beliefs and attitudes that accompany them. Ultimately, for most conservationists, pragmatic arguments win the day. However odd the behaviour and attitudes of hunters, the effects (land set aside for wildlife and revenues generated) are beneficial to many other conservation goals. We have already seen the importance of private game farms, many of which depend on hunting, for the protected area estate of South Africa. When the bill to ban hunting with dogs in the UK was being debated in Parliament, researchers observed that landowners who practised fox hunting and pheasant shooting were more likely to manage their farms in ways that were beneficial to wildlife than those who did not.[44] Advocates of sustainable use point out that ranching, farming and safari hunting have saved crocodile populations in Australia, and that the most populous animals on the planet are the domesticated ones which we use.[45]

As seen in Chapter 3, hunting is endorsed by numerous celebrities, royalty and politicians. Prominent public figures who support the conservation movement (Nelson Mandela, Prince Philip, Theodore Roosevelt) have also been hunters. Hunting can be just part of the lifestyle of the privileged. It is not an integral part of celebrity. However embarrassing the antics of celebrity hunters, they are rarely prejudicial to the conservation movement as a whole.

Self-promotion and hypocrisy

Celebrities promoting conservation often enjoy a pretty good deal. They can enjoy holidays in luxurious eco-lodges, surrounded by beautiful landscapes, and then bask in favourable news reports of their endorsement of conservation projects. The benefits of good publicity often form a particular bone of contention. Celebrity endorsement of good causes, including conservation, can simply be another aspect of their self-promoting lifestyles. For example, Angelina Jolie is prominent for her work with refugees, and claims to give a third of her income to good causes. Conservation causes have benefited from her largesse. She has offered considerable funds to support a wildlife sanctuary in Cambodia[46] and during a stay in Namibia she became patron of the Harnas Wildlife Sanctuary. Observers have noted that her charitable work has helped to reshape her earlier wild girl image and she has been charged with seeking attention through this work.

Celebrities, of course, do not see it that way. For many their work is a means of doing something good with the strange power that they find themselves wielding. They are merely seeking a way of giving something back, using their power for the wider good, not just personal benefit.[47] This is altruistic behaviour.

There may be truth in both explanations but neither provides a complete picture. Recall that it is a celebrity's job to stay in the limelight. A celebrity who avoids publicity is being unprofessional. They might be able to give quietly and anonymously, and many doubtless do, but in doing so they would be indulging in yet another luxury. It is certainly not their duty; it fails to provide their causes with the added value afforded by their fame.

Public giving is part of the celebrity industry. Celebrity endorsement can require agents' agreements, contracts and careful negotiation. The BBC offers this advice to causes seeking celebrity endorsement:

> Remember that the celebrity has something to gain as well from the exchange ... bear in mind ... their own need for promotion at the time. This could be a welcome return to the limelight for one or a way of drawing attention to themselves or their films or books for another. This may sound cynical but sincerity and self-promotion can exist side-by-side. (www.bbc.co.uk/dna/actionnetwork/A2062531#1)[48]

Rojek argues that the best measure of celebrity endorsement is what it does to the cause. One should not get side-tracked into its effect on the celebrity. Of the late Princess Diana and her campaign against landmines he comments that she had:

> dramatically raised public awareness of the issue and mobilized resources. Whether this outcome was the accomplishment of an essentially meretricious and self-serving personality is beside the point. The campaign helped to relieve suffering, and this relief could not have been accomplished so readily by other available means. (Rojek 2001: 91)

It is the same with conservation. If celebrities enjoy good publicity from their benevolence, if indeed they are primarily motivated by the desire

121

for public approbation, then that matters little. After all, is it wrong to derive pleasure from giving? I do not think that this sort of criticism of Jolie and her like has any substance.

A more substantial accusation levelled against celebrity endorsement is that it is hypocritical.[49] The public figures who support conservation with their words, pictures, spare time and cash spend much more energy and resources indulging in lavish and conspicuous consumption which not only threatens the planet itself, but also encourages others to do the same.[50] Celebrities and the wealthy are continually blazing new trails of conspicuous consumption. In some senses it is their job to do so, for through such means they can keep in the public eye and maintain their news (and hence commercial) value. However, does this not mean, as Miller so ably demonstrated at the start of this chapter, that they are completely unsuitable vehicles for promoting the conservation movement, which hinges on reducing consumption?

A number of critics have complained about conservation NGOs forming excessive links with such celebrities, and even adopting their lifestyles in pursuit of celebrity endorsement and backing. For example Christine MacDonald, a former fundraiser for Conservation International, queries the amount of time its chairman Peter Seligmann spends hobnobbing with the extremely wealthy, escorting them, at considerable cost and carbon production, to some of the world's great beauty spots.[51] She argues that this behaviour is emblematic of, and integral to, a set of larger compromises that the US environmental movement has made with corporate America.

If the environmental movement were seriously promoting widespread reductions in resource use these arguments would have a point, but it is not. Most mainstream environmentalist manifestos hinge on continued economic growth. Only a few voices in the wilderness like George Monbiot are urging that we leave the carbon unburnt in the ground, as a simpler alternative to digging it up, burning it and offsetting its use. Conspicuously, consuming celebrities are the public image of a deeper set of contradictions in the global economy. Contemporary environmentalism is largely about altering consumption patterns and not reducing them, and celebrities are some of the best people to make that happen. Criticizing them for their lifestyle substantially misses the point that they are ambassadors for our own. So do critiques of Seligmann's lifestyle. After all, someone has to give up their time to persuade these people to spend money on conservation, and unfortunately that involves mixing with the jet set and taking the flak that results.

Sachedina's analysis of the problems created by proximity to donors' wealth is a more telling criticism.[52] He shows that the real danger of wealth is not that some employees spend too much time in the company of moneyed donors; most NGOs would, rightly, welcome that. The problems come when those close to the donors have too much influence within the NGO, resulting in the orientation of the NGO switching towards the donors rather than the constituents whom the NGO is meant to serve. They become less able to listen to the rural poor and understand their lives. This becomes a more serious issue if the boards governing these NGOs, and holding them to their mission, are themselves out of touch with the realities of life for most of the world, and particularly their target areas, because the board members themselves are rich and privileged. Given the trends in foundational giving towards larger grants, and the conservation NGO sector's structure with larger organizations handling ever increasing sums, it is likely to become an ever more pressing issue.

The consumerist stance is a fundamental aspect of contemporary environmentalism. It has best been examined by Lionel Sklair in his book *The Transnational Capitalist Class*.[53] Sklair's book concerns the activities of an international elite composed of corporate executives, bureaucrats and politicians, professionals, merchants and the media who collectively act to promote global economic growth based on the 'cultural-ideology of consumerism'. He argues that this class is effectively in charge of globalization but also has to resolve crises which arise from its global growth strategy. With respect to environmental problems, he argues, following Gramsci, that corporations and the environmental movement have colluded to form a 'sustainable development historical bloc'.[54] This historical bloc offers solutions to the environmental crises that are inherent to global consumer capitalism, while all the time maintaining and strengthening an accompanying 'consumerist ideology'. Indeed, increased consumption becomes central to the solutions.[55]

Is it possible to escape these contradictions by adopting a more radical line? Two radical celebrity environmentalists have become prominent in Britain in recent years. 'Swampy' (real name Daniel Hooper) became famous in the late 1990s after sealing himself in tunnels to resist road builders in England and defying attempts to remove him. George Monbiot is a vociferous writer on diverse aspects of social and environmental justice and is particularly concerned with global warming. Monbiot presents himself as an uncompromising anti-establishment critic. His book *No Man's Land* (1995), about the problems facing East African pastoralists, promotes Monbiot's personal, heroic stand on environmental issues, declaring that he was *'persona non grata* in seven countries and has a life sentence *in absentia* in Indonesia'.[56] Monbiot directly opposed some of the forms of conservation other celebrities champion, criticizing the eviction, exclusion and marginalization of people from national parks and, as we have seen, authorities like David Attenborough for being silent about the social origins of so many pristine wildernesses.[57] For Monbiot, establishing reserves was akin to road building (another cause he opposes), for both are forms of state-led planning that end up separating people from their environment.

Radical celebrities can insist on no-compromise solutions which do not pander to the legitimated consumption of sustainable development. Monbiot, for example, advocates managed economic recession to combat global warming. However, it is hard to be a radical celebrity conservationist. Their audiences live vicariously the lives of the radicals, as they do with other celebrities. They can subscribe to their arguments, and support their work, simply by buying the book, watching the film, or reading the article. The celebrity in the limelight fights the battle, and they, by watching, are supporting them. Except of course, that the radicals require much more than passive participation for their ideals to be fulfilled. Because of the relationship with their fans that celebrity involves, a radical celebrity conservationist is an oxymoron.

There is in fact a strong sense in which radical environmentalists and the establishment need each other. The radicals need a powerful system in place to speak out against; the system can thrive on that sort of criticism, if it is offered in the manner of a celebrity. Monbiot launched *No Man's Land* at the prestigious Royal Geographical Society's main hall in London. With wonderful irony he regaled his audience for over an hour with opinions which the first explorers would have deplored, while speaking from their lectern and beneath the roll-call of their names. Yet he served a similar function to them. He entertained his audiences with exotic and dramatic stories, showed harrowing pictures and confronted them with horrible injustices. And in speaking thus he allowed his audience assurance and comfort. Something was being done, the truth was being exposed, and, if they overlooked Monbiot's exhortations to act, all they needed to do was buy the book.[58]

Conclusion

Celebrity is a product of the market. What celebrities say and how they say it is strongly shaped by what their audiences demand. It should not be surprising, therefore, that celebrities per se are rarely the main cause of problems that arise from their interaction with the environmental movement. They are part of a much larger system, and it is within the system as a whole that the faults lie. Their conspicuous consumption is performed for societies that are already wedded to consumerist ideologies; their hunting enacted continually on private lands, and its ideologies repeated at campfires all over the world. Their self-promotion is required of them, indeed it would be selfish to demand anonymity.

There are more substantial charges to be laid against the work of celebrity in conservation. As we have seen time and again in this book, celebrity works through the vicarious enjoyment of nature; it is about para-social relations. How can conservation be promoted through such armchair enjoyment, when for decades the movement (and the careers of celebrity conservationists and wildlife presenters) have hinged on close personal interactions with nature? How can the conservation movement reproduce itself in such circumstances? And what are the implications for democracy of ever greater invasion of celebrity into environmental affairs? If so many issues are mediated by celebrity presentation what does this portend for the broader democratic character of the environmental movement as a whole? To these questions we now turn.

8 | Saving the world

People need dramatic examples to shake them out of apathy. I can't do that as Bruce Wayne. As a man I'm flesh and blood, I can be ignored, destroyed. But as a symbol – as a symbol, I can be incorruptible. I can be everlasting. (*Batman Begins*)

I hope that celebrity conservation has appeared thus far to be an intriguing, complex and sometimes amusing phenomenon that helps raise awareness about the world, albeit occasionally on false pretences and using dubious images. Now I must be less equivocal, for there are elements of celebrity conservation that I find disturbing. In this chapter I explain why.

I shall examine first the role of symbols and icons in capitalism, arguing that they obscure important complexities and perpetrate a simplified vision of the world to which the world is expected to conform. I then examine some of the distortions that are commonly encountered in mediagenic conservation, and why they can be so damaging to different people's interests. Finally, I consider the impact of celebrity conservation on conservation itself, and ask what all this vicarious interaction with nature might portend for the movement more generally.

Capitalism, symbol and democracy

What do the symbols of celebrity mean for social movements and good causes? Do they help in ways beyond the obvious benefits of attention and publicity? Do they somehow make it easier for marginalized but important causes to speak truth to power? Do they give voice and political space to the unutterable? If they do, then the anxieties can be allayed. The concentration of wealth and power described in Chapter 6 could still be challenged by the symbolic power of rebellious celebrities who refuse to be marshalled to serve the establishment. If they do not, or worse, give only the appearance of challenging authority, then these are unhappy developments. Examining the work of the symbols of celebrity in capitalist democracies is a vital task.

Celebrities can bring profound social change. As we saw in Chapter 2 (page 12), Street has documented instances where rock stars have become the voices of freedom movements in Eastern Europe.[1] These are unusual cases, but there are others cases in the world of celebrity conservation where the famous have championed marginal causes. Women like Goodall, Fossey or Earle inspire others to strive within patriarchal academes. Grey Owl used his access to prominent politicians to lobby for First Nations' needs. Van der Post championed the decidedly unpopular cause of a post-apartheid South Africa divided into many states; he even opposed Nelson Mandela. Less publicly, celebrities can use their privileged access to the decision-makers and power brokers to persuade them to act on conservation issues. Al Gore organized a dinner in London attended by James Murdoch (son of media mogul Rupert Murdoch) who was seated next to a prominent British wildlife presenter.[2] The meeting and conversations appear to have proved influential as shortly afterwards Rupert Murdoch announced to all his News Corporation staff that they and the company had to take the problem of global warming seriously.

More generally, celebrities serve to condense the barrage of information with which we can be overloaded; they simplify things in what they say and stand for. The global warming debate is complex and hard to understand. It takes a lifetime of reading and expertise to get to the bottom of some of the issues. Things like Al Gore's film or KT Tunstall's directness (see pages 32–3) make all that easier to deal with, and more interesting.

Alternatively, why should one expect celebrity conservationists always to make a difference in the world and to transform it by their actions? Many would like to make a difference and many have, but is it fair to demand such engagement in politics? These people are balladeers and entertainers, performing on nature's stage to keep us happy. When Mark Tennant crawls up to lions for the benefit of correspondents in the *Daily Telegraph*, or when Mark Shand describes the moment when he fell in love with an elephant in India, that is precisely what they are doing.[3] Their biographies and autobiographies attempt to make sense of rapid change in an unstable world, and are just the entertaining stories of harmless eccentrics doing their bit for nature against ridiculous odds.[4]

Perhaps their work is done if they have just inspired a new generation of conservationists. The importance of these individuals' lives for the movement is recognized explicitly. In a review of *Tigerland and Other Unintended Destinations* Stuart Pimm marvelled at the exotic life of the chief scientific officer of the WWF, Eric Dinerstein, whose experiences the book reports.[5] As Pimm read about tigers in Nepal, snow leopards in Asia, bats in Costa Rica, the Orinoco, New Caledonia, Galapagos and the prairies, he insisted that more of this kind of marvellous life history was needed to inspire and entice a new generation of conservation activists who wanted to see and experience the world in such a way. The fascinating lives of leading individuals add to the appeal of the stories they tell, for the listener and, I presume, the teller.

From the perspective of the celebrity conservationists themselves their work is good for popular participation in conservation causes. They see thousands of people energized and excited, giving money and time, responding to the wake-up calls.[6] The celebrities' own view is important; they are uniquely placed to hear about what impact they have on people's lives from their fans. The fact that their day-to-day interactions can be so energizing and stimulating should not be taken lightly. On the other hand, however, it is hard for these people to escape from the celebrity bubble. In some respects celebrities can never find out for themselves what impacts they have because their presence will distort the data they receive. Assessing the impact of celebrity conservation requires not looking at the world through the lens and filters of celebrity encounters. Properly to evaluate the excitement of celebrity encounters we would need reliable data on how long the impacts last, which are unavailable.

All this, however, misses the point about what is dangerous and problematic about the role of celebrities as signs, and the symbolic value of the conservation stories they take part in. These are not just stories about places and people. Ultimately they can govern what we know about the world, how we know it to be true, what we expect to believe and what we think can be done.

To understand these arguments we must first recall that images are commodities in and of themselves. A few particularly iconic places produce pictures and stories which sustain conservation more generally. In the quintessential icons (such as Kruger, Amboseli, Uluru, Amazonian rainforest, Yosemite and Ranthambore) there are especially close links between the visions, the spectacles and their habitat. The industry of nature's image-making, the coffee table books, posters, calendars, post-cards, *National Geographic* articles, tourist brochures, wildlife documentaries and artistic works that represent wild nature require these places to make their images. The image consumers then support the places themselves, by purchasing the images, or by supporting conservation organizations working there, or visiting the parks. Each reinforces the other in a virtuous loop.[7]

Furthermore the ideas and values that these images connote, are also valuable to other commodities. Images of nature, landscape and wildlife can be used to sell cars, beauty products or alcohol, because they signify beauty, strength, rarity, speed, pristineness, isolation or a hundred other things. In other words the sign value of the image (the ideas that they signify) can be attached to other commodities and help to sell them.

This much is straightforward, but the key insight of writers like Barthes, Baudrillard and Debord (French critics) is in what happens when consumer societies are saturated with images, each proclaiming its meaning, and drawing on other signs and symbols to do so. These authors have argued that after a point, the link between the image and the reality breaks down. Signs refer to each other. Authenticity is accorded to the most realistic representation of another sign, not what the sign originally referred to. Signified and signifier switch. This is what Barthes called hyperreality, and Baudrillard called the third order of simulacra. Goldman describes the situation as follows:

> The principles of photographic and commodity abstraction have been carried to such extremes that cultural meanings become more and more thoroughly disjointed and separated from our activities in the lifeworld, but float before our eyes in the service of commodities. (Goldman, R. 1994: 190)

In this context the symbols and signs that proliferate in celebrity conservation are problematic. Most obviously, they simplify complex situations, and present simplistic solutions to them. Nugent, examining the work of Sting in the Amazonian rainforest, complained that Sting's representation (in popular magazines) missed the 'complicated social landscape' of the region, and did not deal with issues of unequal land distribution, or failures of governance.[8] He continued:

> [t]he overriding problem ... is that this particular rendition of the crisis of Amazonia produces a completely mystifying discussion in which comforting but ineffective formlae are recited – save a tree and save the world ... and people believe that somehow, magically, it will happen. (Nugent 1994: 181–2)

Conservation's iconography conceals, obscures and erases. Conservation images can be silent about the impacts of conservation policies on the rural poor. They exclude peoples' histories from manufactured wildernesses. They hide the awkward and unpleasant implications of conservation compromises.[9] Indeed, not only do they say nothing about these problems, they make it impossible for these problems to appear at all. There is no conceptual space for them. We are presented with a series of images of wildlife, of happy children accepting their well/school/ vaccination programme near a national park, of convincingly simple maps of protected area advances and corridors, with no place to examine the problems and difficulties that must inevitably be present. Win-win solutions are the order of the day. Far from giving voice to the unutterable, celebrity conservation may silence it all the more effectively.

Katja Neves-Graca and Jim Igoe have argued that the circulation and consumption of these images in conservation can best be understood as instances of Debordian spectacle.[10] The spectacle is manifest in images consumed in ignorance of the forces producing them and taken at face value. The spectacle, however, is not just the multitude of images, but 'a social relationship between people that is mediated by images'.[11] In other words, how people act on environmental problems, how they affect the lives of distant strangers in conservation projects or in areas of conservation concern is governed by the images at work.

Katja Neves-Graca has shown, in her analysis of Knut the polar bear, how the signs at work in the climate change debate 'iconify complex relationships' and then banalize them into mundane consumption.[12] They make it possible to make a difference by buying a stuffed polar bear toy, or as the *Vanity Fair* website had it, 'click a button to save the world'. Jim Igoe has examined in detail iconification at work on the website of the African Wildlife Foundation:

> Helping people and the environment ... becomes a simple proposition. The ... African Wildlife Foundation 'engaging you' web page presents a variety of ways that individuals can help, all of which involve giving money so experts can fix the problem. Through images they can connect special people in their lives ... to people and wildlife in Africa who are the putative beneficiaries of their largesse and who most of them will never see in real life ... At the 'adopt an animal' web site they are presented with a gallery of African animals with names and personalities like the characters in Disney's Lion King. Auntie Botle is a lioness who 'adopted' two cubs when their parents were killed by poison. 'Charles, a wise mountain gorilla' is devoted to the safety of his family. To adopt one of these virtual animals, a person puts it into her/his virtual shopping cart, enters a series of numbers representing virtual value into a web site, and then s/he presses a virtual button. A short time later the person receives a certificate of adoption; a fact sheet about her/his adopted animal, and a plush toy representing the adopted animal. The donation, minus the value of the plush toy, is tax deductible.[13] (Brockington et al. 2008: 196)

What are the implications of the power of images, and their problematic representations for a conservation sector which prides itself on its authenticity? If conservationists rejoice in wildernesses without saying whose homes these places were, if they celebrate the distribution of aid and good works near parks, without considering whether these benefits outweigh the costs conservation has brought, then they are, sometimes unintentionally, peddling misrepresentations. However, in other respects this lack of truth cannot be an issue in the realm of celebrity conservation. Celebrities are attributed greatness, and part of the greatness we attribute to them is authenticity. We are saturated in the values and landscapes which celebrities endorse. They forge the very expectations of what we think landscapes should look like.

This is the final turn of the screw. Spectacular conservation visions do not just misrepresent the world and make it difficult to understand its problems and complexities. They change the world to fit its imaginary image. They act in other words as 'virtualisms'.[14] They are a model to which we expect the world to conform.[15] They are influential ideas which shape expectations, raise money and alter reality to fit their mould. As I and colleagues have documented elsewhere, tourist lodges, conservation projects and the like physically and sometimes radically redesign the landscape that they are designed to preserve.[16]

The world of images, icons and signs is a strange and deceptive one, once again proving Wilde right: 'the true mystery of the world is the visible, not the invisible'.[17] The beguiling power of images suggests that, contra Batman, symbols are not simple motivating forces. They shape our expectations of what reality is like, they shape the way we interact with other people and distant strangers, they shape our conservation interventions.

In the following two sections I describe some of the more salient distortions of conservation's virtualisms. I hope to show that the work of celebrity conservation can sometimes be just a little Walter Mittyish: indulging in extended fantasies about saving the world while ignoring the realities around them.[18] These sections deliberately focus on the negative aspects of mediagenic conservation. This is not because there are only negative things to mention; far from it. Conservation has all sorts of good effects on people and on the environment. However, mediagenic conservation is known only for these good things. My purpose here is to explore the problems because they are not normally known.

Creating a mediagenic world

A central feature of the North American conservation movement is its concern for pristine, unspoilt wilderness free from human interference, residence and resource use. Only carefully regulated tourism is allowed. This has been the rallying cry of environmentalism in the region since its inception, with John Muir, who worshipped untouched scenery, famously confronting advocates of sustainable use such as Gifford Pinchot. It is enthusiastically endorsed by Robert Nash, in his popular book *Wilderness and the American Mind* in which he envisaged a time when most of America would return to untouched wilderness with people concentrated in a few cities.[19]

Partly under the influence of the North American conservation movement, the values of wilderness, and lobbying for it, cover the globe. African national parks were designed on the US model as places where (local) people were not allowed in order that Edens might be preserved. There are strong wilderness movements in Australia and New Zealand and it is growing in Scotland.

The trouble with wilderness, as William Cronon observed, is that it offers no room for people in nature.[20] We have already seen in Chapter 2 (page 20) how their eviction and exclusion from protected areas is damaging to livelihoods and welfare and excludes people's conceptions of belonging to the land. Writers commenting on African, Latin American and Australian environmental history have observed that the idea of people-less wildernesses has little historical support and is a poor basis on which to base conservation policy.[21]

The conceptual exclusion of people from wilderness is damaging. It is not just that it denies the belonging that many people feel to lands designated as wild, but also that beautiful and wild aspects of anthropogenic landscapes are somehow also tainted, spoilt and less worth fighting for. Some authors have argued that a concentration of wilderness can act to the detriment of wild species. Proctor and Pincetl examined the spotted owl debate in California and noted that the fight for old growth habitat, which was often found in colder, unproductive places, meant that timber companies were not encouraged to manage their stands (found on warmer more productive territories) in a way that could have strengthened ecological corridors for the owl between islands of old growth.[22] Wilderness can impede conservation's vision.

Wildernesses are also inadequate for nature's conservation. Most protected areas are too small, individually and collectively, to preserve species that have large ranges, or migration routes. These depend upon land outside protected areas to survive.[23] For many conservationists one of the main challenges is how to keep valuable habitat intact beyond the boundaries of existing protected areas, to focus not on saving 10–30 per cent of tropical biodiversity in 1–2 per cent of its land, but saving 80–90 per cent on 5–15 per cent of the land.[24]

Yet it is precisely the mediagenic wilderness which attracts celebrities. Conservation's endorsers desire mutually beneficial publicity and this is much more readily offered with easy-to-recognize wilderness images to display before the public. Celebrity support for wild places with people in them, practising slash and burn agriculture or hunting with traps, nets and snares, is harder to spin positively in the public gaze, even if the impact on biodiversity is slight.

Besides, every Westerner recognizes wilderness. They are brought up on it from an early age, for it is popularized by the same media, news and information networks that sell celebrities. Disney's cartoon *Lion King* epitomizes its ubiquity. The film's portrayal of wild Africa showed an ordered hierarchy of nature in which people are absent. African voices grace the soundtrack but otherwise the only reference to humanity is a baboon dressed as a witchdoctor who chants 'thank you very much squashed banana' in a mixture of English and Swahili.[25]

Are wildernesses necessary for the preservation of biodiversity? In some cases undoubtedly they are. Some large and rare animals range over significant territories and do much better without human interference. Many human activities, and the changes that increasing human populations inevitably bring, are a threat to biodiversity. Sometimes wilderness has to be created for conservation's cause.[26] However, too often people can be moved from places without clear evidence that their actions and livelihoods are the cause of the problem.[27] They are simply moved because people in parks are a category error.[28]

Not all people are bad for nature. As we have seen in Chapter 5, heroes are allowed in, for they are intimate with nature. Another permitted group can be indigenous people, who are well known to be authentically close to nature. They also, with their exotic dress and customs, make excellent mediagenic allies to celebrities' causes. Indeed they can become celebrities in their own right. Vivanco notes that the Kayapo, an indigenous group from Panama, and the Penan of Sarawak, Malaysia, won international media celebrity by playing on popular perceptions of the ecologically noble savage.[29] Sting was anointed with paint on stage at one of his concerts by Raoni, one of the leaders of the Kayapo.[30]

Placing land in the care of indigenous groups, however, is no guarantee that they will conserve it.[31] No one is a natural conservationist. They may well be better placed to guard and care for the land than many others, and are often excellent allies to the conservation cause, but this is not automatically the case just because of indigenous peoples' closeness to nature. Promoting conservation on indigenous peoples' lands requires painstaking work, through participation and adequate devolution of power and authority to them.[32]

Being indigenous also has its exclusions. As Igoe has argued, it requires a passport, and access to and recognition from the organizations that recognize indigeneity.[33] It requires a distinctive speech, or dress or culture. The category 'indigenous' excludes the majority of the rural poor, many of whom could also be adversely affected by the creation of protected areas. Michael Goldman has documented a case where rural groups, who were not classified as indigenous, were denied special consideration before being removed from a dam site in Laos.[34] Their case was particularly tragic because the original consultants who worked with them concluded that two of the groups were speaking languages completely new to linguists. The consultants argued that these people should be considered indigenous. However the IUCN, which was working with the World Bank in preparation for the dam, objected because they did not want those people affected to come under the Bank's Operational Directive on Indigenous People which could have delayed the schemes and the IUCN's own negotiations for a US$60 million project (also part funded by the Bank) to set up a series of National Biodiversity Conservation Areas enclosing more than 15 per cent of the nation's territory. The consultants' report was not circulated. Another consultant was hired who was prepared to say that these ethnic groups could be considered 'as a whole, a melting pot culture'.[35]

The point I am making is that the mediagenic wildernesses and peoples that the rich and famous support can often conceal exclusion and marginalization. In order to be endorsed by celebrities, the conservation project has to be a good cause. The good publicity must be mutual. This leaves inadequate conceptual space for understanding conservation as a process that distributes fortune and misfortune across the landscape. The complexities are ignored.

The world of the rich and famous is not just a land of pristine perfection and exotic people, it is also densely populated with large rare charismatic animals, in particular big cats, pandas, seals, apes and elephants. The power of celebrity conservationists is strengthened by the appeal and charm of these animals. They lend their aura of strength, agility and poise (cats), beauty and cuddliness (baby seals), resilience, intelligence and wisdom (apes and elephants).

Conservationists who speak for these animals are therefore particularly popular on the fundraising circuits of conservation organizations. Not all of these animals are widely shared conservation priorities, although some scholars have suggested that flagship species can be useful to conservation because of the attention they can generate.[36] In some cases, such as Care for the Wild's elephant sponsorship, money raised to support flagship species is then spent, with sponsors' agreement, on a much broader range of conservation needs, such as educating wildlife rangers or supporting local communities.[37] The conservation cause will only be advanced, however, if the funds raised can be moved to more pressing needs.

We can capture the character of celebrity conservation by examining one group who epitomize publicity-driven conservation. The company Wildlife Works, based in California, pursues 'consumer-powered conservation'.[38] The idea is simple. It sells products such as clothes with pro-conservation labels and designs, and goods that are sourced from craft industries attached to conservation projects.[39] It then returns a proportion of the profits back into conservation projects. The causes the company supports provide a good idea of what consumers want to pay for. Currently Wildlife Works supports the release of a single circus elephant on to a wildlife sanctuary in Tennessee, the Humane Society's campaign against seal culling and, perhaps its biggest work, the Rukinga Wildlife Sanctuary. This is an 80,000 acre private ranch near the borders of the Tsavo National Park in Kenya which the company has turned into a wildlife sanctuary. It serves as an elephant migration corridor between Tsavo East and Tsavo West National Park. One of the company's garment-making factories is located near it. They hope to set up similar projects to conserve the red panda in Nepal, mountain gorilla in Uganda as well as forests on the Brazilian Atlantic Coast, Canadian Pacific Coast and in Madagascar. The patterns from this are clear: this brand of consumer-driven conservation focuses on highly visible mammals; it facilitates the restoration of wilderness to animals and animals to wilderness; supports communities outside these designated spaces, and promotes non-consumptive use of animals.

Mediagenic conservation does not accurately describe the world. Its imaginations can cause injustice and unhappiness. Eviction in the name of imagined wilderness, and on the basis of dubious ecological imperatives, without adequate compensation, is unfair. The cult of the hero denigrates the everyday actions of multitudes precisely at a time when it is the actions of millions of consumers of resources and energy which are driving environmental change. The celebration of indigeneity allows injustices to be inflicted on less 'authentic' rural groups. A mediagenic world does not accord well with current conservation priorities. Moving elephants to Tennessee, or expanding the already large wildlife estate of Tsavo, is not the best use of scarce conservation resources. Conservationists need to work hard to turn the money raised by mediagenic causes to good effect.

Making a good and valuable world

A world of unspoilt pristineness populated by rare, exotic people and animals guarded by heroes is clearly two-dimensional, but there are other aspects of conservation commonly associated with the rich and famous which can more insidiously work their way into our values and beliefs. The first of these is the idea that good wins out in the end; evil does not triumph; the battle belongs to the righteous. This is particularly prevalent in projects that seek to enrol community support for conservation goals. It is commonly stated in the community conservation literature that conservation that is not just is not sustainable, and that conservation has to win local support if it is to survive.[40]

I call this the principle of local support.[41] There is some good sense in this thinking, for many protected areas have suffered as a result of local opposition.[42] However, it is nonsense to suggest that local resistance will eventually, in every case, triumph over oppressive conservation policy.[43] It is not realistic to suggest that unarmed, disorganized, fractious local groups can fight effectively well organized and armed rangers. The dictum that parks must fail in the face of local opposition obscures the processes and timing of the failure. We cannot learn what makes for effective resistance, or strong conservation, through such thinking.

The rich and famous can be one of the means by which unjust situations can be perpetrated. Their money can enable conservation projects to defy local resistance more effectively. The illusion that injustice is unsustainable adds a further veneer of respectability to such situations. It allows observers to think that, if there were something wrong, the protest would unsettle the good work being done. In fact the good work (particularly investment in security and law enforcement) can do a good job of unsettling the resistance so that it is no longer effective. The exclusions enforced at, for example, the Gir Lion Sanctuary in India, the Mkomazi National Park in Tanzania and the Royal Chitwan National Park in Nepal are sustained in part by the high international profile of these protected areas, their rare species and the funds these generate, not because of the justice of the policies imposed.[44]

Second, conservation by the rich and famous is often associated with the commodification of nature. This means the growth of market value and market relations as a means of valuing nature and managing and ordering society. It requires the translation of nature into a commercial product subject to market forces, with attendant privatization and commercialization of natural resource use.[45]

Making nature into a commodity is central to many conservation solutions. Ted Turner's extensive rewilded ranches can be fished and hunted for a price, and his private herd of buffalo feed customers eating at a chain of restaurants across sixteen US states. Many community conservation initiatives, strongly advocated in Southern and Eastern Africa, promote the right of rural groups to manage hunting or photographic safaris for wildlife found on their lands. A great deal of energy has been expended trying to ensure that the revenues are appropriately distributed to local groups, and not central government.[46] One of the more successful community conservation schemes in Tanzania was able to channel US$50,000 per year into a village fund. This is extraordinary wealth in these societies; it is popular with villagers and appears to have facilitated greater accountability over village affairs.[47] Unwelcome though commodification can be, some rural people need the money. In some respects it is only reasonable that if the wealthy are to gain exclusive access to these resources they ought to pay as much as possible for it. There are terrible inequalities here which could in part be addressed with their money.[48]

One has to marvel at the sheer inventiveness of wildlife entrepreneurs. Consider elephants. It used only to be possible to hunt African elephants with rifles and kill them. Now it is possible to undertake humane hunting safaris in which hunters shoot their elephant with a camera gun, and are rewarded with a picture showing where their bullet would have struck. Other ethical hunters shoot elephants with tranquillizing darts. They can then be photographed with their foot on the vanquished prey and plaster cast moulds are taken of the tusks for them to hang on their walls back home. This allows enterprising wildlife ranches to make a profit from capturing animals from which they can then earn more money when they sell them on. The disadvantage of tranquillizing elephants is that it cannot be done too frequently lest the animals be harmed. One company in Zimbabwe found a way around this problem by experimenting, briefly, with elephant paintball.[49] Clients could waste elephants with live paint ammunition, and then come back and attack the same beast after lunch. Elephant hair is sold as jewellery, elephant dung made into paper, and in Thailand elephants are trained to paint pictures and fabrics which sell for thousands of dollars.

Inventive and lucrative, these are not simply 'market solutions'; they are profound social changes, which will require forgoing other forms of resource use and interactions with nature. Too often, market solutions are seen as the answer to conservation problems, rather than a situation with winners and losers which alters our interactions with nature.[50] The problematic consequences of these changes are not adequately appreciated.

Sian Sullivan observes that the success of community wildlife management in Southern Africa based on selling tourist safaris is considerable. These initiatives have enabled rural groups to 'access monetary, employment and other opportunities ... [t]hey have also generated important institutional frameworks for building and enhancing local infrastructural and governance structures related to livelihood activities connecting people and landscapes'.[51] Sullivan also insists we have to recognize that this is not some simple improvement in people's situations. It introduces a new commodified and commercialized way of managing nature and relating to the environment. This has to be recognized explicitly, lest we fail to note how it drives out the 'joy, magic and contemplation' of other forms of interacting with nature.[52] Moreover, as she has argued elsewhere, these initiatives promote hunting of large mammals and marginalize other forms of resource use by members of the community.[53] Restricting access to hunting to wealthy outsiders means that local hunting, and enjoyment of the same, is marginalized or excluded. Ken MacDonald has documented a similar process in the creation of sports hunting of ibex in Pakistan. Here, existing forms of hunting, and social networks and prestige reinforced by the distribution of meat from hunting, were replaced by the commodification of trophy hunting.[54]

Faith in the market characterizes the world of the rich and famous. Stanley Fink (retired deputy chairman of the Man Group) gave a speech at a dinner at the Mansion House in London at which Prince Charles's Rainforests Project courted the help of financial institutions in the fight against tropical deforestation. Fink insisted that the services forests provided to the planet (clean water, air and particularly carbon offsetting) could all, somehow, be valued and so conservation earn its way in the world. He called it the eighteen trillion dollar challenge.[55] When the African Parks Foundation's work at Nechisar in Ethiopia experienced bad publicity because of the impact on the local Mursi people, Paul van

Vlissingen defended its activities in a letter to a critic, arguing that the market, and product substitution, could effectively alter things for the better:

> Recently I visited the Mursi again and together with the Elders we made a list of what their major concerns are and how we could help them solving these. To give you some examples: they said their wish to hunt antelope was not based on the hunt but on the skin for their wives. Asked if they would be happy with impala skins from South Africa it was affirmative. As giraffe have been nearly exterminated they agreed we should find alternatives for the tail hairs. All zebras ... are gone and they regretted that, but explained it was hunger that made them kill these. They would like to see them back as they saw them – and so much more game – in their youth. We can and will do that. Yes, we can do something about hunger by introducing better inventory systems and help develop markets. Nothing will be easy but it can be done. We have done it in Barotseland, Zambia, also very remote and very difficult to manage, but the Lozis will tell anybody that the best thing that happened there in the last 50 years was the arrival of African Parks. (van Vlissingen to Sheridan, 28 October 2005)

I would be surprised if it was as easy as this to substitute goods; the Mursi do not live in a world of alienated, interchangeable commodities. However, I am not in a position to say whether van Vlissingen was right or wrong. The point is rather that his faith in the market to deliver solutions appeared to reduce his sensitivity to the problems market-based solutions can bring.

The world of the rich and famous is vulnerable to sugary representations of projects and ventures. It is a domain where positive stories abound of local people harmoniously curbing the excesses of their use of natural resources to become conservationists. Equally, fortress conservation supporters doing their bit for needy local neighbours by building clinics and teaching them about the value of their environments, can appear as win-win solutions. I cannot see how celebrity conservation can help us to see through such representations and understand conservation as an exercise which distributes fortune and misfortune, and which promotes and privileges particular values, attitudes and beliefs in the process.

Vicarious environmentalism and sofa-based conservation

Carrier and West, surveying a variety of conservation endeavours and organizations, noted that it could be too easy to assert that virtualisms are at work transforming the world, without paying attention to how they work, and what changes they actually achieve. They suggest that:

> virtualism in practice is more problematic than critics seem to assume ... [t]hey appear to ignore the relationship between what those models portray and the world revealed by field work and case studies, between virtualism and governance on the one hand and execution on the other. (Carrier and West 2009)

They argue that this does not mean that conservation's visions cannot have powerful effects; they plainly can. However, the manner in which these are achieved, and the actual existing work of conservation organizations, requires careful observation. One cannot extrapolate from a series of powerful images reproduced in multiple media to assume it creates a passive consenting public.

The difficulty of understanding how spectacle works as a virtualism quickly becomes apparent if we consider wildlife film. There is great potential for wildlife films to be an important element of conservation. They raise awareness of important causes, and endear wildlife, science, ecology and conservation to their audiences. Attenborough considers that one of his main tasks is to 'persuade the public that animals are interesting and beautiful'.[56] In some respects films already play that role as one of the most readily available and entertaining forms of knowledge about nature. Television is widely recognized to be one of the most important ways by which many people learn about the world around them, and, amid general cynicism about the media, wildlife films remain 'on something of a pedestal' among audiences, respected for their authenticity and adherence to truth.[57] Nevertheless what wildlife films actually do is the subject of considerable uncertainty.

We know that they can be effective means of conservation advocacy. Mitman argues that wildlife films after the Second World War played a major role in turning nature 'into a commodity with a set of values pertaining to democracy and morality which appealed to the American public', thus counteracting the elitism of some conservation NGOs.[58] Bernard and Michael Grzimek used film to great effect in their lobbying for the Serengeti National Park in Tanzania. According to Mitman, the Oscar-winning '*Serengeti Shall Not Die* (1959) became the first propaganda film in a mass public outreach campaign'.[59]

More recently, Mike Pandey's *Vanishing Vultures* (2006) encouraged the Indian government to make good its threat to ban the veterinary drug diclofenac which is thought to be responsible for a 95 per cent decline in vulture populations in the region. In the UK *Are We Changing Planet Earth* (2006) rode a wave of public concern about global warming to achieve high viewing figures and helped to catalyse a mood swing in Britain over climate change. The programmes were presented by David Attenborough whose high credibility with the British public combined with the effective promotion of the programmes in newspapers, television news and radio to make these high-impact conservation films.[60] The programmes were also aired in the US, using a different presenter also famous for his impartiality; they won an Emmy award there. One could also point to Channel 4's sceptical documentary *The Great Global Warming Swindle* (2007) as contributing to a decline in public enthusiasm for action on climate change.

Despite this evidence of influence, there is a great deal of angst in the wildlife film industry as to the value of wildlife films for conservation. Some insider critics feel that natural history programmes put more energy into sustaining the wildlife film industry than wildlife itself. They accuse colleagues of exploiting the natural world without investing anything in maintaining the resource on which their livelihoods depend, and love of which drove many to struggle through poorly paid, hard-working jobs and difficult conditions to establish themselves in the industry. Monbiot's attack on Attenborough also criticized him for failing to show the environmental destruction in the idyllic images of wild nature he presents.[61] The organization Filmmakers for Conservation exists precisely to promote a better conservation message in wildlife films and greater receptivity to the films among television companies.[62]

Using natural history programmes on television as a means of conservation advocacy is paradoxical. While television is ubiquitous, and a vital source of information for many people, it will not necessarily produce more conservationists. There are several basic problems. Some researchers have found that audiences do not clearly understand the scientific messages.[63] Television for many people is a form of escapism, and a way of relaxing. They switch off, or change channels, when programmes get moralistic or depressing. Many people in the industry feel that conservation messages can only come across in well-told or entertaining stories.

Research into the impact of conservation messages and environmental content on television, either in natural history programmes or as part of the more general content of television, does not produce particularly clear findings.[64] Television does not challenge the general consumerism of society. Environmental matters are usually side issues. Moreover, when conservation sentiment and action are formed it can often be hard to say precisely what role television had in producing them. There are, after all, so many factors influencing our behaviour towards the environment. Webber, in an accomplished summary of the state of research for Filmmakers for Conservation, found most encouragement in anecdotal evidence, noting that films about dolphin deaths in tuna nets resulted in consumer pressure to produce dolphin-friendly tuna and that some wildlife programmes encourage audience participation in wildlife surveys.[65]

This does not mean that film cannot be made to work for conservation causes. The filmmakers I spoke to demonstrated frequently that they had done so. However, these films were not generally aimed at large audiences. In fact these were often tiny, even minuscule. The target audience might be the board of a company, or a single minister reviewing a mining application. Sometimes it might be a larger rural community who become involved in making the film, and whose participation is part of the script.[66] Such films, unfortunately, are far removed from the high-profile, award-winning work to which the wildlife film industry is so orientated. At the last Wildscreen (a wildlife film festival held at Bristol) in 2008 there was a prestigious Panda Awards ceremony, known in the trade as the 'Green Oscars'. It was a sumptuous affair with much razzmatazz, but posed a stark contrast to the thinly attended sandwich lunch of the annual meeting and award ceremony of Filmmakers for Conservation held the day before in a café beneath the Wildscreen venue. The kudos, money and attention of the wildlife film industry are not directed to working for conservation.

Perhaps the bigger problem is the type of nature which wildlife films perpetrate. Both Mitman and Bousé are unsettled by the nature they see presented in films and on television and with which people fall in love. Bousé sees only 'sound and fury' on the screen, and cannot find the 'stillness and calm' that he sees outside his window.[67] Mitman makes a similar point: '[c]onditioned by nature on screen, we may fail to develop the patience, perseverance, and passion required to participate in the natural world with all its mundanity and splendour.'[68] He sees animals and wildlife turned into a spectacle, devoid of meaningful relationship. His argument merits quoting in full:

> By making animals into a spectacle, rather than beings we engage with
> in work and play, nature films and other recreations of nature reinforce
> this dichotomy of humans and nature. In nature as spectacle, the animal
> kingdom exists solely to be observed, objectified, and enjoyed. We have

our world and they have theirs. This voyeurism precludes any meaning-ful exchange because we remain at a physically and emotionally safe distance, far removed from the shared labour of animals and humans, whose interactions have made such vicarious experiences possible. We no longer work with animals, we predominantly watch them. And film – as a technology of art, science and entertainment, but above all vision – overwhelmingly has come to mediate our relationship with animals and the natural world. (Mitman 1999: 206)

Mitman's description is not confined to wildlife films. It neatly sum-marizes the condition of the world of celebrity as a whole. It highlights the irony and contradiction at work when filmmakers communicate the intimacy they enjoy with nature. We, their audiences, may wish to know that intimacy and friendship for ourselves, but we have to be content for others to experience it for us and tell us about it.

Bill Adams, in *Against Extinction*, surveyed the achievements of the twentieth century and concluded that for conservationists to win their battles in the long run, they needed to win more people's hearts. 'The challenge', he said, 'is not to preserve (or even restore) "the wild", but people's *relationships* with the wild' for the 'future of conservation will turn on the extent to which a strong individual connection to nature and natural processes is maintained for the world's people in the 21st century'.[69] Kay Milton concurred. In her book *Loving Nature* she asked a question that has long troubled her: 'Why isn't everyone an environmen-talist? ... Why do some people actively protect nature while others, by indifference or intent, are prepared to see it destroyed?'[70] Her answer to her questions is that people who love nature are survivors of the process of falling out of love with nature and being diverted to other interests.[71] The corollary is that conservation will flourish if more people can be enabled to love nature.

I agree with both authors. When I lived and worked in Oxford my fam-ily delighted in the boggy meadow behind our house, which filled with buttercups in May and water and swans in the winter. My elder daugh-ter learned to pick blackberries in it, while we watched out for adders and listened to green woodpeckers yammering. Now, having moved to Manchester, we live on the edge of the Pennines, a range of low hills running down northern England. I can put up red grouse running over heather moorlands and serenade peregrines in the morning sky with Hopkins's verse. My daughters can bounce down peaty slopes, swim in red-brown streams and get lost in bracken. My wife can perch on crags and contemplate the moors in warm sunshine. We can all climb above the fog on wintry days to watch the sunset, pretending we have reached a magical land floating above the clouds. Through such a life, I hoped, my family and I could build a relationship with the wild.

I fear, however, that I may have been conflating *interacting with* and *relating to* the wild. The disturbing conclusion I had to reach on reading about celebrity and conservation was that relationships are not built on physical interaction. Indeed, in a world of para-social relations they cannot be. Rather, when people consume celebrities' support for conservation, when they watch Steven Leonard on television, attend a concert by Sting, buy an acre of Africa online, send an email to their senator which Robert Redford wrote, listen to Leonardo DiCaprio's website video on global warming and enthuse about the patronage of wild Africa by diverse European royalty, at these moments they are restoring their relationship with the wild.

We have already seen, in the success of books like *Born Free*, that many people yearn for the intimacy with wonderful animals which the Adamsons enjoyed. It is also apparent that they are content to let others achieve that sort of relationship, if they themselves cannot, provided that they can enjoy the spectacle of it – read the books, look at the pictures, watch the films and catch up with the follow-up work in *Hello!* magazine. Dedicated wildlife film channels allow constant vicarious interaction with the wild.

In a dominantly urban society, conservationists enjoy unusually close relationships with nature. Most people in the West interact with nature infrequently and irregularly.[72] In these circumstances conservationists, and particularly celebrity conservationists, play an important role by getting close to nature in ways that most of us cannot, and allowing us to participate vicariously by watching them in close-up, on camera. After all, the results of their work, distilled from hours of waiting, filming and careful editing, and occasionally cheating, are more exciting than our own visits to these places.[73] Similarly, the lives of conservationists in the field can be lived in remote places and in close proximity to wildlife, surrounded by beauty, with little humdrum and routine. A substantial element of the attraction of celebrity conservation derives from the exotic appeal of their lifestyles, and supporters' desire to participate vicariously in them.[74] Celebrity conservation fulfils a structural role in predominantly urban societies, allowing people to connect with nature and the excitement of life in the wilds from the comfort of their living rooms.

There is already evidence of the ways in which the consuming public's tastes, habit and knowledge are being altered by the easy pleasures celebrity conservation affords. Zaradic and Pergams have found that visits to national parks in some Western countries are declining after decades of growth.[75] They found that these trends were correlated with various indices that characterize sedentary lifestyles, such as Internet usage and watching films and video games. They suggest that biophilia (E. O. Wilson's term for 'an innate focus on life and lifelike processes') could be being replaced with videophilia, defined as 'the new human tendency to focus on sedentary activities involving electronic media'.[76]

I believe this is a common trend. I have walked in bright morning sunshine on snow-covered hills which have been proclaiming their beauty for a week to the vast conurbation of Manchester. I was utterly alone and I saw few footprints. On a windy day you can fly a kite high on the moors amid swards of dancing cotton grass and see no one. I have camped in accessible public campsites on the Bogong High Plains in the height of the Australian summer holidays beneath a full moon, and shared the experience with only one other (park ranger's) family. I have listened to national park managers in New Zealand describe a steady decline in tramping clubs' 'missions' (long explorations of valleys and hills with or without footpaths), and the concentration of people on to well-defined walking tracks for shorter periods of time.

Para-social relations with nature and the environment are not necessarily bad for conservation. A contentment to let others achieve and enjoy intimacy with nature might reduce footpath erosion in the Pennines. Indian conservationists were delighted when I suggested to them that vicarious enjoyment of celebrities in the wild might reduce some of the pressure on their national parks which the growing middle class are invading in numbers. However accepting para-social relations with environment as normal and exploiting them for the returns they can yield to conservation causes, is risky. Enjoying celebrities' endorsement of conservation results in an impoverished life and experience of nature. After all, we do not vicariously enjoy celebrities reading *Hello!* magazine's travel section. Their enviable lives involve being there and doing it. Not being there, just watching others do it, is neither desirable nor enviable.

Even if they are less exciting, will para-social relations foster the fundamental love of nature that underpins conservation? This is an important question, but not one I can answer. I used to think that celebrity conservation might, in the long run, threaten to break the deep personal connections with nature upon which love for nature and the conservation movement as a whole had depended for so long.[77] Now I think that what we currently see in conservation, and in the movement away from first-hand experience of nature, is the product of two generations of vicarious conservation sentiment. Celebrity does not threaten the future of conservation. It has already infested it for decades, and is now working out its consequences on new generations of conservationists.

'But,' you may protest, 'what about *Springwatch*?'[78] This British programme runs for three weeks over the spring (paralleled by *Autumnwatch* later in the year). It plots the advent and progress of the season with cameras in nest boxes, studies of insect life close up, and plants growing, leafing and flowering. Its impact on audiences and the growth of a '*Springwatch* community' is remarkable. In 2005 it promoted an audience-led phenological survey, following which the number of observers recording the events of spring increased from just over 4,000 to over 132,000.[79] Tourist boards speak of 'the *Springwatch* effect' to describe the influx of visitors who turn up at places featured in the programmes. When *Springwatch* promotes bumble bee nesting boxes public demand is such that, overnight, supplies on shop shelves are exhausted. Its festivals of action and engagement with nature pull in 250,000 people, who are not at all passive escapists. Nor are these the already converted. Many are young families who go because their children want to. The core audience of nature lovers might make up to 2 million of *Springwatch*'s audience, but that leaves an additional 2 million converts.

Springwatch certainly bucks the trend, defying all previous observations on the passivity of audiences. Its leitmotif is participation – viewers' surveys of wildlife, wildlife gardening and diverse forms of action. Part of its success is due to its innovative use of multi-platform broadcasting (so called '360 degree commissioning') in which the web, local radio, different television programmes and a host of other outlets are enrolled to promote awareness of the programme. That, however, is probably not the fundamental reason for its success. At bottom *Springwatch* is about everyday wildlife, the animals and birds which the British public see every day and identify with – robins, blue tits, rabbits, foxes, etc. It is about the insects in their gardens. It pursues storylines which most viewers can easily see carrying on outside their windows when the television is turned off. It also promotes easily accessible, achievable actions to make a difference. It works, in other words, with uncharismatic, unexotic, undramatic wildlife that is not normally associated with the world of celebrity conservation.

The importance of these is demonstrated by the failure of the US version of *Springwatch*. This focused on the drama of getting spy cameras into the nests and dens of large rare and dangerous creatures, not on everyday wildlife with which people might identify or interact. Its emphasis was surveillance, not connection. It was not broadcast live, so could not respond to audience interest and demand, nor did it create the fora for audience participation. It imagined its audience as passive and reaped the consequences.

To be sure *Springwatch* has its celebrity presenters, but these are not the stars of the show. They are glorified continuity announcers, preserving the identity of the brand across its different platforms. The stars of the show are the public and their participation. The real achievement of *Springwatch* takes place on its message boards, websites and festivals. *Springwatch* celebrates the everyday and the ordinary, the myriad actions of individuals. Far from refuting the thesis of this book, *Springwatch*'s success endorses it: celebrity conservation does not build connection with nature. Rather, when people are given the space to celebrate and dwell on their own interactions with the wild, then connection with nature is forged.[80]

A perfect world or just the end?

'You're quite perfect, Miss Fairfax.'

    'Oh! I hope I am not that. It would leave no room for developments, and I intend to develop in many directions.' (Oscar Wilde: *The Importance of Being Earnest*)

To reiterate: mediagenic conservation and commodification can have good effects. They are endorsed by many players, transforming the world in ways that many participants find welcome. The danger, however, is that we perceive these developments only as they are served up to us as spectacles – alienated images whose verisimilitude and consequences we are unable, and do not wish, to question. Viewed thus, these images can rarely have a negative side.

When considered less credulously, the distortions of mediagenic conservation make unhappy reading. It seems unlikely that most consumers of spectacle will ever be in a position to challenge or question it. However, these images and their consumers do not have it all their own way; the world is not being remade that easily. It is kicking and struggling, and the people losing the battle can be on the rich and famous side. When rural people resist eviction and exclusion, when they deny attempts to commodify wildlife and make their lives and sacred places a spectacle, when they are not satisfied with inadequate development projects in lieu of access to protected resources, when figureheads and heroes cannot be found in mass protest, when wildlife depends on lands beyond the boundaries of secluded sanctuaries, this is when the oversimplified representations of conservation break down.

There is a growing body of activism and scholarship that is challenging the comfortable truths of conservation, and particularly 'feel good' celebrity conservation, from within and without the movement.[81] This can be exhilarating and riveting work, but one has to be sanguine about the nature of this struggle. Challenges to the spectacle of celebrity conservation are taking on the industrial might and slick media machines of a multibillion-dollar growth industry, which has all the force of the moral majority that conservation's cachet and kudos afford it. The odds are stacked against the challengers.

Unfortunately, the power of celebrity conservation is not only its industrial might. It is much more strongly rooted than that. To appreciate properly how difficult the task is we have to consider how deeply set celebrity is in our political systems. This will make it painfully clear why it is hard to imagine any alternative to the power and authority celebrity conservation enjoys.

Rojek argues that celebrity is the inevitable consequence of democracy itself. He notes that the growth of modern democracy initiated the possibility of achieved celebrity. It marked the waning of ascribed celebrity, of Court and Royalty, and allowed the development of societies where anyone could achieve greatness, regardless of birth. Celebrities are symbols and manifestations of that change.[82]

Democracies, however, do not actually deliver on their promises:

> The universal choice and equality implied by democratic theory is not accomplished in practice. In as much as this is so, it implies that the social and psychological condition of democracy consists of a generalised lack of fulfilment and satisfaction, since the cultural and economic promise implied by the political system is not experienced in the lived relations of culture and economy. (Rojek 2001: 182–3)

Instead, he observes, democracy is afflicted by a crucial paradox: 'the system formally delivering the means of equality and freedom to all cannot survive without generating structured inequalities of status and wealth' (Rojek 2001: 190). Our societies are divided between those who sell their labour and those who provide the means of production. Honour and prestige are unequally distributed. Many of the vital roles without which modern societies would not function, be clean, built, serviced and pampered are accorded the lowest honour. The least essential – actors, models, explorers, athletes and academics – receive the greatest. This explains part of the attraction and the contradiction of celebrity. The attraction is that it is still theoretically possible for anyone to achieve the equality and greatness democracy enshrines. A celebrity embodies what democracies promise everyone can become: an important individual. Following celebrities accepts that some people will be more equal than others, but retains the dream of future success. The contradiction is tragic:

> democracy, the system which claimed moral superiority on the basis of extending equality and freedom to all, cannot proceed without creating celebrities who stand above the common citizen and achieve veneration and god-like worship. (Rojek 2001: 198)

Celebrity conservation is as strong and as powerful as democracy in western cultures. Rojek's argument suggests that there is no alternative to it. I cannot see how conservation could be different from the music trade or film industry. Some people are wonderful musicians and actors; some are not but have wonderful agents. Either way these people will always be the few. Likewise a few of us will always enjoy life outdoors and relationships with wildlife, and some will want to tell other people about them. And their stories may be told in such an exciting way that they can command a large market.

It is hard to predict what the world of celebrity conservation will be like in years to come. In the first instance we are only just getting to grips with the nature of the work of celebrity within conservation. We need to talk to more people about their perceptions of celebrity, the environment and conservation in order better to understand the para-social relations involved if we are to form clear judgements about them. The conservation movement, and particularly conservation organizations using celebrities, need this research if they are to understand the implications of their marketing. All I can do here is highlight the need for more careful ethnography.

The technology of celebrity will change enormously. A generation ago there was no Internet, and the major celebrity magazines had not been launched. There were far fewer television channels, especially in the UK. It is unlikely that current levels of interest will be maintained, which means there will still be celebrities, but perhaps fewer of them.[83] Recall also how few people read celebrity news and gossip (page ix), and that many of the few who are interested are not at all swayed by the authenticity of the material in front of them (page 10). They know it is a charade and enjoy pulling it apart. It was reassuring to read Boorstin's condemnation of celebrity's shallownesses (written nearly five decades ago) and still find his concerns fresh and contemporary. Despite decades of ever increasing celebrity productivity, our minds have not become dulled into accepting it.

From another perspective, things are less bright. The constant refrain of people analysing conservation images is that they capture their contexts inadequately. Many academics insist that until consumers find those contexts, and understand the background of the images they are consuming, there will continue to be a risk of perpetrating injustice. I am not sure that this complaint is reasonable. We simply cannot decode the images coming before us all the time; it took many years of research for the current decoders to produce their findings. Many people buy into these spectacles in order to worry less about the poverty and degradation of their lives, not more. I cannot see how this will change.

My forecast presents several different challenges. To celebrities I would say this. You will find it hard to suffer bad publicity through your conservation work. Almost regardless of what you or the cause actually do, you are likely to be seen to be doing good. Does this comfort you? I suspect not. The interviews I had with celebrity agents suggested that the public reception of their charitable work was not as important to them as their own opinions of it.[84] Their agents gave them a free hand regarding whom to help, and support for conservation causes tended to be offered carefully, because they believed in them, not because of publicity concerns. It follows that more vigilance on celebrities' part concerning the impacts of the conservation projects they support may deal with some of the more significant problems conservation can create. Given their concern to make a positive difference, celebrities themselves may well be in the best position to explore the substance behind the images that proliferate around conservation.

The challenge facing the conservation establishment is how it can institutionalize critiques of its celebrity-ridden practices so that it does not let the commodified and iconified relationships they entail do violence to the ecosystems and societies conservation is trying to serve. This will require a new sort of engagement between conservation and its critics which is yet to emerge. It need not be a populist movement. The key decision-makers (NGO boards and funders, fieldworkers, producers, presenters, celebrities, volunteers and scientists) need to understand better the distortions of representation with which their worlds are filled. As the conservation movement expands and philanthropic giving becomes yet more monolithic these needs can only increase. The world's wealthiest people, and those channelling and courting their largesse, will find it ever harder to see behind the spectacles presented to them. My hope is that an independent standard of evaluation will emerge which would offer rigorous independent assessments of the images at work, and their consequences, and to which donors, and celebrities, could go to examine the effects and grounding of the representations that surround them.[85] I realize that this could take decades to emerge.

In the meantime the future appears bright indeed for celebrity conservation. We shall have many ways of enjoying its products. We are steadily creating more stages upon which it can perform. We shall still desire to experience the amazing world we know exists somewhere out there. If we can only visit it rarely, we can still enjoy its wonderfully imagined representation. This is indeed a growth industry, with plenty of room for developments.

Notes

1 Introduction

1 Jones 2001. *Storyteller* was authorized by van der Post's family and published five years after his death.

2 It would not be easy to write a particularly salacious account of conservation. There is nothing remarkable, as far as I can tell, about social mores in conservation circles. Van der Post was unusual.

3 I was struck by the following event in van der Post's life and one reaction to Jones's book. In 1952 when van der Post was forty-five he was asked to escort a fourteen-year-old girl from Cape Town to London. While they were at sea he seduced her. He kept her as his mistress in London, sending her back to South Africa as soon as he realized she was pregnant (at fifteen) with no explanation. The girl, and her family, only discovered she was pregnant later. In his response to Jones's book, Christopher Hope protested that 'Van der Post was an indefatigable seducer with a spectacular weakness for younger women: that is not in doubt. But Jones's need to huff and puff each time he turns up evidence of some fresh betrayal is baffling' (Hope 2001).

4 Booker 2001.

5 Birkett 2001. Wilde would doubtless have concurred. The context of the epigraph to this chapter reads as follows: 'Bored by the tedious and improving conversation of those who have neither the wit to exaggerate nor the genius to romance, tired of the intelligent person whose reminiscences are always based upon memory, whose statements are invariably limited by probability, and who is at any time liable to be corroborated by the merest Philistine who happens to be present, Society sooner or later must return to its lost leader, the cultured and fascinating liar. Who he was who first, without ever having gone out to the rude chase, told the wandering caveman at sunset how he had dragged the Megatherium from the purple darkness of its jasper cave, or slain the Mammoth in single combat and brought back its gilded tusks, we cannot tell, and not one of our modern anthropologists, for all their much-boasted science, has had the ordinary courage to tell us. Whatever was his name or race, he certainly was the true founder of social intercourse. For the aim of the liar is simply to charm, to delight, to give pleasure. He is the very basis of civilized society' (Wilde 2003: 1081). Wilde also insisted, however, that the highest form of lying was for Art's sake. It would be hard for van der Post to show that he lied solely for such a higher cause.

6 Booker 2001.

7 After all, why should you have heard of any of them?

8 They are taken from *Complete Works of Oscar Wilde* (2003), with some help from Keyes 1996, and Mikhail 1979.

9 Wilde's writings on fame in his fictional worlds did not deal with the

publicly attributed celebrity we know now. In his world, people had influence because of their character ('I had come face to face with someone whose mere personality was so fascinating that, if I allowed it to do so, it would absorb my whole nature, my whole soul, my very art itself' [*Dorian Gray*]), and because they belonged to the English aristocracy, where fame is ascribed by birth in the first instance, before any further renown can be achieved. A diary could only become 'something sensational to read' (*The Importance of Being Earnest*) if one was already somebody. He had low views of public taste, and the art and culture demanded by it. For him the People were 'despots' and 'tyrants', they 'bribe[d] and brutalize[d]', '[t]heir authority is a thing blind, deaf, hideous, grotesque, tragic, amusing, serious and obscene' (*The Soul of Man Under Socialism*).

10 This is what he told Prince Charles (Smith, D. 2002).

11 Keyes 1996.

2 Combining celebrity and the environment

1 My main sources for this section have been Cooper 2007; Boorstin 1992 (1961); Gamson 1994, 2001; Marshall 1997; Turner et al. 2000; Schickel 2000 (1985); Rojek 2001; Turner 2004 and Richey and Ponte 2006. Ferris (2007) provides an excellent overview of most of these authors and others.

2 Turner 2004: 3.

3 Boorstin 1992 (1961): 57.

4 Rojek 2001: 31.

5 Schickel 2000 (1985).

6 Rojek 2001: 19.

7 Schickel 2000 (1985): 35.

8 *Twelfth Night*.

9 Boorstin 1992 (1961): 45.

10 Rojek 2001: 12.

11 Weber 1968 (1914).

12 Source 31, 20 March 2008.

13 One of the earliest movie stars was Florence Lawrence. Once known simply as 'the Biograph Girl' for the company she worked for, she was signed by another producer, Carl Laemmle, who leaked news that she had been killed in an accident. A few days later, shortly before the new film starring her came out, Laemmle denounced the story of her death as a hoax perpetrated by his rivals and staged her reappearance. The media attention resulting was immense (Schickel 2000 [1985]).

14 Schickel 2000 (1985).

15 For the most illuminating accounts see Gamson (1994), Turner et al. (2000) and Turner (2004).

16 Turner 2004: 38–9.

17 Rojek 2001: 33.

18 Ibid.

19 Wilde was so fond of this idea that his characters can be found voicing this phrase in at least two of his major works: *The Picture of Dorian Gray* and *A Woman of No Importance*.

20 Rojek 2001: 74.

21 Ibid.: 43.

22 Gamson 1994.

23 Schickel 2000 (1985).

24 Gamson 2001. Since Gamson wrote this, the rise of reality TV shows and programmes like *Pop Idol*, *X Factor* etc. (brilliantly portrayed in Ben Elton's novel *Chart Throb*) suggests a new development, namely a more active audience participation in celebrity production (cf Holmes, S. 2005).

25 Ferris 2007.

26 Turner 2004: 4.

27 Rojek 2001: 90–1.

28 Hartley 1999.

29 I could say the same of most

prominent politicians, but it is their job to know about the issue and their failure to understand it is interesting for that reason, whereas Ms Westwood is not an elected representative, and her opinions are less interesting.

30 Meyer and Gamson 1995: 184.

31 Street 2004.

32 *The Importance of Being Earnest.*

33 Street 2004: 447.

34 Turner 2004: 82.

35 This thesis is most thoroughly explored in *Nature Unbound* (Brockington et al. 2008).

36 Guha and Martinez-Alier 1997; Adams, W. M. 2001.

37 West et al. 2006.

38 Chape et al. 2005. These are not all the strictly protected areas of the Yellowstone model. Only about half of existing protected areas are found in the stricter categories which restrict human resource use.

39 The WWF's Panda Ball sponsorship page boasts that the organization is 'one of the world's largest independent global conservation organizations and one of the most respected and well-known brands (no. 2 in Europe and in the top ten in the U.S. according to the Edelman 2003 study, presented at the World Economic Forum in Davos)'. www.panda.org/how_you_can_help/donate/panda_ball/sponsorship/index.cfm (accessed 22 August 2008).

40 West and Carrier 2004.

41 Sarkar et al. 2006.

42 James et al. 2001; Bruner et al. 2004.

43 Not all scientists are comfortable with this state of affairs. Wilde quipped, 'Science can never grapple with the irrational. That is why it has no future before it, in this world' (*An Ideal Husband*). I find it, however, entirely logical that where ideas are both false and powerful it is impossible to explain their power by studying their veracity.

44 Fairhead and Leach 1996.

45 Eckholm 1976.

46 Thompson et al. 1986.

47 It was realized only later, for example, that some local farmers will deliberately trigger landslides, mix up the leached surface soils with richer subsoils, and then re-terrace the disturbed slopes. Erosion scars of landslides do not necessarily represent the failure and retreat of agriculture, but rather can signify its renovation and renewal.

48 Ives and Messerli 1989.

49 Richards 1985; Mortimore 1998.

50 Brockington 2002.

51 Later analyses of the satellite data showed that the cattle were having some impact on the vegetation but not one which needs necessarily to be solved by evictions (Canney 2001). The scientific basis of the theories, which predict that arid and semi-arid rangelands could be degraded by overgrazing, is being substantially challenged (Sullivan and Rohde 2002, Gillson and Hoffman 2007).

52 Tiffen et al. 1994. Other studies have shown that wealthier families were best placed to benefit from these changes; poorer families could lose out (Rocheleau et al. 1995; Murton 1999).

53 Boerma 1999.

54 Brockington et al. 2008.

55 MacDonald has shown how a conservation project in Pakistan to save the ibex was launched in the absence of any population data about ibex numbers (MacDonald, K. 2004).

For an excellent account of extinction and its varieties see Ladle and Jepson 2008. For a review of the evidence of extinction see Brockington et al. 2008, chapter 3.

56 The predictions of high annual losses made by most observers are yet to be recorded. In the last ten years at least 12,000 species should have become extinct according to the most conservative of the predictions made (Dirzo and Raven 2003), and 260,000 according to the Conservation International website. Actual species known to have become extinct from the late 1990s to 2004 were just twelve (Baillie et al. 2004). But up to 122 further species of amphibian are listed as possibly extinct, with the decline occurring since 1980 (Stuart et al. 2004; Pimenta et al. 2005; Stuart et al. 2005; Mendelson et al. 2006).

57 About 15–20,000 new species are still being described annually (Dirzo and Raven 2003: 148). It is very hard to know how these species are faring given that they have only just been discovered. Moreover extinction is difficult to prove even in well-known taxa. A species has to be known, and missing, for a long time to qualify. Some commentators believe that it is best to consider the more threatened species to be 'committed to extinction' (Heywood et al. 1994).

58 Balmford, Green et al. 2003; Jenkins et al. 2003; Balmford et al. 2005.

59 Butchart et al. 2004; Butchart et al. 2005; Butchart et al. 2006.

60 The failures of environmental predictions are sometimes used to denigrate validity of environmental movement and conservation concerns. By proving environmentalists wrong in some instances detractors cast doubt on the broader movement. One of the most recent manifestations of this trend is Bjorn Lomborg's book *The Skeptical Environmentalist* (2001) in which he reviews a 'litany' of environmental ills and proclaims the planet healthy in every case. The problem with Lomborg's book is that it is not a work of very good scholarship (Brockington 2003a). He simply does not know enough about the problems he reviews to have the authority to make any public pronouncements about them. This does not mean that he is wrong, simply that we can never really be sure whether anything he says is right or not.

61 The rewriting of West African forest history which Fairhead and Leach attempt is challenged. Some scholars have pointed to quite different case studies close to the Guinean example (Nyerges and Green 2000).

62 Leach and Mearns 1996.

63 Foucault 1977; Ferguson 1990.

64 For example the idea of nature as a pristine Eden spoilt by people is tremendously evocative in the West and elsewhere. The idea of a pristine wilderness in Africa or Latin America may be a myth (Adams and McShane 1992; Gomez-Pompa and Kaus 1992; Denevan 1992) but it is an immensely appealing one.

65 Redford and Fearn 2007a.

66 Spence 1999.

67 Brockington and Igoe 2006.

68 Shahabuddin and Shah 2003; Buergin and Kessler 2000; Anderson and Ikeya 2001; Hitchcock 2002; Sato 2002; Buergin 2003; Goenewald and Macleod 2004; Pearce 2005a, 2005b; Sunseri 2005; Anon. 2006; Nyenyembe 2006.

69 Cernea 2005.

70 Brockington 2002.

71 Emerton 2001.

72 Brockington and Schmidt-Soltau 2004; Brockington et al. 2006.

73 Brosius 2004; Terborgh 2004.

74 Fairhead and Leach 2000; Chapin 2004; Dowie 2005; Dowie 2006.

75 Ghimire and Pimbert 1997; Brockington 2002; Chatty and Colchester 2002; Colchester 2003; Igoe 2004; Brockington et al. 2008.

76 Recommendations (R 1–32). These may be viewed at: www.iucn.org/themes/wcpa/wpc2003/English/outputs/recommendations.htm.

77 COP 7 Decision VII/28 page 354.www.biodiv.org/doc/decisions/COP-07-dec-en.pdf (accessed 14 July 2004).

78 Balmford and Whitten 2003.

79 Redford and Fearn 2007a, 2007b.

80 Jacoby 2001.

81 Wolmer 2003; Duffy 2006.

82 Upton et al. 2008.

83 Strkalj 2008.

84 Gamson 1994.

3 Conserving celebrities

1 The public service announcement described here was devised and promoted by Conservation International. The video is hosted on their website and they have made much of this promotion, even hosting another video about the making of the first. See www.conservation.org/FMG/Pages/Videos.apx (accessed 19 September 2008).

2 This is the 'boisterously democratic approach' to fame that Holmes observed of *Heat* magazine (Holmes, S. 2005: 9).

3 www.tusk.org/calendar.asp?page=29 (accessed 26 August 2006).

4 Bristow 2002.

5 Bonner 1993.

6 Street 2004.

7 www.brickbond.co.za:16081/ (accessed 24 August 2006).

8 www.ippmedia.com/ipp/observer/2006/09/03/73714.html (accessed 3 September 2006).

9 www.simr.org.uk/pages/celebrity_support/index.html (accessed 24 August 2006).

10 www.forbes.com/2006/06/12/06celebrities_ money-power-celebrities-list_land.html (accessed 22 August 2006).

11 Boykoff and Goodman forthcoming.

12 www.vanityfair.com (accessed 22 August 2006).

13 Nielsen 2007.

14 Club4Climate is run by the flamboyant Andrew Charalambous (a businessman also known as Dr Earth). In addition to the Surya eco-club he also has plans to develop an ecotourist island resort where it will be possible to 'save the world lying down drinking cocktails next to the pool'. The Club4Climate website reports that profits go to the environmental NGO Friends of the Earth. Friends of the Earth has issued a statement disassociating itself from Club4Climate, saying that it will not accept financial contributions, see www.foe.org/friends-earth-does-not-support-club4climate (accessed 20 February 2009). Club4Climate have added a disclaimer stating that 'Friends of the Earth in no way supports or endorses the activities of Club4Climate, but we're going to give them the money anyway.' www.club4climate.com (accessed 21 February 2009).

15 Adams, W. M. 2004.

16 www.conservation.org/fmg/pages/videoplayer.aspx?videoid=29 (accessed 23 January 2009).

17 Blashford-Snell and Lenska 1996: 147.
18 Boykoff and Goodman 2008.
19 Meyer and Gamson 1995.
20 Hutchins and Lester 2006; Lester 2006.
21 Lester 2006: 918.
22 Turner et al. 2000.
23 Lester 2006.
24 Hutchins and Lester 2006: 447.
25 Ibid.: 446.
26 Castells 1997.
27 Hutchins and Lester 2006: 437.
28 Burgess et al. 1991: 501, italics in the original.
29 Cf Castells 1997: 131.
30 Giles 2000: 8.

4 Wildlife presenters and wildlife film

1 Letter in possession of the author.
2 Bousé 2000; Mitman 1999; Beinart 2001; Vivanco 2002.
3 Bousé 2000: 5.
4 Both Bousé and Mitman observe that the concerns for authenticity in wildlife films built on an earlier debate by leading conservationists and authors on the authenticity of popular writing in nature that embroiled the works of Ernest Thompson Seton, Jack London, William Long, John Burroughs and President Theodore Roosevelt.
5 Mitman 1999: 50.
6 This account is based on Mitman 1999: 35-58.
7 Attenborough 2004.
8 Philo and Henderson 1998: 33.
9 Gray 2002.
10 Knowing what is happening to the lemmings makes watching these scenes from *White Wilderness* distinctly unpleasant. See www.youtube.

com/watch?v=xMZlr5Gf9yY (accessed 9 May 2009).
11 Vivanco 2002: 1196.
12 Bousé 2003.
13 Mitman 1999: 127.
14 Vivanco 2002.
15 Ibid.: 1199.
16 Ibid.
17 Cubitt observed of Attenborough that 'it is possible to be irritated by the lack of concern for the human populations of exotic countries, symbolised by the absence of local musics from the soundtrack'. www.museum.tv/archives/etv/A/htmlA/attenborough/attenborough.htm (accessed 24 August 2006).
18 Monbiot 2002.
19 Beinart 2001.
20 Ibid.
21 Vivanco 2002: 1199-1200.
22 Cf Adams, C. 2003.
23 Vivanco 2002: 1202.
24 Bousé 2000: 14-15.
25 Ibid.: 8-9.
26 Ibid.: 42.
27 Mitman 1999: 208.
28 This section draws on Brockington 2008a.
29 Jeffries 2003.
30 Philo and Henderson 1998.
31 Ibid.: 27.
32 Bousé 2000: 53-4.
33 Parsons 1982.
34 Source 34, May 2008.
35 Parsons 1982.
36 Philo and Henderson 1998: 23.
37 Accessed 24 August 2006. Attenborough himself noted the value of 'bring[ing] the excitement of dramatic landscapes into the series and [taking] viewers, vicariously, to little known corners of the world' (Attenborough 2002: 351). Irwin's films made exotic places comprehensible with his simplifications. Vivanco, analysing a film in which

Irwin rescues some crocodiles held in captivity in East Timor, argued that the film reduced complex political situations and local beliefs and culture to become just another backdrop to Irwin's work (Vivanco 2004, 2006).

38 Attenborough 2002.

39 Cottle 2004.

40 Philo and Henderson 1998: 29.

41 Bousé 2000.

42 Aldridge and Dingwall 2003; Dingwall and Aldridge 2006.

43 Mitman 1999: 127.

44 Cottle 2004: 97.

45 Attenborough 2002.

46 Source 23, February 2008.

47 Bousé 2000: 82.

48 Basset et al. 2002.

49 Cottle 2004.

50 Ibid.

51 Bassett et al. 2002: 169.

52 Cottle 2004: 87.

53 Warren 2002.

54 Quoted in Cottle 2004: 85.

55 Martin, Dattatri, Whitaker pers comm. 2008.

56 The intelligence of wildlife films is a sensitive issue. While working on this book I attended the Wildscreen film festival in Bristol. Part of the experience of that festival is to try to pitch film ideas to as many commissioning editors as possible, and in the spirit of anthropological participant observation, I joined in, based on ideas in this book about the problems celebrity poses for conservation. Most pitches are only a minute long, but I was able to develop the idea over coffee to a Wildscreen grandee of many years' experience. She did not commission films but she knew the industry well and who might be interested. Having listened to it, she called over an old friend, again of many years' experi-

ence, and summed up the pitch in one word. 'Jane,' she said, 'Dan wants to make an intelligent film. Do you know anyone who would do it?' Jane paused and thought silently for a long time. 'No,' she said, 'I don't.'

57 Quoted in Bousé 2000: 86.

58 Source: www.jonathanangela scott.com/safaris.html (accessed 22 January 2008).

59 Cottle 2004.

60 Turner 2004. The outpourings of grief that celebrities' deaths occasion is hard for the analysts to understand. Turner admits these responses demonstrate that critics are missing some of the role that celebrities play in people's lives and identities, which concepts like 'parasocial relations' cannot capture. But Turner also insists that these are identities built up by cultural consumption. The grief displayed at these (real) media events is the personal grief of consumers.

5 Celebrity conservation

1 He may even have influenced the future careers of Richard Attenborough (film director) and his brother David who attended one of his talks in London. My source for Grey Owl is Smith's comprehensive biography (Smith, D. B. 1990).

2 And perhaps also as a result of the Whig histories that have been written of these conservation movements which privilege the work of great men and women.

3 Principal works include Hornaday 1931; Carson 1962; Leopold 1989 (1949); Thoreau 1991 (1854).

4 Hornaday 1931.

5 Carson 1962.

6 He meant we should adopt a long-term perspective and recognize that prey species, however valuable to

human hunters, need to be limited by wild predators to prevent them overrunning their range, see Leopold (1989 [1949]).

7 Thoreau made his claims about the importance of wildness in his essay on walking. He has been misquoted by such luminaries as Martin Holdgate, for example, Director of the IUCN from 1988 to 1994, see Holdgate 1999: 4.

8 Schama 1996.

9 Nash 2001.

10 Gordon 2006: 9

11 Quammen 2008.

12 Wilson 1992; Igoe 2004.

13 NGO Source 21, 12 January 2006.

14 The film is notable for not lionising Treadwell as a celebrity conservationist.

15 thecanadianencyclopedia. com/index.cfm?PgNm=TCE&Para ms=M1ARTM0012020 (accessed 1 September 2008).

16 www.museum.tv/archives/etv/ A/htmlA/attenborough/attenborough. htm (accessed 24 August 2006).

17 Beinart 2001.

18 Ibid.

19 Mitman 1999: 200.

20 Milton 2002.

21 Ibid.: 73, italics in the original.

22 I am paraphrasing Wilde; he made the remark of Whistler (an artist).

23 Leakey and Morell 2001: 35. For another example, consider the title of ecologist Stuart Pimm's book about the impact of people on the world; it is called *The World According to Pimm*, which probably indicates some self-confidence.

24 Ibid.: 79.

25 This was my perception after my interview with him in 2008. Other discussions I had with other tiger

experts in the country, notably Ullas Karanth, had a more upbeat tone, despite the announcement that tiger numbers had reached a historic low, of just over 1,400, half those of previous estimates.

26 Hughes 2006.

27 Boorstin 1992 (1961).

28 Ibid.: 63.

29 LaBastille 1992.

30 Garland 2006, 2008.

31 Theroux 1997 (1967).

32 Ibid.: 48, 49.

33 Do they provide them still?

34 Theroux 1997 (1967): 52.

35 This list is expanded from that presented in Garland's dissertation (2006). See also Garland's excellent exploration of the whiteness of East African conservation in her paper in *African Studies Review* (2008).

36 Garland 2008: 67, and cf Neumann 2004.

37 House 1993: 365.

38 Garland 2006.

39 Bonner 1993.

40 Quammen 2008: 47.

41 Milton 2002; Adams, W. M. 2004.

42 Brockington and Igoe 2006; Scholfield and Brockington 2009.

43 Darlington 1998.

44 Weber 1968 (1914).

45 The Wildlife Conservation Network finds inspiration in Margaret Mead's aphorism: 'Never doubt that a small group of thoughtful, committed citizens can change the world. Indeed, it's the only thing that ever has.'

46 Note Malcolm Draper's careful discussion of the complexities of the masculinities of some of the men – Ian Player and Nick Steele – who have played a defining role in conservation circles in South Africa (Draper 1998).

47 Steinhart 2006. House uses stories of these three to set the scene

of what Kenya was like for readers of his biography of the Adamsons (1993).

48 Steinhart 2006: 133–4.

49 Cf Balmford, Gaston et al. 2003.

50 www.owens-foundation.org (accessed 28 August 2006).

51 www.owens-foundation. org/docs/biograph2.htm#honors (accessed 28 August 2006).

52 Ward 1997.

53 Adams and McShane 1992.

54 Wilde understood the appeal of the wicked: 'Well, ever since dear Uncle Jack first confessed to us that he had a younger brother who was very wicked and bad, you of course have formed the chief topic of conversation between myself and Miss Prism. And of course a man who is much talked about is always very attractive. One feels there must be something in him, after all. I daresay it was foolish of me, but I fell in love with you, Earnest' (*The Importance of Being Earnest*).

55 Brockington 2004.

56 *A Woman of No Importance.*

57 Bourdieu 1998: 45.

58 Smith, D. B. 1990: 85.

6 Concentrations of wealth and power

1 www.iccfoundation.us/aboutus. htm (accessed 22 August 2008). This echoes Nash's view that national parks are the USA's best idea.

2 In both countries the violence and legality of the procedures used to evict residents from these areas, not to mention the social consequences, have caused alarm and controversy.

3 Turner et al. 2000.

4 Cooper 2007; Richey and Ponte 2006.

5 Barrett 2000.

6 www.celebrityoutreach.com (accessed 30 August 2006).

7 Although Pringle's investigation into the benefits of celebrity advertising warned that it is no guarantee of success (Pringle 2004).

8 Beinecke pers. comm. 30 August 2006.

9 www.youtube.com/watch?v= VSZR13_f6KA (accessed 21 February 2009).

10 Igoe and Kelsall 2005.

11 Edwards and Hulme 1995; Hulme and Edwards 1997; Bebbington et al. 2007.

12 Scholfield and Brockington 2009.

13 www.charity-commission.gov. uk/registeredcharities/factfigures. asp#intro. (accessed 8 May 2009).

14 Khare and Bray 2004; Dowie 2005.

15 www.sas.com/success/ worldwildlifefund.html (accessed 21 August 2006).

16 Dowie pers. comm. 6 August 2006.

17 Source 38, October 2008.

18 Pamphlet in the possession of the author.

19 www.wildnet.org/expo2006_ weekend.htm (accessed 26 August 2006).

20 Source 38, October 2008; Source 27, October 2008; Source 25, July 2008; Source 35, August 2008.

21 Source 8, August 2008.

22 Source 35, August 2008.

23 Scholfield and Brockington 2009.

24 www.leonardodicaprio.org/ index.html (accessed 22 August 2006).

25 www.turnerfoundation.org/ grants/fa.asp (accessed 22 August 2006).

26 Sachedina pers. comm. May 2008.

27 Edwards 2008. The credit crunch must dampen the enthusi-

asm of these authors. Many foundations are facing 25–30 per cent losses in endowment income which could take years to recover.

28 Foundations are not yet connecting with conservation and environmental NGOs in all contexts. US conservation NGOs are much more reliant on foundations than their colleagues in Canada and the UK. In the latter country environmental NGOs earned just 2.7 per cent of their income from foundations, and accounted for 1.6 per cent of £2 billion of foundation giving; in Canada 2 per cent of environmental NGOs' income is derived from foundations, whereas in the USA it is between 20 and 40 per cent. Many conservation NGOs in Canada and the UK are keen to increase their revenues from foundations (Cracknell and Godwin 2007).

29 Bonner 1993.

30 www.celb.org/xp/CELB/about/ (accessed 18 September 2008).

31 Goldman, M. 2005.

32 MacDonald, C. 2008.

33 Rothkopf 2008.

34 Ibid.

35 Pharoah reports that giving to charities in the UK increased in real terms in the 1990s as a result of more giving by a few large donors (2002). At the same time she notes that the poor are giving away proportionally four times more of their income than the rich.

36 Rangarajan 2001.

37 George Holmes's work on the transnational conservationist class, which draws on Sklair's idea of the transnational capitalist class (2001), was coming into the public domain as this book went to press. For more information about his ideas see his paper in *Antipode* and his doctoral thesis.

38 Poole 2006.

39 Macleod 2003.

40 Bonner 1993.

41 www.ecoclub.com/news/051/ interview.html (accessed 30 August 2006).

42 www.savechinastigers.net/ about.html (accessed 3 September 2006).

43 www.csmonitor.com/2006/ 0823/p15s01-lign.html (accessed 3 September 2006).

44 My source for this paragraph is Draper and Mare 2003.

45 Through Sir James, Aspinall met Mangosuthu Buthelezi (President of the Zulu-based Inkatha Freedom Party of South Africa) in 1986. As South Africa moved towards independence Aspinall championed an independent Zulu nation and urged Zulu nationalists to 'sharpen their spears and fall on the Xhosas', another ethnic group in South Africa (Draper and Mare 2003: 555).

46 Pasquini 2007.

47 Jacoby 2001: 39.

48 Similarly the 14,000 hectares of land he purchased in Wyoming formed the basis, after much local resistance, of the Grand Teton National Park (Jacoby 2001). He also donated land that formed the basis of a national park on the island of St John in the Caribbean, and which has been sustained by the support of its wealthy neighbours since (Fortwangler 2007).

49 Pearce 2005b: 48.

50 Goenewald and Macleod 2004.

51 Luck 2003; McIntosh Xaba and Associates 2003.

52 Connor 2006.

53 Langholz and Kerley 2006.

54 Rothkopf 2008.

55 Sklair 2001; Rothkopf 2008.

7 Criticisms

1 Wikipedia reports: 'In 1999, he published *The Biggest Secret*, in which he wrote that the secret world government consists of a race of reptilian humanoids known as the Babylonian Brotherhood, and that many prominent figures are, in fact, reptilian, including George W. Bush, Queen Elizabeth II, Kris Kristofferson, and Boxcar Willie. Icke has further claimed that a small group of Jews, namely the Rothschild family – who are really a "reptilian humanoid bloodline" – secretly financed Adolf Hitler and supported the Holocaust … Icke has strongly denied that he is an anti-Semite, stressing that the Rothschilds are reptiles, not Jews.' en.wikipedia.org/wiki/David_Icke (accessed 22 August 2006).

2 www.whitelions.org/ (accessed 22 August 2006).

3 MacKenzie 1988.

4 www.rainforestfoundation. com/html/info-center.htm (accessed 22 August 2006).

5 Source 28, August 2008.

6 Charity Navigator is a US-based charity evaluator that compares the efficiency of US charitable organizations based on analyses of their financial reports. They assess the efficiency and capacity of each charity by comparing, for example, how efficiently they raise money, and other such indices. See www.charitynavigator. org/ (accessed 10 February 2009).

7 Castro and Locker 2000; Halpern et al. 2006; Mansourian and Dudley 2008. There is one exception to this pattern, namely an analysis of conservation expenditure in sub-Saharan Africa which I carried out with Katherine Scholfield (Scholfield and Brockington 2009), which found a strong correlation between levels of biodiversity and conservation expenditure. But it is less clear why they should be so well matched. We cannot infer cause from correlation.

8 Christensen 2003; Wilson et al. 2006; Murdoch et al. 2007; Wilson et al. 2007.

9 Dowie 1996.

10 MacDonald, C. 2008.

11 Ottaway and Stephens 2003.

12 Rothkopf 2008: 178.

13 Chapin 2004.

14 Price et al. 2004; Romero and Andrade 2004, Dowie 2005, 2006.

15 Sachedina 2008.

16 Neumann 1998; Brockington 2002; Colchester 2004; Pearce 2005a; Brockington and Igoe 2006; Cernea and Schmidt-Soltau 2006; Schmidt-Soltau and Brockington 2007.

17 Ghimire and Pimbert 1997; Igoe and Croucher 2007.

18 Rodriguez et al. 2007.

19 Lees 2007.

20 Igoe 2003.

21 *The Picture of Dorian Gray.*

22 Weber and Vedder 2002.

23 Bonner 1993.

24 Clynes 2002.

25 Adams and McShane 1992.

26 Adams, W. M. 2001: 166–7.

27 Clynes 2002. This is an incident that has attracted academic attention elsewhere (Igoe 2002; Neumann 2004; Ferguson 2006).

28 Shanahan 2005.

29 Ibid.: 254.

30 Cartmill 1993.

31 MacKenzie 1988.

32 MacKenzie 1987: 50.

33 Hurt and Ravan 2000: 296.

34 www.nitroexpresssafaris.com (accessed 18 August 2008). There is a salient theme in Mark Sullivan's videos of his work. They are called *Sudden Death, Death Rush, Death at My Feet, Death by the Ton, Shot to*

Death, Death on the Run, In the Face of Death, Death and Double Rifles and Africa's Black Death. These disturbing videos allow armchair hunters the pleasure of vicariously experiencing highly dangerous hunting activity. This work does not enjoy the broader approval of the hunting community in East Africa. Sullivan's work recalls Wilde's quip: 'The English country gentleman galloping after a fox – the unspeakable in full pursuit of the uneatable' (A Woman of No Importance). However, Sullivan's philosophy is but an extension of the codified forms of hunting big game that have long characterized hunting.

35 Neumann 2004: 825.

36 Steinhart 2006.

37 Ibid.: 121.

38 Hurt and Ravan 2000.

39 Lindsey et al. 2007 and www. usatoday.com/news/nation/2007-10-22-Hunter_N.htm (accessed 19 August 2008).

40 Hulme and Murphree 2001.

41 Cartmill 1993: 154.

42 See entries in Prins et al. 2000 for a discussion of the impacts of hunting in Kenya.

43 Cartmill 1993.

44 Oldfield et al. 2003.

45 Bradshaw et al. 2007.

46 www.cambodianvision.com/angelina.html (accessed 24 August 2006).

47 Angelina Jolie, Bono and Harrison Ford all explain their charitable work in terms of their desire to give something back to the world.

48 Accessed 18 August 2006.

49 Hypocritical in Wilde's sense: 'I hope that you have not been leading a double life, pretending to be wicked and being really good all the time. That would be hypocrisy' (The Importance of Being Earnest).

50 Goldman, R. (1994) argues that mass advertising developed to cope with 'crises of overproduction and underconsumption', such that products became makers of lifestyles and personal identity, thus increasing the pressure to consume generally, rather than meeting particular needs. He notes that advertising has had to work harder to legitimate itself. Although Goldman does not touch on the issue I suspect that celebrity, particularly in recent years, has been integral to the development of advertising and the continuing consumerist ideology.

51 MacDonald, C. 2008.

52 Sachedina 2008.

53 Sklair 2001.

54 Ibid.: 8.

55 Ibid.: 216.

56 Monbiot 1995: iii.

57 Monbiot 2005.

58 It is perhaps in recognition of this that Monbiot subsequently promoted environmental causes that required more active participation, such as The Land is Ours (www.tlio.org.uk/index.html) and declines to lead protest against global warming which is not defined by such active involvement. Swampy, after a brief period in the limelight, vowed not to speak to the media. www.guardian.co.uk/uk_news/story/0,3604,994224,00.html (accessed August 2006).

8 Saving the world

1 Street 2004.

2 Source 17, January 2009. I will not name the presenter because this person has not sought any publicity for the influence they wielded on this occasion.

3 On Mark Tennant see www.telegraph.co.uk/travel/destinations/africaandindianocean/botswana/731770/Botswana-The-mane-man.html

(accessed 6 August 2008). Mark Shand writes: 'It was a long love affair with a country that ignited my passion for elephants. Fifteen years ago, I decided to write my next book about a journey across India. Purely on a whim, I decided to buy an elephant ... After many weeks of searching for available elephants, fate led me to my future paramour, late one monsoon night on the outskirts of a village, in the eastern state of Orissa. There standing quietly, illuminated by the glow of the campfire were three elephants.

My mouth went dry. I felt giddy, breathless. With one hind leg crossed over the other, she was leaning nonchalantly against a tree, the charms of her perfectly rounded posterior in full view, like a prostitute on a street corner. I knew then that I had to have her and I realised, with some surprise that I had fallen in love with a female Asian elephant.' www.kiplingcamp.com/markshand.html (accessed 30 January 2009).

4 Some can be less harmless than others. This sort of writing of encounters with exotic locales and peoples can provide 'an effective alibi for the perpetuation or reinstallment of ethnocentrically superior attitudes to "other" cultures, peoples and places' (Holland and Huggan 1998: viii).

5 Dinerstein 2005; Pimm 2006.

6 Source 12, January 2009; Source 29, March 2007. My sample size on which I base this claim is not large (just two wildlife presenters), but I suspect that it will prove representative of broader experience.

7 Indeed the social relations of production of this industry are intimately intertwined with these same protected areas. The photographers, artists, researchers, presenters and documentary writers who create the images of spectacle share field stations, meals and life-changing experiences. Celebrity conservationists, filmmakers and scientists meet and mingle at field stations in remote parts of the world. They discover new talent there. They intermarry.

8 Nugent 1994: 183.

9 See Sachedina 2008.

10 Debord 1995 (1967).

11 Debord 1995 (1967): thesis four.

12 Neves-Graca forthcoming.

13 shop.awf.org/adopt/ (accessed 18 September 2008).

14 Carrier 1998.

15 West and Carrier 2004; West et al. 2006.

16 Brockington et al. 2008.

17 *The Picture of Dorian Gray.* I wonder whether Wilde would not welcome a world where image and symbol are so free from their referents. In *The Decay of Lying* he wrote that 'And when that day dawns, or sunset reddens, how joyous we shall all be! Facts will be regarded as discreditable, Truth will be found mourning over her fetters, and Romance, with her temper of wonder will return to the land. The very aspect of the world will change to our startled eyes. Out of the sea will rise Behemoth and Leviathan, and sail round the high-pooped galleys, as they do on the delightful maps of those ages when books on geography were actually readable. Dragons will wander about the high places, and the phoenix will soar from her nest of fire in the air. We shall lay our hands on the basilisk, and see the jewel in the toad's head. Champing his gilded oats, the Hippogriff will stand in our stalls, and over our heads will float the Blue Bird singing of beautiful and impossible things, of things that are lovely and that never happen, of

things that are not and that should be. But before that comes to pass we must cultivate the lost art of Lying' (Wilde 2003: 1090–1). One could argue that the extraordinary success of the Harry Potter series, in which most of these wonderful myths and characters have been revived, heralds the arrival of this glorious day. The freedom of images allows us to lie with real grandiosity. But I think Wilde would mourn the mundane commonplaceness of the lies spectacles conjure up. For lies can only work in the presence of truth, and where truth is so hard to see, or so tangential to consumer needs, then how can we celebrate lying?

18 *The Secret Life of Walter Mitty* is a popular short story by James Thurber written in 1941 and made into a film six years later. Walter Mitty is a weak, ineffectual and hen-pecked office clerk who escapes a dull, boring and subservient existence by imagining himself the hero of an increasingly improbable set of adventures.

19 Nash 2001.

20 Cronon 1995.

21 Adams and McShane 1992; Denevan 1992; Gomez-Pompa and Kaus 1992; Rose 1996; Neumann 1998.

22 Proctor and Pincetl 1996.

23 Homewood and Rodgers 1991; Western 1994.

24 Hutton and Leader-Williams 2003: 220.

25 Bill Adams has analysed the symbolism deeply engrained in the film's narratives and devices, and its resonances with colonial visions for Africa (Adams, W. M. 2003).

26 When they are, it needs to be with adequate compensation for all the impoverishment and risks which displacement can cause (Cernea 2005; Cernea and Schmidt-Soltau 2006).

27 Homewood and Brockington 1999; Shahabuddin et al. 2005.

28 Brockington et al. 2006.

29 Vivanco 2002.

30 Sting and Dutilleux 1989.

31 Redford 1990; Brockington et al. 2008.

32 Igoe 2004, 2005.

33 Nugent 1994; Kuper 2003; Igoe 2006; Brockington et al. 2008.

34 Goldman, M. 2001.

35 Ibid.: 200–1.

36 Walpole and Leader-Williams 2002.

37 www.careforthewild.org/ adoptions.asp?S_ID=5&pageName= Adoptions (accessed 27 October 2006).

38 www.wildlifeworks.com/ (accessed 21 February 2009).

39 A better known, and similar exercise, is Bono's Product (RED)™, on which see Richey and Ponte 2006.

40 Barrow and Fabricius 2002; Borrini-Feyerabend et al. 2002.

41 I have discussed this issue in more depth elsewhere; see Brockington et al. 2008 and Brockington 2004.

42 Brockington et al. 2008.

43 Brockington 2003b; Brockington 2004.

44 Brockington 2002; McLean and Straede 2003; Ganguly 2004.

45 Bakker 2005; Castree 2007a, b.

46 Murombedzi 2001; Murphree 2001; Dzingirai 2003; Murombedzi 2003.

47 Nelson and Makko 2003; Nelson 2004.

48 Brockington et al. 2008.

49 My thanks to Professor Duffy for this information. Unfortunately I have been unable to locate any pictures of this activity.

50 Brockington et al. 2008.

51 Sullivan 2006: 112.

52 Ibid.: 120. Perhaps Wilde

might say that such changes calculate the cost of everything, but know the value of nothing (*Lady Windermere's Fan*).

53 Sullivan 2000.

54 MacDonald, K. 2004; MacDonald, K. 2005.

55 www.princesrainforests project.org/images/stories/pdfs/18trilliondollarvision.pdf (accessed 5 February 2009). The dinner is described thus on the Rainforests Project website: 'The evening was supported by the Steering Group of The Prince's Rainforests Project, comprising 16 of the world's largest companies including the Man Group, who underwrote the event. It included addresses by The Prince of Wales, Sir David Attenborough and Stanley Fink, recently retired Deputy Chairman of Man Group. Entertainment was provided by Sarah Brightman, who sang Nella Fantasia, the theme tune from the film "The Mission", which was deliberately chosen as a hymn to the forests.'

56 Quoted in Bousé 2000: 30.

57 Philo and Henderson 1998: 32.

58 Mitman 1999: 123–4.

59 Ibid.: 197. It was followed by *Wild Gold* (1961) and *The Dying Plains of Africa* (1961), both of which preached the dangers local people posed to wildlife. All were produced in the context of uncertainty and fear as to what future the colonial legacy of nature conservation faced from independent African governments. Mitman notes that by the end of the 1950s 'the media consistently portrayed freedom for Africans as a threat to the freedom of wildlife' (page 190).

60 Source 17, January 2009.

61 Monbiot 2002.

62 See www.filmmakersforconservation.org/.

63 Burgess et al. 1991.

64 Shanahan and McComas 1997; Shanahan et al. 1997; McComas et al. 2001.

65 Webber 2002.

66 Source 1, March 2008; Source 4, October 2008; Source 7, October 2008; Source 9, October 2008; Source 10, October 2008; Source 15, October 2008; Source 18, October 2008; Source 20, October 2008.

67 Bousé 2000: 192. Note however there are new companies like Earthtouch, which keep camera crews permanently in the field, streaming much more mundane events continually to their audiences. www.earth-touch.com/ (accessed 21 February 2009).

68 Mitman 1999: 207

69 Adams, W. M. 2004: 235, 236.

70 Milton 2002: 1.

71 Ibid.: 72.

72 Dunn et al. 2006.

73 Gray 2002.

74 Moreover African celebrity conservationists enjoy the special privilege of being perceived to be in touch with the real Africa that is popularly believed to have existed before it was spoilt by exploration and development.

75 Pergams and Zaradic 2006, 2008; Zaradic and Pergams 2007.

76 Pergams and Zaradic 2006: 392.

77 This view is published in Brockington 2008b.

78 The material in these paragraphs is principally derived from Sources 3 and 30, January 2009.

79 Source 30, February 2009. Phenology is the recording of the timing of key natural events. Before *Springwatch* the UK Phenology Network's survey run by the Woodland Trust was suffering from the ageing and dying off of the recorders on

which it had relied. As *Springwatch* has changed its interests the number of recorders has declined to just over 5,000, but this is still a significant increase on previous levels, and the main point remains. *Springwatch* encourages audience participation in ways in which other nature programmes do not.

80 In this sense the activities of *Springwatch* and associated initiatives like the BBC's *Breathing Places* resemble the Natural History Field Clubs which sprang up throughout Britain in the Victorian era (Allen 1994 [1976]). The historian of Natural History in Britain, David Allen, notes that in natural history societies (and I would add their associated conservation NGOs) there needs to be a healthy tension between professionals and amateurs. Too many of the former can stifle the 'volunteer dynamism' (p. 243). He notes that the growth of scientifically trained professionals after the Second World War could have its dangers for the movement as a whole. His final paragraph (first published in 1976) bears repeating: 'with the means of influencing public taste now so powerfully heightened, the possibilities of being deceived in this respect are greater than ever before. The more impressive the inflation, the even more extreme and prolonged now the potential aftermath of revulsion. We do well to greet the newfound respect for natural history in Britain with a continuing degree of wariness' (p. 244). If we read the 'means of influencing the public' to refer to the alliance of science and wildlife film then this seems prescient. The role of *Springwatch* may also be to give space for the amateur, even if it means that the scientists may have some

problematic data to cope with, as one commentator quipped, 'we can find that Spring may be seen to arrive a week earlier than normal if the BBC brings its schedule forward' (Source 30, February 2009).

81 For the scholarship examine the work of Bill Adams, Grazia Borinni-Feyerabend, Steven Brechin, Shirely Books, Lisa Campbell, James Carrier, Michael Cernea, Dawn Chatty, Marcus Colchester, Catherine Corson, Michael Dorsey, Tim Doyle, Rosaleen Duffy, Vupenyu Dzingirai, Christo Fabricius, Taghi Favor, Colin Filer, Crystal Fortwrangler, Krishna Ghimire, George Holmes, Kathy Homewood, Jon Hutton, Jim Igoe, Geoff Kinch, Ashish Kothari, Annette Leese, Ken MacDonald, Lorraine Moore, Marshall Murphree, James Murumbedzi, Katja Neves-Graca, Michel Pimbert, Mahesh Rangarajan, Maano Ramutsindela, Dilys Roe, Hassan Sachedina, Kai Schmidt-Soltau, Katherine Scholfield, Kartik Shanker, Marja Spierenburg, Sian Sullivan, Harry Wels, Paige West, Pete Wilshusen, Will Wolmer and Zoe Young.

82 Rojek 2001: 121.

83 We have seen interest in celebrity wax and wane before, in the 1930s for example.

84 Sources 31, 36, October 2008.

85 This would add to the work of Charity Navigator because it looks not just at the financial returns, but at the substance of the programmes that NGOs are undertaking. Organizations like New Philanthropy Capital and GiveWell are doing that, but their work with environmental and conservation organizations is limited. See www.philanthropycapital. org/ and givewell.net/ (accessed 9 February 2009).

Bibliography

Adams, C. (2003). 'Pitfalls of Synchronicity: A Case Study of the Caicaras in the Atlantic Rainforest of South-Eastern Brazil', in D. G. Anderson and E. Berglund, *Ethnographies of Conservation: Environmentalism and the Distribution of Privilege*. New York: Berghahn Books, 19–31.

Adams, J. S. and T. O. McShane (1992). *The Myth of Wild Africa: Conservation without Illusion*. Berkeley: University of California Press.

Adams, W. M. (2001). *Green Development*. London: Routledge.

— (2003). 'Nature and the Colonial Mind', in W. A. Adams and M. Mulligan, *Decolonizing Nature: Strategies for Conservation in a Post-Colonial Era*. London: Earthscan, pp. 16–50.

— (2004). *Against Extinction: The Story of Conservation*. London: Earthscan.

Aldridge, M. and R. Dingwall (2003). 'Teleology on Television? Implicit Models of Evolution in Broadcast Wildlife and Nature Programmes', *European Journal of Communication* 18 (4): 435–53.

Allen, D. E. (1994 [1976]). *The Naturalist in Britain: A Social History*. Princeton, NJ: Princeton University Press.

Anderson, D. G. and K. Ikeya (2001). 'Introduction: Hunting Culture and Mining Knowledge', *Senri Ethnological Studies No. 59. Parks, Property and Power: Managing Hunting Practice and Identity within State Policy Regimes*. Osaka: National Museum of Ethnology, 59: 1–5.

Anon. (2006). 'Education on Environmental Protection Viable for Sustainability', *Guardian*, Dar es Salaam: Editorial, 27 June 2006.

Attenborough, D. (2002). *Life on Air: Memoirs of a Broadcaster*. London: BBC Books.

— (2004). 'Only the Eagle-Eyed Will Spot a Fake ... Natural History Film-Makers Should be Allowed to Manipulate Images but Not Distort the Truth, Says David Attenborough'. *Daily Telegraph*, London, 29 January 2004.

Baillie, J. E. M., C. Hilton-Taylor and S. N. Stuart (2004). *2004 IUCN Red List of Threatened Species(™): A Global Species Assessment*. Gland: IUCN.

Bakker, K. (2005). 'Neoliberalizing Nature? Market Environmentalism in Water Supply in England and Wales', *Annals of the Association of American Geographers* 95 (3): 542–65.

Balmford, A. and T. Whitten (2003). 'Who Should Pay for Tropical Conservation, and How Could These Costs be Met?', *Oryx* 37 (2): 238–50.

Balmford, A., K. J. Gaston, S. Blyth, A. James and V. Kapos (2003). 'Global Variation in Terrestrial Conservation Costs, Conservation Benefits, and Unmet Conservation Needs', *Proceedings of the National Academy of Sciences of the United States of America* 100 (3): 1046–50.

Balmford, A., R. E. Green and M. Jenkins (2003). 'Measuring the Changing State of Nature', *Trends in Ecology & Evolution* 18 (7): 326–30.

Balmford, A., L. Bennun, B. ten Brink, D. Cooper, I. M. Cote, P. Crane, A. Dobson, N. Dudley, I. Dutton, R. E. Green, R. D. Gregory, J. Harrison, E. T. Kennedy, C. Kremen, N. Leader-Williams, T. E. Lovejoy, G. Mace, R. May, P. Mayaux, P. Morling, J. Phillips, K. Redford, T. H. Ricketts, J. P. Rodriguez, M. Sanjayan, P. J. Schei, A. S. van Jaarsveld and B. A. Walther (2005). 'The Convention on Biological Diversity's 2010 Target', *Science* 307 (5707): 212–13.

Barrett, W. P. (2000). 'Sweet Charity', *Forbes* 165 (7): 180, 182.

Barrow, E. and C. Fabricius (2002). 'Do Rural People Really Benefit from Protected Areas: Rhetoric or Reality?', *Parks* 12: 67–79.

Bassett, K., R. Griffiths and I. Smith (2002). 'Cultural Industries, Cultural Clusters and the City: The Example of Natural History Film-Making in Bristol', *Geoforum* 33: 165–77.

Bebbington, A. J., S. Hickey and D. C. Mitlin (2007). *Can NGOs Make a Difference? The Challenge of Development Alternatives*. London: Zed Books.

Beinart, W. (2001). 'The Renaturing of African Animals: Film and Literature in the 1950s and 1960s', *Kronos: The Journal of Cape History* 27: 201–26.

Birkett, D. (2001). 'Storyteller: The Many Lives of Laurens Van Der Post by JDF Jones. Soldier, Explorer, Philosopher, Author, Liar'. *Independent*, London, 11 October.

Blashford-Snell, J. and R. Lenska (1996). *Mammoth Hunt: In Search of the Giant Elephants of Nepal*. London: HarperCollins.

Boerma, P. A. (1999). 'Seeing the Wood for the Trees: Deforestation in the Central Highlands of Eritrea since 1890', University of Oxford. D.Phil. thesis, School of Geography and the Environment.

Bonner, R. (1993). *At the Hand of Man: Peril and Hope for Africa's Wildlife*. London: Simon and Schuster.

Booker, C. (2001). 'Small Lies and the Greater Truth', *Spectator*, London, 20 October.

Boorstin, D. J. (1992 [1961]). *The Image: A Guide to Pseudo-Events in America*. New York: Vintage Books, Random House.

Borrini-Feyerabend, G., T. Banuri, T. Farvar, K. Miller and A. Phillips (2002). 'Indigenous and Local Communities and Protected Areas: Rethinking the Relationship', *Parks* 12: 5–15.

Bourdieu, P. (1998). *On Television and Journalism*. London: Pluto Press.

Bousé, D. (2000). *Wildlife Films*. Philadelphia: University of Pennsylvania Press.

— (2003). 'False Intimacy: Close-Ups and Viewer Involvement in Wildlife Films', *Visual Studies* 18 (2): 123–32.

Boykoff, M. and M. K. Goodman (forthcoming). 'Conspicuous Redemption: Promises and Perils of Celebrity Involvement in Climate Change', *Geoforum*.

Bradshaw, C. J. A., B. W. Brook and C. R. McMahon (2007). 'Dangers of Sensationalizing Conservation Biology', *Conservation Biology* 21 (3): 570–1.

Bristow, M. (2002). 'The Future of the Industry', in *Careers in Wildlife*

Film-Making. P. Warren. UK: Wildeye.

Brockington, D. (2002). *Fortress Conservation: The Preservation of the Mkomazi Game Reserve, Tanzania.* Oxford: James Currey.

— (2003a). 'Myths of Sceptical Environmentalism', *Environmental Science and Policy* 6: 543–6.

— (2003b). 'Injustice and Conservation: Is Local Support Necessary for Sustainable Protected Areas?', *Policy Matters* 12: 22–30.

— (2004). 'Community Conservation, Inequality and Injustice: Myths of Power in Protected Area Management', *Conservation and Society* 2 (2): 411–32.

— (2008a). 'Celebrity Conservation: Interpreting the Irwins', *Media International Australia* 127: 96–108.

— (2008b). 'Powerful Environmentalisms: Conservation, Celebrity and Capitalism', *Media Culture & Society* 30 (4): 551–68.

Brockington, D. and J. Igoe (2006). 'Eviction for Conservation: A Global Overview', *Conservation and Society* 4 (3): 424–70.

Brockington, D. and K. Schmidt-Soltau (2004). 'The Social and Environmental Impacts of Wilderness and Development', *Oryx* 38 (2): 140–2.

Brockington, D., J. Igoe and K. Schmidt-Soltau (2006). 'Conservation, Human Rights, and Poverty Reduction', *Conservation Biology* 20 (1): 250–2.

Brockington, D., R. Duffy and J. Igoe (2008). *Nature Unbound: Conservation, Capitalism and the Future of Protected Areas.* London: Earthscan.

Brosius, J. P. (2004). 'Indigenous Peoples and Protected Areas at the World Parks Congress', *Conservation Biology* 18 (3): 609–12.

Bruner, A. G., R. E. Gullison and A. Balmford (2004). 'Financial Costs and Shortfalls of Managing and Expanding Protected-Area Systems in Developing Countries', *Bioscience* 54 (12): 1119–26.

Buergin, R. (2003). 'Shifting Frames for Local People and Forests in a Global Heritage: The Thung Yai Naresuan Wildlife Sanctuary in the Context of Thailand's Globalization and Modernization', *Geoforum* 24: 375–93.

Buergin, R. and C. Kessler (2000). 'Intrusions and Exclusions: Democratization in Thailand in the Context of Environmental Discourses and Resource Conflicts', *Geojournal* 52 (1): 71–80.

Burgess, J., C. Harrison and P. Maiteny (1991). 'Contested Meanings: The Consumption of News About Nature Conservation', *Media Culture & Society* 13: 499–519.

Butchart, S. H. M., H. R. Akcakaya, E. Kennedy and C. Hilton-Taylor (2006). 'Biodiversity Indicators Based on Trends in Conservation Status: Strengths of the IUCN Red List Index', *Conservation Biology* 20 (2): 579–81.

Butchart, S. H. M., A. J. Stattersfield, J. Baillie, L. A. Bennun, S. N. Stuart, H. R. Akcakaya, C. Hilton-Taylor and G. M. Mace (2005). 'Using Red List Indices to Measure Progress Towards the 2010 Target and Beyond', *Philosophical Transactions of the Royal Society B-Biological Sciences* 360 (1454): 255–68.

Butchart, S. H. M., A. J. Stattersfield, L. A. Bennun, S. M. Shutes, H. R. Akcakaya, J. E. M. Baillie, S. N. Stuart, C. Hilton-Taylor and

G. M. Mace (2004). 'Measuring Global Trends in the Status of Biodiversity: Red List Indices for Birds', *Plos Biology* 2 (12): 2294–304.

Canney, S. (2001). 'Satellite Mapping of Vegetation Change: Human Impact in an East African Semi-Arid Savanna', University of Oxford, D.Phil. thesis, Department of Zoology.

Carrier, J. G. (1998). 'Introduction', in *Virtualism: A New Political Economy*. J. G. Carrier and D. Miller. Oxford: Berg, 1–24.

Carrier, J. G. and P. West (2009). 'Introduction', in J. Carrier and P. West, *Virtualism, Governance and Practice: Vision and Execution in Environmental Conservation*. New York: Berghahn.

Carson, R. (1962). *Silent Spring*. New York: Fawcett Crest.

Cartmill, M. (1993). *A View to a Death in the Morning: Hunting and Nature through History*. Cambridge, MA: Harvard University Press.

Castells, M. (1997). *The Power of Identity*. Oxford: Blackwell.

Castree, N. (2007a). 'Neoliberalizing Nature: Processes, Effects and Evaluations', *Environment and Planning A* 40: 153–71.

— (2007b). 'Neoliberalizing Nature: The Logics of De- and Re-Regulation', *Environment and Planning A* 40: 131–52.

Castro, G. and I. Locker (2000). *Mapping Conservation Investments: An Assessment of Biodiversity Funding in Latin America and the Caribbean*. Washington, DC: Biodiversity Support Program.

Cernea, M. M. (2005). '"Restriction of Access" Is Displacement: A Broader Concept and Policy', *Forced Migration Review* 23: 48–9.

Cernea, M. M. and K. Schmidt-Soltau (2006). 'Poverty Risks and National Parks: Policy Issues in Conservation and Resettlement', *World Development* 34 (10): 1808–30.

Chape, S., J. Harrison, M. Spalding and I. Lysenko (2005). 'Measuring the Extent and Effectiveness of Protected Areas as an Indicator for Meeting Global Biodiversity Targets', *Philosophical Transactions of the Royal Society B* 360: 443–55.

Chapin, M. (2004). 'A Challenge to Conservationists', *World Watch Magazine* Nov/Dec: 17–31.

Chatty, D. and M. Colchester (2002). *Conservation and Mobile Indigenous Peoples: Displacement, Forced Settlement and Sustainable Development*. New York: Berghahn Books.

Christensen, J. (2003). 'Auditing Conservation in an Age of Accountability', *Conservation in Practice* 4: 12–18.

Clynes, T. (2002). 'They Shoot Poachers, Don't They?' *National Geographic Adventure Magazine*, October.

Colchester, M. (2003). *Salvaging Nature: Indigenous Peoples, Protected Areas and Biodivesity Conservation*. Moreton-in-Marsh, World Rainforest Movement: Forest Peoples Programme.

— (2004). 'Conservation Policy and Indigenous Peoples', *Cultural Survival Quarterly* 28 (1).

Connor, T. K. (2006). 'Opportunity and Constraint: Historicity, Hybridity and Notions of Cultural Identity in the Sundays River Valley (Eastern Cape) and Pafuri (Mozambique)', Rhodes University, PhD thesis, Department of Anthropology.

Cooper, A. F. (2007). *Celebrity Diplomacy and the G8: Bono and Bob as Legitimate International Actors*. Working Paper 29, The Centre for International Governance Innovation, University of Waterloo.

Cottle, S. (2004). 'Producing Nature(s): On the Changing Production Ecology of Natural History TV', *Media Culture & Society* 26 (1): 81–101.

Cracknell, J. and H. Godwin (2007). *Where the Green Grants Went*. London: Environmental Funders Network.

Cronon, W. (1995). 'The Trouble with Wilderness; or Getting Back to the Wrong Nature', in W. Cronon, *Uncommon Ground: Rethinking the Human Place in Nature*. New York: W. W. Norton, pp. 69–90.

Darlington, S. M. (1998). 'The Ordination of at Tree: The Buddhist Ecology Movement in Thailand', *Ethnology* 37 (1): 1–15.

Debord, G. (1995 [1967]). *Society of the Spectacle*. New York: Zone Books.

Denevan, W. M. (1992). 'The Pristine Myth: The Landscape of the Americas in 1492', *Annals of the Association of American Geographers* 82 (3): 269–85.

Dinerstein, E. (2005). *Tigerland and Other Destinations*. Washington, DC: Island Press.

Dingwall, R. and M. Aldridge (2006). 'Television Wildlife Programming as a Source of Popular Scientific Information: A Case Study of Evolution', *Public Understanding of Science* 15: 131–52.

Dirzo, R. and P. H. Raven (2003). 'Global State of Biodiversity and Loss.' *Annual Review of Environment and Resources* 28: 137–67.

Dowie, M. (1996). *Losing Ground: American Environmentalism at the Close of the 20th Century*. Cambridge, MA: MIT Press.

— (2005). 'Conservation Refugees: When Protecting Nature Means Kicking People Out', *Orion* Nov/Dec: 16–27.

— (2006). 'Problems in Paradise: How Making New Parks and Wildlife Preserves Creates Millions of Conservation Refugees around the World', *San Francisco Chronicle*, 11 June

Draper, M. (1998). 'Zen and the Art of Garden Province Maintenance: The Soft Intimacy of Hard Men in the Wilderness of Kwazulu-Natal, South Africa, 1952–1997', *Journal of Southern African Studies* 24 (4): 801–28.

Draper, M. and G. Mare (2003). 'Going In: The Garden of England's Gaming Zookeeper and Zululand', *Journal of Southern African Studies* 29 (2): 551–69.

Duffy, R. (2006). 'Global Governance and Environmental Management: The Politics of Transfrontier Conservation Areas in Southern Africa', *Political Geography* 25 (1): 89–112.

Dunn, R. R., M. C. Gavin, M. C. Sanchez and J. N. Solomon (2006). 'The Pigeon Paradox: Dependence of Global Conservation on Urban Nature', *Conservation Biology* 20 (6): 1814–6.

Dzingirai, V. (2003). 'The New Scramble for the African Countryside', *Development and Change* 34 (2): 243–63.

Eckholm, E. (1976). *Losing Ground: Environmental Stress and Food Problems*. New York: W. W. Norton.

Edwards, M. (2008). *Just Another Emperor: The Myths and Realities of Philanthrocapitalism*. New York: Demos.

Edwards, M. and D. Hulme (1995). *Non-Governmental Organisations – Performance and Accountability: Beyond the Magic Bullet*. London: Earthscan.

Emerton, L. (2001). 'The Nature of Benefits and the Benefits of Nature: Why Wildlife Conservation Has Not Economically Benefited Communities in Africa', in D. Hulme and M. Murphree, *African Wildlife and Livelihoods*. Portsmouth: Heinemann, pp. 208–26.

Fairhead, J. and M. Leach (1996). *Misreading the African Landscape*. Cambridge: Cambridge University Press.

— (2000). 'The Nature Lords: After Desolation, Conservation – and Eviction. The Future of West African Forests and Their Peoples', *Times Literary Supplement*, 5 May (5066): 3–4.

Ferguson, J. (1990). *The Anti-Politics Machine: 'Development', Depoliticisation and Bureaucratic State Power in Lesotho*. Cambridge: Cambridge University Press.

— (2006). *Global Shadows: Africa in the Neoliberal World Order*. Durham, NC: Duke University Press.

Ferris, K. O. (2007). 'The Sociology of Celebrity', *Sociology Compass* 1 (1): 371–84.

Fortwangler, C. (2007). 'Friends with Money: Private Support for a National Park in the U.S. Virgin Islands', *Conservation and Society* 5 (3): 504–33.

Foucault, M. (1977). *Discipline and Punish: The Birth of the Prison*. London: Penguin.

Gamson, J. (1994). *Claims to Fame: Celebrity in Contemporary America*. Berkeley: University of California Press.

— (2001). 'The Assembly Line of Greatness: Celebrity in Twentieth-Century America', in C. L. Harrington and D. D. Bielby, *Popular Culture: Production and Consumption*. Oxford: Blackwell.

Ganguly, V. (2004). *Conservation, Displacement and Deprivation: Maldhari of Gir Forest of Gujarat*. New Delhi: Indian Social Institute.

Garland, E. (2006). 'State of Nature: Colonial Power, Neoliberal Capital and Wildlife Management in Tanzania'. University of Chicago, PhD thesis, Department of Anthropology.

— (2008). 'The Elephant in the Room: Confronting the Colonial Character of Wildlife Conservation in Africa', *African Studies Review* 51 (3): 51–74.

Ghimire, K. B. and M. P. Pimbert (1997). *Social Change and Conservation*. London: Earthscan.

Giles, D. (2000). *Illusions of Immortality: A Psychology of Fame and Celebrity*. London: Macmillan.

Gillson, L. and M. T. Hoffman (2007). 'Rangeland Ecology in a Changing World', *Science* 315: 53–4.

Goldman, M. (2001). 'The Birth of a Discipline: Producing Authoritative Green Knowledge, World Bank-Style', *Ethnography* 2 (2): 191–217.

— (2005). *Imperial Nature: The World Bank and Struggles for Social Justice in the Age of Globalisation*. Yale, CT: Yale University Press.

Goldman, R. (1994). 'Contradictions in a Political Economy of Sign Value', *Current Perspectives in Social Theory* 14: 183–211.

Gomez-Pompa, A. and A. Kaus (1992). 'Taming the Wilderness Myth', *Bioscience* 42 (4): 271–9.

Gordon, R. J. (2006). 'Introduction',

Bibliography

in L. A. Vivanco and R. J. Gordon, *Tarzan was an Eco-Tourist ... And Other Tales in the Anthropology of Adventure*. New York: Berghahn Books: 1–23.

Gray, J. (2002). *Snarl for the Camera: Tales of a Wildlife Cameraman*. London: Judy Piaktus.

Groenewald, Y. and F. Macleod (2004). 'Park Plans Bring "Grief"', *Weekly Mail and Guardian*, 25 June.

Guha, R. and J. Martinez-Alier (1997). *Varieties of Environmentalism*. Earthscan: London.

Halpern, B. S., C. R. Pyke, H. E. Fox, J. C. Haney, M. A. Schlaepfer and P. Zaradic (2006). 'Gaps and Mismatches between Global Conservation Priorities and Spending', *Conservation Biology* 20 (1): 56–64.

Hartley, J. (1999). *Uses of Television*. London: Routledge.

Heywood, V. H., G. M. Mace, R. M. May and S. N. Stuart (1994). 'Uncertainties in Extinction Rates', *Nature* 368 (6467): 105.

Hitchcock, R. (2002). 'Removals, Politics and Human Rights', *Cultural Survival Quarterly* 26 (1): 25–6.

Holdgate, M. (1999). *The Green Web: A Union for World Conservation*. London: Earthscan.

Holland, P. and G. Huggan (1998). *Tourists with Typewriters: Critical Reflections on Contemporary Travel Writing*. Ann Arbor: The University of Michigan Press.

Holmes, G. (forthcoming). 'The Rich, the Powerful and the Endangered: Conservation Elites, Networks and the Dominican Republic', *Antipode*.

Holmes, S. (2005). '"Starring ... Dyer?": Re-Visiting Star Studies and Contemporary Celebrity Culture', *Westminster Papers in Communication and Culture* 2 (2): 6–21.

Homewood, K. M. and D. Brockington (1999). 'Biodiversity, Conservation and Development', *Global Ecology and Biogeography Letters* 8: 301–13.

Homewood, K. M. and W. A. Rodgers (1991). *Maasailand Ecology: Pastoralist Development and Wildlife Conservation in Ngorongoro, Tanzania*. Cambridge: Cambridge University Press.

Hope, C. (2001). '"It's a Stitch-Up." Laurens Van Der Post May Have Fudged the Truth, Says Christopher Hope, but He Deserves Better than This: Storyteller: The Many Lives of Laurens Van Der Post', *Guardian*, 6 October.

Hornaday, W. T. (1931). *Thirty Years War for Wild Life: Gains and Losses in the Thankless Task*. Stamford, CT: The Gillispie Bros, Inc.

House, A. (1993). *The Great Safari: The Lives of George and Joy Adamson*. London: HarperCollins.

Hughes, J. (2006). 'Who Watches the Watchmen?: Ideology and "Real World" Superheroes', *Journal of Popular Culture* 39 (4): 546–57.

Hulme, D. and M. Edwards (1997). *NGOs, States and Donors: Too Close for Comfort?* London: Macmillan.

Hulme, D. and M. Murphree (2001). *African Wildlife and Livelihoods: The Promise and Performance of Community Conservation*. Portsmouth: Heinemann.

Hurt, R. and P. Ravan (2000). 'Hunting and Its Benefits: An Overview of Hunting in Africa with Special Reference to Tanzania', in H. H. T. Prins, J. G. Grootenuis and T. T. Dolan, *Wildlife Conservation by Sustainable Use*. Boston, MA: Kluwer Academic Publishers, pp. 295–313.

Hutchins, B. and L. Lester (2006).

'Environmental Protest and Tap-Dancing with the Media in the Information Age', *Media, Culture & Society* 28 (3): 433–51.

Hutton, J. and N. Leader-Williams (2003). 'Sustainable Use and Incentive-Driven Conservation: Realigning Human and Conservation Interests', *Oryx* 37 (2): 215–26.

Igoe, J. (2002). 'Book Review of "Fortress Conservation"', *International Journal of African Historical Studies* 35 (2–3): 594–6.

— (2003). 'Scaling up Civil Society: Donor Money, NGOs and the Pastoralist Land Rights Movement in Tanzania', *Development and Change* 34: 863–85.

— (2004). *Conservation and Globalisation: A Study of National Parks and Indigenous Communities from East Africa to South Dakota*. Belmont, CA: Wadsworth and Thomson Learning.

— (2005). 'Global Indigenism and Spaceship Earth: Convergence, Space, and Re-Entry Friction', *Globalizations* 2 (3): 1–13.

— (2006). 'Becoming Indigenous Peoples: Difference, Inequality, and the Globalisation of East African Identity Politics', *African Affairs* 105 (420): 399–420.

Igoe, J. and B. Croucher (2007). 'Poverty Alleviation Meets the Spectacle of Nature: Does Reality Matter?', *Conservation and Society* 5 (4): 534–61.

Igoe, J. and T. Kelsall (2005). 'Introduction: Between a Rock and a Hard Place', in *African NGOs, Donors, and the State: Between a Rock and a Hard Place*. J. Igoe and T. Kelsall. Durham, NC: Carolina Academic Press, pp. 1–33.

Ives, J. D. and B. Messerli (1989). *The*

Himalayan Dilemma: Reconciling Development and Conservation. London: Routledge.

Jacoby, K. (2001). *Crimes against Nature: Squatters, Poachers, Thieves and the Hidden History of American Conservation*. Berkeley: University of California Press.

James, A., K. J. Gaston and A. Balmford (2001). 'Can We Afford to Conserve Biodiversity?', *Bioscience* 51 (1): 43–52.

Jeffries, M. (2003). 'BBC Natural History Versus Science Paradigms', *Science as Culture* 12 (4): 527–45.

Jenkins, M., R. E. Green and J. Madden (2003). 'The Challenge of Measuring Global Change in Wild Nature: Are Things Getting Better or Worse?', *Conservation Biology* 17 (1): 20–23.

Jones, J. D. F. (2001). *Storyteller: The Many Lives of Laurens Van Der Post*. London: John Murray.

Keyes, R. (1996). *The Wit and Wisdom of Oscar Wilde: A Treasury of Quotations, Anecdotes, and Observations*. New York: Gramercy Books.

Khare, A. and D. B. Bray (2004). *Study of Critical New Forest Conservation Issues in the Global South*. Final report submitted to the Ford Foundation.

Kuper, A. (2003). 'The Return of the Native', *Current Anthropology* 44 (3): 389–402.

LaBastille, A. (1992). *Mama Poc: An Ecologist's Account of the Extinction of a Species*. New York: W. W. Norton and Co.

Ladle, R. J. and P. Jepson (2008). 'Toward a Biocultural Theory of Avoided Extinction', *Conservation Letters* 1 (3): 111–18.

Langholz, J. and G. H. Kerley (2006). *Combining Conservation and Development on Private Lands: An Assess-*

ment of Eco-Tourism Based Private
Game Reserves in the Eastern Cape.
Port Elizabeth: Centre for African
Conservation Ecology, Nelson
Mandela Metropolitan University.

Leach, M. and R. Mearns (1996).
'Challenging Received Wisdom
in Africa', in M. Leach and
R. Mearns, The Lie of the Land.
Oxford: James Currey, pp. 1–33.

Leakey, R. and V. Morell (2001).
Wildlife Wars: My Fight to Save
Africa's Natural Treasures. New
York: St Martin's Press.

Lees, A. (2007). Review and Analysis of
Fiji's Conservation Sector. Waita-
kere City: The Austral Foundation.

Leopold, A. (1989 [1949]). A Sand
County Alamanac: And Sketches
Here and There. Oxford: Oxford
University Press.

Lester, L. (2006). 'Lost in the Wilderness? Celebrity, Protest and the
News', Journalism Studies 7 (6):
907–21.

Lindsey, P. A., P. A. Roulet and
S. S. Romanach (2007). 'Economic
and Conservation Significance
of the Trophy Hunting Industry
in Sub-Saharan Africa', Biological
Conservation 134: 455–69.

Lomborg, B. (2001). The Skeptical
Environmentalist: Measuring the
Real State of the World. Cam-
bridge: Cambridge University
Press.

Luck, K. (2003). 'Contested Rights:
The Impact of Game Farming on
Farm Workers in the Bushman's
River Area', Rhodes University,
MA thesis, Department of Antro-
pology.

MacDonald, C. (2008). Green, Inc.:
An Environmental Insider Reveals
How a Good Cause Has Gone Bad.
Guilford, CO: The Lyons Press.

MacDonald, K. (2004). 'Developing

"Nature": Global Ecology and
the Politics of Conservation in
Northern Pakistan', in J. Carrier,
Confronting Environments: Local
Environmental Understanding in a
Globalising World. Lanham, MD:
AltaMira Press, pp. 71–96.

— (2005). 'Global Hunting Grounds:
Power, Scale and Ecology in the
Negotiation of Conservation',
Cultural Geographies 12: 259–91.

MacKenzie, J. M. (1987). 'Chivalry,
Social Darwinism and Ritualised
Killing: The Hunting Ethos
in Central Africa up to 1914',
in D. Anderson and R. Grove,
Conservation in Africa: People,
Policies and Practice. Cambridge:
Cambridge University Press,
pp. 41–61.

— (1988). The Empire of Nature:
Hunting, Conservation and British
Imperialism. Manchester: Man-
chester University Press.

Macleod, F. (2003). 'Makro King
in Parks Rescue Plan', Mail and
Guardian, 10 June.

Mansourian, S. and N. Dudley (2008).
Public Funds to Protected Areas.
Gland: WWF International.

Marshall, D. P. (1997). Celebrity and
Power: Fame in Contemporary
Culture. Minneapolis: University
of Minnesota Press.

McComas, K. A., J. Shanahan and
J. S. Butler (2001). 'Environmental
Content in Prime-Time Network
TV's Non-News Entertainment
and Fictional Programs', Society
and Natural Resources 14: 533–42.

McIntosh Xaba and Associates
(2003). The Investigation in the
Effects of Conservation and Tourism
on Land Tenure and Ownership
Patterns in Kwazulu-Natal Part 1.
Bishopsgate. Durban: McIntosh
Xaba and Associates.

McLean, J. and S. Straede (2003). 'Conservation, Relocation and the Paradigms of Park and People Management: A Case Study of Padampur Villages and the Royal Chitwan National Park, Nepal', *Society and Natural Resources* 16: 509–26.

Mendelson, J. R., K. R. Lips, R. W. Gagliardo, G. B. Rabb, J. P. Collins, J. E. Diffendorfer, P. Daszak, R. Ibanez, K. C. Zippel, D. P. Lawson, K. M. Wright, S. N. Stuart, C. Gascon, H. R. da Silva, P. A. Burrowes, R. L. Joglar, E. La Marca, S. Lotters, L. H. du Preez, C. Weldon, A. Hyatt, J. V. Rodriguez-Mahecha, S. Hunt, H. Robertson, B. Lock, C. J. Raxworthy, D. R. Frost, R. C. Lacy, R. A. Alford, J. A. Campbell, G. Parra-Olea, F. Bolanos, J. J. C. Domingo, T. Halliday, J. B. Murphy, M. H. Wake, L. A. Coloma, S. L. Kuzmin, M. S. Price, K. M. Howell, M. Lau, R. Pethiyagoda, M. Boone, M. J. Lannoo, A. R. Blaustein, A. Dobson, R. A. Griffiths, M. L. Crump, D. B. Wake and E. D. Brodie (2006). 'Biodiversity: Confronting Amphibian Declines and Extinctions', *Science* 313 (5783): 48.

Meyer, D. S. and J. Gamson (1995). 'The Challenge of Cultural Elites: Celebrities and Social Movements', *Sociological Inquiry* 65 (2): 181–206.

Mikhail, E. H. (1979). *Oscar Wilde: Interviews and Recollections*. New York: Harper and Row.

Milton, K. (2002). *Loving Nature: Towards an Ecology of Emotion*. London: Routledge.

Mitman, G. (1999). *Reel Nature: America's Romance with Wildlife on Film*. Cambridge, MA: Harvard University Press.

Monbiot, G. (1995). *No Man's Land: An Investigative Journey through Kenya and Tanzania*. London: Macmillan.

— (2002). 'Planet of the Fakes', *Guardian*, 17 December.

— (2005). 'And Still He Stays Silent', *Guardian*, 6 September.

Mortimore, M. (1998). *Roots in the African Dust: Sustaining the Drylands*. Cambridge: Cambridge University Press.

Murdoch, W., S. Polasky, K. A. Wilson, H. P. Possingham, P. Kareiva and R. Shaw (2007). 'Maximizing Return on Investment in Conservation', *Biological Conservation* 139 (375–88).

Murombedzi, J. (2001). 'Committees, Rights, Costs and Benefits: Natural Resource Stewardship and Community Benefits in Zimbabwe's Campfire Programme', in D. Hulme and M. Murphree, *African Wildlife and Livelihoods: The Promise and Performance of Community Conservation*. Oxford: James Currey, pp. 244–55.

— (2003). 'Devolving the Expropriation of Nature: The Devolution of Wildlife Management in Southern Africa', in W. M. Adams and M. Mulligan, *Decolonizing Nature: Strategies for Conservation in a Post-Colonial Era*. London: Earthscan, pp. 135–51.

Murphree, M. (2001). 'Community, Council and Client: A Case Study in Ecotourism Development from Mahenye, Zimbabwe', in D. Hulme and M. Murphree, *African Wildlife and Livelihoods*. Portsmouth: Heinemann, pp. 177–94.

Murton, J. (1999). 'Population Growth and Poverty in Machakos District, Kenya', in *The Geographical Journal* 165: 37–46.

Nash, R. (2001). *Wilderness and the American Mind*. New Haven, CT: Yale Nota Bene.

Nelson, F. (2004). *The Evolution and Impacts of Community-Based Ecotourism in Northern Tanzania*, Programme Issue Paper 131, IIED Drylands.

Nelson, F. and S. O. Makko (2003). 'Communities, Conservation and Conflicts in the Tanzanian Serengeti', Third Annual Community-based Conservation Network Seminar: Turning Natural Resources into Assets, Savannah, Georgia, 14–17 October.

Neumann, R. P. (1998). *Imposing Wilderness: Struggles over Livelihood and Nature Preservation in Africa*. Berkeley: University of California Press.

— (2004). 'Moral and Discursive Geographies in the War for Biodiversity in Africa', *Political Geography* 23: 813–37.

Neves-Graca, K. (forthcoming). 'Taking the Heat with Iconized Nature: The Human-Environmental Conundrums of Two Bare Lives'.

Nielsen, A. (2007). *Global Omnibus Survey*. Oxford: AC Nielsen.

Nugent, S. (1994). *Big Mouth: The Amazon Speaks*. San Francisco, CA: Brown Trout Press.

Nyenyembe, C. (2006). 'Wanaoishi Eneo La Hifadhi Waondoke Haraka', *Daima*: www.freemedia. co.tz/daima/2006/9/19/habari31. php (accessed 7 May 2009).

Nyerges, A. E. and G. M. Green (2000). 'The Ethnography of Landscape: GIS and Remote Sensing in the Study of Forest Change in West African Guinea Savanna', *American Anthropologist* 102 (2): 271–89.

Oldfield, T. E. E., R. J. Smith and N. Leader-Williams (2003). 'Field Sports and Conservation in the United Kingdom', *Nature* 423: 531–3.

Ottaway, D. B. and J. Stephens (2003). 'Nonprofit Land Bank Amasses Billions: Charity Builds Assets on Corporate Partnerships', *Washington Post*, 4 May.

Owens, D. and M. Owens (1992). *The Eye of the Elephant*. Boston, MA: Mariner Books.

Parsons, C. (1982). *True to Nature: Christopher Parsons Looks Back on 25 Years of Wildlife Filming with the BBC Natural History Unit*. Cambridge: Patrick Stephens.

Pasquini (2007). 'Privately-Owned Lands and Biodiversity Conservation: Analysing the Role of Private Conservation Areas in the Little Karoo, South Africa'. University of Sheffield, PhD thesis, Department of Geography.

Pearce, F. (2005a). 'Big Game Losers', *New Scientist* 16 April 2005: 21.

— (2005b). 'Laird of Africa', *New Scientist* 13 August 2005: 48–50.

Pergams, O. R. W. and P. Zaradic (2006). 'Is Love of Nature in the US Becoming Love of Electronic Media? 16 Year Down Trend in National Park Visits Explained by Watching Movies, Playing Video Games, Internet Use and Oil Price', *Journal of Environmental Management* 80: 387–93.

— (2008). 'Evidence for a Fundamental and Pervasive Shift Away from Nature-Based Recreation', *Proceedings of the National Academy of Sciences of the*

United States of America 105 (7): 2295–2300.

Pharoah, C. (2002). 'How Much Do People Give to Charity and Who Are the Donors?', in C. Walker and C. Pharoah, *A Lot of Give: Trends in Charitable Giving for the 21st Century*. Bath: Hodder and Stoughton, pp. 23–42.

Philo, G. and L. Henderson (1998). *What the Audience Thinks: Focus Group Research into the Likes and Dislikes of UK Wildlife Viewers*. Glasgow: Glasgow Media Group.

Pimenta, B. V. S., C. F. B. Haddad, L. B. Nascimento, C. A. G. Cruz and J. P. Pombal (2005). 'Comment on "Status and Trends of Amphibian Declines and Extinctions Worldwide"', *Science* 309 (5743).

Pimm, S. (2006). 'The Perfect Gift to Inspire Your Students and Make Your Mother Love You Even More', *Conservation Biology* 20 (3): 920.

Poole, R. M. (2006). 'Heartbreak on the Serengeti', *National Geographic* February.

Price, S. V., S. Reichle, R. E. Rice, E. T. Niesten, C. Romero and G. I. Andrade (2004). 'Letters Concerning ICO Approaches to Tropical Forest Conservation', *Conservation Biology* 18 (6): 1452–5.

Pringle, H. (2004). *Celebrity Sells*. Chichester: John Wiley and Sons.

Prins, H. H. T., J. G. Grootenuis and T. T. Dolan (2000). *Wildlife Conservation by Sustainable Use*. Boston, MA: Kluwer Academic Publishers.

Proctor, J. D. and S. Pincetl (1996). 'Nature and the Reproduction of Endangered Space: The Spotted Owl in the Pacific Northwest and Southern California', *Environment and Planning D: Society and Space* 14: 683–708.

Quammen, D. (2008). 'An African Love Story', *National Geographic* September: 42–63.

Rangarajan, M. (2001). *India's Wildlife History*. Delhi: Permanent Black.

Redford, K. (1990). 'The Ecologically Noble Savage', *Orion* 9: 25–9.

Redford, K. H. and E. Fearn (2007a). *Protected Areas and Human Livelihoods*. New York: Working Paper 32. New York, Wildlife Conservation Society.

— (eds) (2007b). *Protected Areas and Human Displacement: A Conservation Perspective*. Working Paper 29, New York: Wildlife Conservation Society.

Richards, P. (1985). *Indigenous Agricultural Revolution: Ecology and Food Production in West Africa*. Hemel Hempstead: Allen and Unwin.

Richey, L. A. and S. Ponte (2006). *Better (Red)™ Than Dead: 'Brand Aid', Celebrities and the New Frontier of Development Assistance*. Working Paper 2006/26, Danish Institute for International Studies.

Rocheleau, D., P. Benjamin and A. Diang'a (1995). 'The Ukambani Region of Kenya', in *Regions at Risk: Comparisons of Threatened Environments*. J. X. Kasperson, R. E. Kasperson and B. L. Turner II. Tokyo: United Nations University Press.

Rodriguez, J. P., A. B. Taber, P. Daszak, R. Sukumar, C. Valladares-Padua, S. Padua, L. F. Aguirre, R. A. Medellin, M. Acosta, A. A. Aguirre, C. Bonacic, P. Bordino, J. Bruschini, D. Buchori, S. Gonzalez, T. Mathew, M. Mendez, L. Mugica, L. F. Pacheco,

A. P. Dobson and M. Pearl (2007). 'Environment – Globalization of Conservation: A View from the South', *Science* 317 (5839): 755–6.

Roe, E. (1995). 'Except-Africa: Postscript to a Special Section in Development Narratives', *World Development* 23: 1065–70.

Rojek, C. (2001). *Celebrity*. London: Reaktion Books Ltd.

Romero, C. and G. I. Andrade (2004). 'International Conservation Organisations and the Fate of Local Tropical Forest Conservation Initiatives', *Conservation Biology* 18 (2): 578–80.

Rose, D. B. (1996). *Nourishing Terrains: Australian Aboriginal Views of Landscape and Wilderness*. Canberra: Australian Heritage Commission.

Rothkopf, D. (2008). *Superclass: The Global Power Elite and the World They Are Making*. New York: Farrar, Straus and Giroux.

Sachedina, H. (2008). 'Wildlife are Our Oil: Conservation, Livelihoods and NGOs in the Tarangire Ecosystem, Tanzania', University of Oxford, D.Phil. thesis, Department of Geography.

Sarkar, S., R. L. Pressey, D. P. Faith, C. R. Margules, T. Fuller, D. M. Stoms, A. Moffett, K. A. Wilson, K. J. Williams, P. H. Williams and S. Andelman (2006). 'Biodiversity Conservation Planning Tools: Present Status and Challenges for the Future', *Annual Review of Environment and Resources* 31: 123–59.

Sato, J. (2002). 'Karen and the Land in Between: Public and Private Enclosure of Forests in Thailand', in D. Chatty and M. Colchester, *Conservation and Mobile Indigenous Peoples: Displacement,* *Forced Settlement and Sustainable Development*. New York: Berghahn Books, 277–95.

Schama, S. (1996). *Landscape and Memory*. London: Fontana Press.

Schickel, R. (2000 [1985]). *Intimate Strangers: The Culture of Celebrity in America*. Chicago, IL: Ivan R. Dee.

Schmidt-Soltau, K. and D. Brockington (2007). 'Protected Areas and Resettlement: What Scope for Voluntary Relocation', *World Development* 35 (12): 2182–202.

Scholfield, K. and D. Brockington (2009). *The Work of Non-Governmental Organisations* in African Wildlife Conservation. BWPI Working Paper 80, University of Manchester.

Shahabuddin, G. and A. Shah (2003). 'Relocation of People from Wildlife Areas: Socio-Economic and Ecological Issues', *Economic and Political Weekly* 38 (47): 4945–6.

Shahabuddin, G., R. Kumar and M. Shrivastava (2005). *Forgotten Villages: A People's Perspective on Village Displacement from Sariska Tiger Reserve*. New Delhi: Environmental Studies Group, Council for Social Development.

Shanahan, C. L. (2005). '"(No) Mercy" Nary Patrols: A Controversial, Last-Ditch Effort to Salvage the Central African Republic's Chinko Basin', *Thomas Jefferson Law Review* 27: 223–54.

Shanahan, J. and K. McComas (1997). 'Television's Portrayal of the Environment', *Journalism and Mass Communication Quarterly* 74 (1): 147–59.

Shanahan, J., M. Morgan and M. Stenbjerre (1997). 'Green or Brown? Television and the Cultivation of Environmental

Concern', *Journal of Broadcasting and Electronic Media* 41: 305–23.

Sklair, L. (2001). *The Transnational Capitalist Class*. Oxford: Blackwell.

Small, M. F. (2007). 'From Gombe to the World', *Science* 315: 498–9.

Smith, D. (2002). 'Master Storyteller or Master Deceiver?', *New York Times*, 3 August.

Smith, D. B. (1990). *From the Land of Shadows: The Making of Grey Owl*. Saskatoon, SK: Western Producer Prairie Books.

Spence, M. D. (1999). *Dispossessing the Wilderness: Indian Removal and the Making of National Parks*. Oxford: Oxford University Press.

Steinhart, E. I. (2006). *Black Poachers, White Hunters: A Social History of Hunting in Colonial Kenya*. Oxford: James Currey.

Sting and J.-P. Dutilleux (1989). *Jungle Stories: The Fight for the Amazon*. London: Barrie & Jenkins.

Street, J. (2004). 'Celebrity Politicians: Popular Culture and Political Representation', *British Journal of Politics and International Relations* 6: 435–52.

Strkalj, G. (2008). 'Jane Goodall: The Woman Who Redefined Man', *American Journal of Physical Anthropology* 136 (3): 371–2.

Stuart, S. N., J. S. Chanson, N. A. Cox, B. E. Young, A. S. L. Rodrigues, D. L. Fischman and R. W. Waller (2004). 'Status and Trends of Amphibian Declines and Extinctions Worldwide', *Science* 306 (5702): 1783–6.

Stuart, S. N., J. S. Chanson, N. A. Cox, B. E. Young, A. S. L. Rodrigues, D. L. Fischman and R. W. Waller (2005). 'Response to Comment On "Status and Trends of Amphibian Declines and Extinctions Worldwide"', *Science* 309 (5743): 1999c.

Sullivan, S. (2000). 'Gender, Ethnographic Myths and Community-Based Conservation in a Former Namibian "Homeland"', in D. Hodgson, *Rethinking Pastoralism in Africa: Gender, Culture and the Myth of the Patriarchal Pastoralist*. Oxford: James Currey, pp. 142–64.

— (2006). 'The Elephant in the Room? Problematising "New" (Neoliberal) Biodiversity Conservation', *NUPI Forum for Development Studies* 2006 (1): 105–35.

Sullivan, S. and R. Rohde (2002). 'On Non-Equilibrium in Arid and Semi-Arid Grazing Systems', *Journal of Biogeography* 29: 1595–618.

Sunseri, T. (2005). '"Something Else to Burn": Forest Squatters, Conservationists, and the State in Modern Tanzania', *Journal of Modern African Studies* 43 (4): 609–40.

Terborgh, J. (2004). 'Reflections of a Scientist on the World Parks Congress', *Conservation Biology* 18(3): 619–20.

Theroux, P. (1997 [1967]). 'Tarzan is an Expatriate', *Transition* 75/76: 46–58.

Thompson, M., M. Warburton and T. Hatley (1986). *Uncertainty on a Himalayan Scale: An Institutional Theory of Environmental Perception and a Strategic Framework for the Sustainable Development of the Himalaya*. London: Milton Ash Ethnographica.

Thoreau, H. D. (1991 [1854]). *Walden or, Life in the Woods*. New York: Vintage Books.

Tiffen, M., M. Mortimore and F. Gichuki (1994). *More People, Less Erosion: Environmental Recovery in Kenya*. Chichester: John Wiley.

Turner, G. (2004). *Understanding Celebrity*. London: Sage.

Turner, G., F. Bonner and D. P. Marshall (2000). *Fame Games: The Production of Celebrity in Australia*. Cambridge: Cambridge University Press.

Upton, C., R. Ladle, D. Hulme, T. Jiang, D. Brockington and W. M. Adams (2008). 'Protected Areas, Poverty & Biodiversity: A National Scale Analysis', *Oryx* 42 (1): 19–25.

Vivanco, L. A. (2002). 'Seeing Green: Knowing and Saving the Environment on Film', *American Anthropologist* 104 (4): 1195–204.

— (2004). 'The Work of Environmentalism in an Age of Televisual Adventures', *Cultural Dynamics* 16 (1): 5–27.

— (2006). 'The Work of Environmentalism in an Age of Televisual Adventures', in L. A. Vivanco and R. J. Gordon, *Tarzan Was an Eco-Tourist ... And Other Tales in the Anthropology of Adventure*. New York: Berghahn Books, pp. 125–46.

Wainana, B. (2006). 'How to Write About Africa', *Developments* 34: www.developments.org.uk/data/issue34/Africa.htm (accessed 13 November 2006).

Walpole, M. J. and N. Leader-Williams (2002). 'Tourism and Flagship Species in Conservation', *Biodiversity and Conservation* 11: 543–7.

Ward, S. (1997). 'Boy Tarzan Vs Rambo of the Bush', *The South African Trumpet* 2.

Warren, P. (2002). *Careers in Wildlife Film-Making*. UK: Wildeye.

Watson, K. (2008). 'Lost Land of the Jaguar–BBC1', *Metrolife*, 6 August.

Webber, A. (2002). 'Are Wildlife Programmes on Television Effective in Producing Conservation?', Unpublished report for Filmmakers for Conservation.

Weber, B. and A. Vedder (2002). *In the Kingdom of Gorillas: The Quest to Save Rwanda's Mountain Gorillas*. London: Aurum.

Weber, M. (1968 [1914]). *Economy and Society: An Outline of Interpretive Sociology*. New York: Bedminster Press.

West, P. and J. G. Carrier (2004). 'Ecotourism and Authenticity: Getting Away from It All?', *Current Anthropology* 45 (4): 483–98.

West, P., J. Igoe and D. Brockington (2006). 'Parks and People: The Social Impacts of Protected Areas', *Annual Review of Anthropology* 35: 251–77.

Western, D. (1994). 'Ecosystem Conservation and Rural Development: The Case of Amboseli', in D. Western and R. M. Wright, *Natural Connections: Perspectives in Community-Based Conservation*. Washington, DC: Island Press.

Wilde, O. (2003). *Complete Works of Oscar Wilde*. London: Harper Collins.

Wilson, A. (1992). *The Culture of Nature: North American Landscapes from Disney to the Exxon Valdez*. Cambridge, MA: Blackwell Publishers.

Wilson, K. A., E. C. Underwood, S. A. Morrison, K. R. Klausmeyer, W. W. Murdoch, B. Reyers, G. Wardell-Johnson, P. A. Marquet, P. W. Rundel, M. F. McBride, R. L. Pressey, M. Bode, J. M. Hoekstra, S. Andelman, M. Looker, C. Rondinini, P. Kareiva, M. R. Shaw and H. P. Possingham (2007). 'Conserving Biodiversity Efficiently: What to Do, Where, and When', *Plos Biology* 5 (9): 1850–61.

Wilson, K. A., M. F. McBride, M. Bode and H. P. Possingham (2006). 'Prioritizing Global Conservation Efforts', *Nature* 440 (7082): 337–40.

Wolmer, W. (2003). 'Transboundary Conservation: The Politics of Ecological Integrity in the Great Limpopo Transfrontier Park', *Journal of Southern African Studies* 29 (1): 261–78.

Zaradic, P. and O. R. W. Pergams (2007). 'Videophilia: Implications for Childhood Development and Conservation', *Journal of Development Processes* 2 (1): 130–47.

Index

Index

Index